THE MAN WHO LIVES WITH WOLVES

THE MAN WHO LIVES WITH WOLVES

SHAUN ELLIS

WITH PENNY JUNOR

HarperCollins*Publishers*

HarperCollins*Publishers*
77–85 Fulham Palace Road,
Hammersmith, London W6 8JB

www.harpercollins.co.uk

First published in the United States by
Harmony Books, an imprint of the Crown Publishing Group,
a division of Random House, Inc., New York.
This edition first published in the UK by
HarperCollins Publishers in 2010

1 3 5 7 9 10 8 6 4 2

© Shaun Ellis 2010

Shaun Ellis asserts the moral right to
be identified as the author of this work

A catalogue record of this book is
available from the British Library

ISBN 978-0-00-732715-7

Printed and bound in Great Britain by
Clays Ltd, St Ives plc

Mixed Sources
Product group from well-managed
forests and other controlled sources
www.fsc.org Cert no. SW-COC-1806
© 1996 Forest Stewardship Council
FSC

FSC is a non-profit international organisation established to promote the
responsible management of the world's forests. Products carrying the FSC
label are independently certified to assure consumers that they come
from forests that are managed to meet the social, economic and
ecological needs of present and future generations.

Find out more about HarperCollins and the environment at
www.harpercollins.co.uk/green

CONTENTS

AUTHOR'S NOTE

When you are living with wolves, all that matters is staying alive and protecting the pack; days slip into weeks, weeks into years. Time, as we know it, has no relevance and I want to apologise in advance if I am a little fuzzy about dates and times. I have never kept a diary, never been a letter-writer, and have never hung on to anything. For much of my life I have lived out of a rucksack so have very few possessions of any sort. There is very little, therefore, to remind me about when the various events that took place in my life actually happened. If I have attributed something to the wrong year, please bear with me. The events themselves I remember as if they were yesterday.

TOUCHING
A NERVE

I was helping out at a wildlife centre in Hertfordshire, just north of London. One day a man appeared outside the wolf enclosure pushing a child in an old-fashioned wheelchair that looked almost Victorian, with a large rectangular tray on the front of it. I was immediately struck by how out of place it looked. He told me that he and his son, who looked about thirteen or fourteen and who I could see at a glance was severely disabled, had driven all the way from Scotland, a distance of around five hundred miles. He had heard that we allowed members of the public to interact with the wolves and he wanted his son to meet one.

I was surprised that this man should have gone to such lengths to show his son a wolf. The child didn't look as though he would get anything out of the encounter. He sat immobile, silent, staring into space, and I doubted that he would even be able to stroke the animal's fur. Normally, I loved this part of the job. Children arrived with such preconceptions. They pulled back and screamed when the wolf came near, convinced by all the stories they'd read, and the cartoons they'd watched, that wolves were sly, vicious creatures that ate grandmothers, blew down the houses of little pigs and ripped the throats out of little girls. I had grown up with exactly the same terror. It had taken me many years to discover that wolves are actually shy, intelligent animals with a very sophisticated social structure, whose bloodthirsty reputation is not deserved. I found nothing more gratifying than watching children touch the wolves and listen to what I had to tell them about these animals, and watch their prejudice and ignorance fade away.

I felt almost evangelical about this. I thought that if children could feel their coats and look them in the eye, they could make up their own minds about them so that, in time, future generations will perhaps be ready to give back to wolves the place in our world that is rightfully theirs.

Once upon a time wolves and men lived alongside one another, each respecting and benefiting from the other's way of life. Sadly, those days are gone and I believe that we are the poorer for that. The natural balance in nature that they promoted has been whittled away and several species, including our own, have been allowed to go unchecked and become diseased – in the truest sense of the word.

This may be a little fanciful, but I believe that having wolves roaming the forests once more would not only restore the balance and heal the natural world but would also benefit human society. We could learn a lot from the loyalty they display to family members, the way they educate and discipline their young, the way they look after their own and the circumstances in which they use their considerable weaponry to kill. The world is not yet ready for that, but I like to think that in some small way my work of the last twenty years might have begun the process.

Whenever I introduced a child to the wolves, it was vital that the child did not become frightened. I had to watch their reaction carefully so that I didn't do more harm with this exercise than good.

This boy didn't speak. His disabilities were clearly mental as well as physical and I guessed he might have been autistic. I could immediately see there would be a problem and asked the father, as tactfully as I could, whether the child would be able to indicate when he no longer wanted to be near the wolf, explaining how important this was. 'He won't be able to,' said the man, bluntly. 'He has never spoken, and never reacted in any way to anything. And he has never expressed an emotion in his life.'

Common sense was screaming at me to tell this man to turn around, to take his poor child all the way back to Scotland – but for reasons I can't explain, and a few I can, I agreed to go ahead.

There was a young wolf in the enclosure called Zarnesti that had been handled a lot in his first few months of life and was perfect, therefore, for introducing to children. His mother had stood on him or rolled on him soon after birth, crushing his jaw. As a result he had been hand-reared and was not as nervous around humans as most wolves. I loved him; he had the most wonderful character, but he looked a bit like Goofy the dog in the Mickey Mouse cartoons.

Questioning my own sanity, I went into the enclosure and came out carrying Zarnesti. He was then about three months old, the size of a spaniel and a wriggling, struggling bundle of energy. It was all I could do to hold him; he was almost flying out of my arms as I put him down on the tray of this old-fashioned wheelchair, in front of the boy. I had the pup in a vice-like grip, but something miraculous happened. The moment Zarnesti saw the child he became still. He looked into the boy's eyes and they stared at each other. Then the pup settled down with his back legs tucked under him and his front legs stretched out in front. I took one hand off him and I realised very quickly that I could take the other hand away too. After a few moments, still looking into his eyes, the cub reached forward and started to lick the boy's face. I lunged to intercept him, terrified that

Zarnesti would nip the boy's mouth with his needle-sharp teeth, which is what cubs do to adult wolves when they want them to regurgitate food. But Zarnesti didn't nip; he just licked, very gently.

The scene was electrifying. As I looked at the boy I saw one single tear welling up in his right eye, then trickle slowly down his cheek. Guessing this had never happened before, I turned to his father. This big, strong, capable Scotsman was standing there, watching what was unfolding in front of him, with tears streaming down his face.

In a matter of seconds, the wolf cub had got through to this boy in a way that no human had managed to do in fourteen years.

Chapter One

A SPECIAL
RELATIONSHIP

It was early morning. I had crept out of my bed, as I often did as a child, and gone out into the nearby barn where the farm dogs slept, to curl up with them – something to which my kindly grandparents turned a tolerant blind eye. I was a loner, the dogs my closest friends, and the nearest thing I had to siblings. I woke up to find the oldest of the dogs standing over me, his head facing the door. When I stirred, he turned to look at me and raised an eyebrow. I could tell immediately that something was wrong. His mouth was open and saliva was dripping from his tongue. The younger dogs were lying curled up by my side, which is where Bess, the eldest, should have been too. I could hear a great commotion in the yard outside and my grandfather was calling my name. I can't have been more than six or seven years old, but it's a memory that has stayed with me, and although I had no notion of it at the time, it was the beginning of a very long journey for me.

Bess had bitten one of the other farm hands. His arm was crudely bandaged with a handkerchief and spots of blood were seeping through the flimsy material. He was complaining bitterly. He had come into the barn to collect a chainsaw that was on a shelf above my head, and without warning the dog, who knew him well, had gone for him. Bess (a male, despite his name) wasn't a vicious dog; he had been on the farm all his life and had never been known to attack before. The man was highly indignant, but my grandfather, a wise and wonderful old man, not given to hysteria, soon managed to calm the situation. He not only worked on the land but had lived in the country alongside animals all his life, as his father had before him, and he knew at once what had happened. My bond with the farm dogs had become so close that Bess, the eldest and most dominant dog, had come to regard me as one of the pack, and a young member at that. When the farm hand burst into the barn, waking Bess and probably the other dogs too, Bess thought I was in danger and he was protecting me in the only way he knew how; the way that his wild relatives might have protected their young.

My grandfather decided that in the interests of safety it was time to ban my night-time excursions to the barn, but he recognised that the dogs played such an important part in my wellbeing that I should be allowed to have one of my own, which could sleep with me in the cottage.

The dog of a neighbouring farmer had had pups, and not long after this incident my grandfather set off on foot to choose one from the litter. We had no car in those days; my grandparents were simple folk who lived from hand to mouth. A lot of what we ate came from the wild. We would shoot rabbits, hares, pigeons and pheasants, but I was always taught to hunt in moderation, to respect nature and never to take more than we needed or than the population could sustain. Whenever I made a kill, I knew to cut the animal open lengthways, remove the innards and throw them into the hedgerow for other creatures to scavenge. I had no qualms about killing or skinning rabbits and hares and preparing them for the pot. Life and death was all part of the natural world, and on the farm we were very much a part of it.

The farmer with the puppies was a neighbour, but the definition of neighbour in our world was someone who lived within a day's walk, and we set off straight after an early breakfast when it was barely light. It was a cold morning, I could see my breath in the frosty air, and I had on a warm coat and boots and carried in a poacher's bag over my shoulder the cold tea and thick cheese sandwiches that my grandmother had made for us. I was used to long walks – I often used to accompany my grandfather when he went to pay his respects or to do business with neighbouring farmers – and I used to relish time spent alone with him. There were no other children around the farm for me to play with, no television, no video games or any of the other things that keep children amused these days. We were some way outside the village; there was just me and my grandparents, the dogs and the farm animals. Occasionally – or so it seemed to me then – my mother would appear; but it was rare, and my father was never mentioned.

But I was not unhappy. I adored my grandparents and never thought for a moment that I was missing out. My grandfather and I would take the dogs with us on our walks, and we would never get far before he'd be stopping to point out something of interest. It might be an abandoned nest in the hedgerow: he would tell me all about the birds that had inhabited it, and how many young they would have produced, how far their territory would have extended. He would dissect the nest, so I could see the skill with which it had been constructed. He'd spot a broken bird's egg lying on the ground, and would explain how it might have got there, stolen from the nest by a predator maybe; or he'd pick up an owl's pellet deposited on a wooden gatepost, and pull it apart, exposing the tiny fragments of bone, all that remained of the rodents the great raptor had feasted on during the night.

He might make me close my eyes and tell him what I could hear. I had thought it was quiet, but once my eyes were closed there would be a deafening noise, with birds singing and chattering, insects rubbing their legs, small mammals scurrying, even sheep bleating in the distance or a cow coughing three fields away – so many different sounds and songs. Or we'd investigate a rabbit burrow for signs of activity or identify the prints left by deer and other animals on the muddy tracks. He made every outing an adventure, made every discovery exciting. I loved listening to him talk, hearing him explain, in his rich Norfolk accent, which birds preferred which berries, or why foxes killed more than they could eat or carry away; and sometimes, if I asked, he would talk about himself and about his childhood and how different life had been when he was my age, when there were no modern conveniences like refrigerators, tractors, or electricity; when they'd harvested with scythes and milked the cows by hand.

When we'd reach our destination, he would never take me inside with him. He would leave me to wait with the dogs a little way off while he went to see whomever he had come to visit. Sometimes he would be gone for several hours while he and his friend shared a bottle or two of stout, but I had been taught to wait patiently. It would never have crossed my mind to complain; I adored this man and I never questioned his authority, enjoying nothing more than his approval. Besides, I knew that no matter how long he was gone, he would always come back. He would suddenly appear, saying, 'Come on then, boy,' and I'd slip my hand into his great rough paw. We'd retrace our steps and find new things to look at and talk about on our way home.

It was just such a trip that we made to choose my puppy. My grandfather and the farmer greeted one another warmly, like long-lost friends, and disappeared into a barn together, where mother and pups were kennelled, leaving me alone in the farmyard. 'Wait there, boy,'

4

he said. 'I won't be long.' And so without question, despite the excitement and my impatience to see the litter, I found myself a comfortable spot and sat down to wait.

After a while I heard the barn door creak as a gust of wind took it and suddenly a large dog escaped through the open gap and came charging towards me, barking ferociously, ears flat against its head. I knew enough to know that this was not a friendly greeting. I sat still, kept my hands by my side and waited; it didn't occur to me to be frightened. Bess and the farm dogs had often charged at me and, however aggressive they sounded in a pack, I always held my ground, and once they had sniffed me they were never anything but friendly. This dog's hackles were raised, her tail was erect and she was growling as she reached me, her teeth bared. I didn't move. I let her sniff my legs, feet, hands and head. Soon the growling stopped and I turned my hands over to expose the palms, which smelt of the cheese sandwich I'd eaten during our walk. She licked them and looked up at my face with soft eyes. I started to scratch the long fur under her chin, which she obviously enjoyed because she sat down and leaned her body into mine, allowing me to rub the rest of her silky body.

The barn door creaked again and, as my grandfather and the farmer emerged, the dog by my side growled deeply, gave a sharp bark and charged the two men. I guessed she was the mother of the pups, and from the panic that ensued, I gathered she did not welcome visitors. The farmer shouted angrily at her, 'Get in that barn, now!' The dog lowered her body and slunk back towards me. 'Keep still, boy,' warned the farmer. 'Don't move and she won't hurt you.' But as he ran over towards me, yelling at the dog to get back to the barn, it was clear he didn't trust the animal an inch. By the time he reached me, the dog had tucked her frightened, shaking body into mine and, ignoring his command to stay still, I had started scratching her again while speaking softly to her.

'Well bless my soul. Come and have a look at this,' said the farmer, cap in his hand as he scratched his head in disbelief. 'I've never seen anything like it. No one has ever been able to get near that bitch. The only reason I keep her is because she's so good with the sheep, but she's always been a real liability with strangers.'

'Ma always said the boy has some sort of gift with dogs,' said my grandfather, still keeping a safe distance. 'She'll swear he knows what they say.'

Not trusting the dog to remain calm, the farmer shut her up while we went into the barn for me to choose one of the puppies. They were fenced in behind straw bales; five in all – four girls and a boy – curled up in one big bundle of black, brown and white fur. They were Lurcher-Collie cross, so would be good hunters. I knew I wanted a female; my grandfather had taught me that bitches were far better than dogs at providing for their family, and I wanted this dog to earn her keep.

The farmer had a rabbit's foot tied on the end of a length of baling twine which he dangled in front of the bundle, while squeaking as an alarmed rabbit might. Immediately the sleeping pups' ears went up and they looked around. When they spotted the foot dangling within their reach, they sprang to life and, sure enough, it was the bitches that were there first, two of them ahead of the others. It was one of those two that I chose to take. I picked her up and held her in my arms, and as my grandfather handed over a couple of large bottles of light ale in payment, I just heard, over the puppy's frantic licking, the farmer say, 'The boy's right, y'know. She's the one I'd've picked.'

'Away y'go, boy,' said the farmer with a cheery smile. 'Take care of her.'

'Don't worry, sir,' I said, grinning from ear to ear, the puppy warm and wriggly in my arms. 'I'll take care of her.'

I named her Whiskey, and in the next thirteen years she scarcely left my side.

Chapter Two

A CHILDHOOD IN RURAL NORFOLK

The English countryside is not an obvious place for a child to develop a passion for wolves, and it wasn't immediate, but animals have been in my life for as long as I can remember.

I grew up on the land and I was fascinated by the natural world. There was no money for outings, treats or toys when I was a child; the hedgerows, fields and forests were my playground, and the dogs were my companions. I roamed for hours; I explored the thickets for birds' nests, I knew when rabbits had young, I watched hares boxing in the springtime, I knew where to look for foxes' dens and badger setts. I could recognise owls in flight and knew the difference between kestrels and sparrow hawks. I would have been lost in a place like London – and to be honest, I still feel uneasy in big cities in my forties – but there was not a lot I didn't know about the world on my doorstep.

My home was north Norfolk, a remote part of a remote county on the most eastern side of England, renowned for its fens, its pheasant shoots and its flat, fertile farmland. Those that own the land are among the richest in the country; those that work it are some of the poorest. My family were the latter. They were farm labourers and we lived from hand to mouth, a very simple life. We caught what we ate and ate what we caught; and my job as the youngest member of the family – when I was too young for gainful employment – was to catch it, with the dogs we had on the farm. They were my friends, but they were working dogs. Apart from Whiskey, they lived outside in the barn, and I was never allowed to be sentimental about them. In our world, every animal had a purpose. We couldn't afford to feed any creature that didn't earn its keep – and Whiskey was a skilful courser (hunting by sight rather than scent) who chased and caught a lot of hares.

Our neighbours lived in the same way. Country folk were caring but not sentimental. I remember going with my grandfather to visit a gamekeeper friend of his when I was about eight. This man had the most beautiful black Labrador. He was his pride and joy. His coat glistened and he had the softest mouth; he could pick up an egg or anything else he was asked to retrieve without leaving so much as a mark on it. He was immaculately trained; he seemed to know this man's every thought. One day the man discovered that his two sons had taken the dog ratting in the barn, and all the work and training that he had so patiently done with the dog was lost in less than a morning. The first time the Labrador went for a rat, the rat bit him on the muzzle and he was so traumatised that he shook from then on. The dog was ruined; so the gamekeeper shot the dog and beat the two boys. He knew that he'd let the dog down, that he'd failed to protect him from his sons, but he couldn't repair the damage and he couldn't afford to keep a dog as a pet. I was horrified; the dog's death seemed so meaningless. But that was the reality of the world in which I grew up.

My grandfather – Gordon Ellis, my mother's father – taught me everything I knew. He was sixty-seven when I was born, but it was he and my grandmother, Rose, who brought me up. Although Shirley, my mother, lived in the cottage with us, it seemed to me as a child that she was never there. As a result, I felt far closer to my grandparents than I ever did to my mother. My grandfather was my hero. He was gentle, wise and wonderful, and if he had asked me to walk over hot coals, I would have done it for him without even asking why. He was a thin, wiry man with a weather-beaten face and hands that were gnarled and leathery from decades of hard, manual work, but inside he was a true gentleman and I revelled in every moment spent by his side. Rose was also a strong character; like my grandfather, she seemed to demand respect without ever needing to say a word. But she was warm and loving and my abiding memory of her is in the kitchen, singing while she baked.

The truth, I discovered when I went back to Norfolk very recently after many years away, is that my mother was simply always out earning our keep. She was up and out of the house in the mornings, often before dawn, to work in the fields, enduring long hard days of backbreaking drudgery for very little money. She would be collected by a gang-master who drove her and the other women of the village to whatever farm had need of labour. Sometimes they might drive for an hour or two to the other side of the county, to harvest peas or potatoes or soft fruit, whatever the season dictated, and be delivered home at the end of the day, exhausted. After a meal she would go straight to bed. If she didn't work, she didn't get paid and we struggled. As a single mother, she had no alternative.

I didn't realise as a child just how unremittingly hard her life was; I didn't appreciate what she did for me – and how I wish I had. All I knew was that she wasn't there and my grandparents were.

My grandparents had had eleven children, six girls and five boys. Most of them had left the village by the time I was born, on 12 October 1964, and I never met them. A few stayed, but apart from one sister, Leenie, who was very close to my mother, I don't remember seeing any of them. I think my arrival, out of wedlock, caused a rift in the family.

The cottage we lived in felt huge to me as a small boy, but in reality it was very modest, with low ceilings that I hit my head on if ever I tried to bounce on my bed. It was a typical tied workman's cottage made of the local red brick, with a couple of outhouses, set back from a narrow lane on the outskirts of the village and looking on to a meadow at the back, with dense forest beyond. At night I would lie in bed with the window wide open and listen to the noises of the night – scarcely any of them man-made. There was no inside sanitation, no hot water and no heating, and the old iron window frames were rusty and ill-fitting. The privy was in the garden, and we bathed once a week in an old copper tub. Sunday nights were bath nights, and the tub would be brought into the living room in front of the fire and filled with water heated in a big copper pan that hung over the coals. We took turns bathing and, being the youngest, I was last.

There were no major roads or motorways and no railway lines within miles. The only thing that sometimes broke the silence was the noise of jets from one of the many airbases in the county screaming overhead. The airbases are still there, but forty years later Norfolk is still one of the least populated counties in England and one of the most inaccessible corners of the country.

In the 1960s, it was like a place that time forgot. While the rest of the country was enjoying post-war prosperity, people in the parish of Great Massingham lived as they had lived centuries ago. There were several farms in the locality, most of them mixed: they had dairy herds, sheep, pigs, and beef cattle as well as cereal crops, vegetables and fruits. The land was broken up at that time into small parcels of land divided by tall, thick hedges and forestry that kept the worst of the Arctic weather at bay – and provided perfect cover for wildlife. And almost all of the farmers laid down pheasant chicks in the spring and ran shoots during the winter months.

Winters were harsh. The cold blew in from the Urals to the east and the Arctic to the north, bringing huge quantities of snow and ice. The hedges stopped most of the snow from drifting, but at times the roads were completely impassable. The landscape would be white for weeks on end, while the ponds in the village turned into skating rinks.

At that time there was very little machinery on the farms, although that changed as I grew older. Tractors had already taken over from the heavy shire horses – but it hadn't been so long ago. The old horses from our farm lived in happy retirement in the meadow at the back of our cottage. There were no combine harvesters, no chemicals. The work was done by hand. Each farmer had his own workers – most of them living in simple cottages, like ours, on the farms – and at harvest time gangs of labourers were driven from farm to farm to weed and pick and bale.

My grandfather worked at Ward's farm, and we lived on the edge of its land. Ward was one of the biggest landowners in the village, and my grandfather had had the cottage for as long as he'd had the job.

There were people living in our village who had never left it. And they had no reason to. The village was self-sufficient. There was a butcher's shop, where my grandparents traded vegetables from the garden for meat, a bakery with delicious fresh bread at any time of the day, a dairy, a shop that sold general provisions, a hairdresser, a primary school, a fire engine, five pubs and a blacksmith, who shod horses and fixed machinery. It was a farming community through and through. It was also the sort of community in which everyone knew everyone else, and knew everything about everyone else.

There were no tourists in those days, no strangers wandering about the village, except when the circus came. Even the gypsies who came at harvest time were the same ones that made the journey year after year. And there was no crime. We all left our houses open – and people would come in without knocking and put the kettle on while they were passing through to say hello. It was a genuine community. The worst that might happen was for someone to have a chicken go missing, in which case they would report it to Phil, the village policeman. He knew everything; he knew exactly where to go to find the culprit, paid a quiet visit, and the next day two chickens would mysteriously be delivered to the aggrieved party.

Shirley, my mother, had given birth to me at the age of twenty-four, knowing that she would have to bring me up on her own. At that time and in that sort of tight-knit community to have a child out of wedlock was not easy, but her parents were apparently very supportive. Sadly, I don't know the story; I don't know whether she was in love with someone who was unattainable for some reason. I don't even know whether my father knows I exist. All I know is that she never had or wanted another partner. So I don't know who my father was. Even now, forty-five years later, my mother won't talk about it.

My guess is that he was a Romany gypsy – not to be confused with the tinkers and travellers who have given gypsies such a bad name over the years. The gypsies we knew were wonderful people, scrupulously clean and honest, with a very strong sense of family and strict codes of morality. They used to travel about the countryside in their traditional, prettily painted caravans, drawn by horses, going wherever there was work. They would pick hops and fruit in Kent and vegetables and soft fruit in Norfolk. Occasionally they would graze their horses on the village green, but they had a permanent site on a piece of common land just outside the village next to an old Roman road called Peddars Way.

Every summer I used to go and play with them. While the farm workers were harvesting we would go out with the dogs and catch rabbits. They had lots of dogs, big Lurchers. One in particular, I remember, was called Scruff; a huge dog, he was crossed with a wolfhound, and he would chase rabbits until he dropped.

A little further up the Way was a caravan set on its own. It belonged to an old gypsy woman who, it was said, bought illnesses. She was very old and wizened, with long grey hair, gold hoop earrings and looked like the old-fashioned gypsies you saw in picture books. People who were ill used to go and see her. I don't know whether she made them better but I don't imagine anyone would have dared say if she hadn't because it was said she would put a curse on anyone who spoke ill of her.

I felt very at home with the gypsies, and although my mother never said anything, I have a strong feeling that she was pleased. I think, in retrospect, she may have been trying to introduce me to my father's family. It was unusual for village children to mix with gypsies. They were never liked by the village people and were made to feel distinctly unwelcome in the shops and pubs. I knew how it felt to be treated like an outcast.

I was a solitary child. I attended the little primary school in Great Massingham until the age of eleven, but I don't remember many friends from that time. I must have had the odd one, I suppose, because I do remember throwing sticks into the horse chestnut tree in the churchyard to get conkers and being told off by the vicar – and I don't imagine I'd have been doing that alone. But with no father, I think I may have been viewed as a bit of an outcast myself. Maybe I felt I didn't need friends; I had Whiskey and the farm dogs and they were much easier than my peers. Dogs don't pick fights or bully or make unkind remarks.

I was drawn to all sorts of animals; not just dogs. I remember my mother coming home from work one summer's evening. She had been pulling carrots or some other vegetable out of the ground all day and was exhausted. 'There's a job waiting for you inside,' said my grandfather. 'Shaun's been busy again.' She opened the door and recoiled in horror. Frogs were hopping, croaking and climbing over every surface in the room. I had spent my afternoon collecting them from the pond up the road, steadfastly walking back and forth with a bucket, and the room was alive with frogs. And I spent that evening going back and forth with the bucket once again, putting them all back.

Another time she went into the coal shed, when night had fallen, to get some fuel for the fire and screamed as five black chickens started flapping and squawking. I had found them on my travels across the fields – and the very next morning I was dispatched to take them back again.

And then there was the time I brought a Muscovy duck home, complete with its nest filled with eggs. My mother was too scared to touch the duck – an ugly brute, she called it – so I carried the duck under my arm, while she carried the nest and the eggs back to the pond where we reinstated the whole lot among the reeds. My poor mother; I was always giving her heart failure, coming home with some creature that I'd find a home for somewhere about the house.

I didn't have much time for friends. While other children hung around together after school, I always had to hurry home to chop wood for the fires, get in coal or feed the animals, and I was often taken out of school for several weeks at a time to help with the harvest or whatever work needed to be done either on Ward's or one of the neighbouring farms. The school never seemed to mind my absence – I was never going to be top of the class, and I wasn't the only child at the school who was taken out to work on the land at busy times. The teachers seemed to focus on those children who obviously had an academic future and didn't pay too much attention to the rest of us. And so I worked hard at the subjects I enjoyed, which apart from art were animal related – biology and science – and sport. That was something I really could do and I was in all the teams for football and rugby and cricket. I loved anything played with a ball or anything athletic, although if there was work to do on the farm, sport, like school, came second to pulling my weight at home.

I also loved fishing. There were three big ponds in the village which the local children used to fish. One of them dried out one summer and we rescued the fish in buckets and ran to put them into the other ponds before they died. North Norfolk has dozens of little ponds, or 'pits' as they were called, often in the middle of fields, with tall trees surrounding them. It was a curious feature of the landscape in that part of the county. There were all sorts of theories about how they came to be there. Some people said they were craters caused by German bombs jettisoned during the Second World War; others said they were left over from some sort of mineral excavation. Whatever caused them, they were full of fish, mostly carp, roach, pike and bream, and provided hours of entertainment for children like me.

Sometimes we would fish further afield. One pit we were particularly fond of was in a field by the side of the road about four miles from Great Massingham. It was full of gold-coloured fish, but every time we got ourselves set up, the farmer would come running out of the farmyard across the field, shouting angrily and waving a stick at us, and we would leap on to our bicycles and race away.

I had a green Chopper which was just the coolest bike at that time. I think my grandfather must have found it on some rubbish tip. It looked as though it had been run over by a steam-roller and was all rusty, but he restored it for me, painted it and found a new seat for it. It became my prize possession.

My bike made trips to the doctor's surgery easier. This was the only facility missing from the village. It was a two-and-a-half-mile walk away in the village of Harpley, where Dr Bowden had his practice. It was a route I knew well. I was seldom ill but I was accident prone and often needed to be stitched up after bad falls or being bashed during football and rugby games.

I didn't care for doctors much, but dentists I loathed with a passion. I have only ever been to a dentist once in my life, for a check-up at a practice in Fakenham, a town about twelve miles away. I would have been about eleven. The dentist said I needed a back tooth removed and, although he gave me a local anaesthetic, I have never felt pain like it. He had his knee in my chest as he wrestled to pull this tooth out. It was the most horrific experience. I couldn't bear it. It hated the smell, I hated the noise, I hated the injection and I couldn't stand the pain. I vowed I would never go near a dentist again, and I haven't. On the positive side, it did make me clean my teeth properly, and the only teeth I've lost since then have been knocked out by over-boisterous wolves.

Hospitals have been less easy to avoid. I fell through a roof in my late teens and broke my wrist, and I went through a car windscreen soon after I learnt to drive; but my first visit was aged nine. I lost my grip on the school climbing frame and fell on to the hard ground beneath, shattering my elbow. I was rushed to hospital in King's Lynn, where I languished in the children's ward with my arm suspended above my head for three weeks. There was a boy in the next-door bed who had slipped and fallen under the wheels of a double-decker bus.

I have no memory of my mother visiting, but she tells me that she gave up work for those three weeks and early every morning took the bus into King's Lynn, which was fifteen miles away, to sit by my bedside until early evening when she took the bus home again.

One day the sister in charge of the ward came up to her and said, 'You've been coming here every day for nearly three weeks and I have never seen you have anything to eat. Today you are going to have some lunch. I have organised it with the kitchen.' The sister had rightly surmised that having been off work all this time, with no wage coming in, my mother couldn't afford to pay for lunch.

At home my grandmother was the cook, and although we ate simply and mostly off the land, we ate well. Sundays were her baking days, when wonderful smells would waft into the yard. In preparation she would buy eggs to supplement those our chickens laid. One Sunday she couldn't find the eggs she had bought and, after looking all over, she had to abandon her cooking. That evening my grandfather came into the house and said, 'I've found your eggs, Ma. They're under the chicken at the top of the garden.' I had taken them and put them under a broody hen to see if she would hatch them.

My grandmother always sang when she baked, and I can still picture her wearing a blue floral dress. There was always a big stew or a casserole on the stove, made with vegetables that my grandfather grew in the garden and game of one sort of another that we had shot or coursed on the land. I learnt to shoot at a very early age, and could always use a knife. I was never squeamish about killing and could skin and gut.

By the age of eight or nine my job was to bring home our meals. My grandmother would make me those coarsely cut cheese sandwiches and some cold tea – we never had hot drinks for some reason – and send me out with a penknife, a piece of string, a 10p piece (although what that was for I have no idea) and tell me I was equipped to conquer the world. And off I would go with the dogs and not come back until I had plenty for everyone to eat.

I didn't kill indiscriminately. My grandfather had taught me which animals to take and which ones to leave. I knew to leave female rabbits that were nursing their young. He could spot 'milky does' as he called them from fifty yards, by their lack of condition and the absence of fur on their underbellies. He knew they had young underground that would die if their mother was killed.

Instead I learnt to go for the young bucks, which would otherwise overpopulate the area.

His whole philosophy was about sustainability and about maintaining a balance in nature. Younger farmers wanted to kill off the rabbits because they were so destructive to the crops, but he wanted to protect them, knowing that if you drastically reduced one species another would take over. He would say that problems only arose when human beings interfered. I learnt so much from my grandfather.

Chapter Three

A WOLF AT THE WINDOW

Ιn bed at night, when I was small and the lights were out, I was convinced I could see a wolf outside my bedroom window. I suppose it must have been the way the branches of a tree fell. As an adult, of course, the idea of a wolf being tall enough to look in through a first-floor window is patently ridiculous, but as a young child I was convinced. And I was terrified. Every night I hid my head under the coarse, black blanket that covered me, to escape, but then I couldn't resist peeping to see if it had gone and scaring myself all over again. It was just the wolf's head, ears erect, looking to its left; but by morning, in the daylight, there was no sign of it.

I knew a lot about the wild animals around my home when I was a small – probably much more than most children of my age – but I knew nothing about those in the wider world. I didn't see wildlife programmes, because we had no television; and I didn't visit a zoo until I was in my late teens because there was no money for that kind of thing. So the only knowledge I had of big and dangerous wild animals was from books and fairy stories. And all I knew about wolves was that they were sly, sinister, fierce and deadly, and the images of the stories my grandmother told me preyed on my imagination. It was a long, long time before I confronted my fear and wolves became my reason for living.

Foxes, on the other hand, were familiar, and although they too had a sinister reputation, I was not scared of them. One night I was startled from sleep by the noise of the old shire horses thundering back and forth across the meadow behind the cottage. There was a full moon, as bright as I'd seen. It was almost like daylight outside, so I pulled on some clothes, told Whiskey to stay under my bed, and crept out of the house. I quietly made my way down towards the edge of the forest to see what was agitating the horses.

What I saw was pure magic. By the time I reached them, the horses had begun to settle, and playing among their giant hooves was the most beautiful vixen with four young kits. They were so busy leaping on each other and tearing round that they seemed quite unaware of my presence, so I sat down a short distance away and watched their game unfold.

It was the most exciting sight. I had never watched a fox at close quarters before. All I had seen were glimpses of reddish brown from afar or a tail, with its distinctive white tip, disappearing into the hedge as the animal ran for safety when I was out with the dogs. Out there in the dark, sitting not more than thirty feet away from them, in their environment not mine, I felt as though I was witnessing another world.

Eventually I dragged myself away and went home to bed. I told no one what I'd seen, but the next night I went back and there they were again. I can only assume their den was just inside the forest and this was their playground. Once again I sat a short distance away and watched, and once again they ignored me, but allowed me to be there. This went on for several months as the kits grew bigger and stronger, preparing to take their part in the world.

Every night I went out for my secret rendezvous – it was intoxicating to find myself welcome among creatures that were instinctively so afraid of man. In time, they were playing in a small semi-circle in front of where I sat. They showed no hint of nervousness; nor did they seem to pay me any attention. Then one night there was a rustling behind me and one of the boldest of the four kits had started to play in the bush behind where I sat. He burst out into the open and raced round me and playfully ambushed one of his siblings. I was no longer an observer; I had become part of their game.

I learnt so much about foxes in that time. I watched the vixen bring food for the kits. It's widely believed that foxes kill for fun, that they go into a hen house and kill far more than they can eat, but it's a myth. What tends to happen is that because of the commotion the fox is caught in the act and frightened away. If left undetected the fox will take one hen from the coop, which is all they can carry at a time, and then go back again and again until they have collected everything they killed. They will eat as much as their family needs that day and bury the remainder in the ground, where it keeps. Nothing is wasted. I know because I saw what they did and saw how well this mother looked after her young and taught them how to take care of themselves.

Six months later I saw a sight that filled me with grief and horror. Walking in the woods with the dogs I came across the limp and lifeless body of this boldest fox kit swinging from a tree. It was held by the leg in a crude trap, having died a painful and lingering death. The fact that this creature that I had come to know so well over the months – one so majestic, so beautiful, so full of energy – could have had its life ended in such a horrible way made me feel sick and angry. I hated whoever who had done it and felt more drawn to the foxes than ever.

Native American Indians would say that that was the moment when my fate was sealed. They say that you sign nature's unwritten contract to work with animals at a very young age, as a result of some experience, either good or bad, that happens in early childhood. Looking back, there is no doubt that the shock of seeing that magnificent young fox – my friend – hanging from that tree left me with a feeling of revulsion for my own kind and a desire to distance myself from the human race.

My concern for foxes put me at odds with the rest of the community. The farmers hated them because a hungry fox will take a new-born lamb, and the gamekeepers hated them because they took pheasants. So the local hunt was given a free rein to go wherever the scent took them, and it was a popular sport. The results were sickening.

Many were the times I came across a den where the vixen had gone to ground and the huntsmen had dug her out and gassed and killed the kits. The deadly smell of poison would still be lingering in the air. Sometimes it was a family I had watched for weeks, seeing the kits grow stronger and more adventurous. All of them gone, wiped out, given no chance of escape – all because of a reputation that the fox didn't deserve and a few people's desire for sport.

My grandmother used to tell a story about how she had been spring-cleaning the cottage one day with both front and back door open, and a fox ran through the yard and straight in one door, through the house and out of the other. Moments later the entire pack of thirty-odd foxhounds followed. They were like a tidal wave sweeping through, jumping up and over tables and chairs as they followed the scent, and they wrecked the place. She had all her best china out of the cupboard and the whole lot was smashed. Shortly afterwards the huntsmen came past on their horses, all dressed up in their pink coats, and when she asked what they were going to do about it, they simply doffed their hats and galloped off.

No one would listen to me when I tried to protest that hunting was cruel. As a young boy it was hard to argue with my elders without being disrespectful, but it seemed to me that if you didn't want foxes to get into your hen house, then you needed to build an enclosure that was fox-proof. It seemed totally unjust to set foxhounds to kill foxes because human beings were too lazy to take proper care of their chickens. Whenever I tried to speak to anyone about it I was told to mind my manners. After all, what did I know? I was just a child.

I very quickly grew to be evasive. I went out with the dogs and, so long as I came home with a couple of rabbits or pigeons, I could be gone from very early morning until after dark and no one asked any questions. I spent my days studying foxes, sitting for hours and hours watching and waiting; and all the wonderful things I saw and experienced and learnt about foxes and their world, I kept to myself. I knew it was dangerous to share it. I felt sure that if I told anyone where I had been watching families at play, it wouldn't have been long before someone went to the den and killed every creature inside it. I retreated ever more inside myself and without knowing it, I became what the American Indians call 'a Keeper of the Wild'.

It was the beginning of a bad time for me. My world that seemed so safe and secure, so happy and so loving, began to fall apart in the most terrifying way. I went off to school one day, and what had started out as a perfectly ordinary day turned into a nightmare. I came home to find the house in turmoil. My grandfather had had a massive stroke which left him paralysed down one side. The doctor had been called and my grandmother was distraught. I had not prepared myself in any way; it had never crossed my mind that he might ever be anything other than fit and strong, teaching me about the lore of the countryside and making the decisions in the family. I couldn't imagine him any other way and didn't want him any other way. But suddenly he was; suddenly he looked old and frail and could no longer do all the things we used to do together. His mind seemed to have gone. Sometimes he remembered who I was; sometimes he seemed to have forgotten. And where once I had depended on him, he now depended upon others.

It wasn't long before he had a second, even bigger stroke and died where he lay on the settee at home. My grandmother covered him with a jacket and sat with him, refusing to move, until the undertakers came to take him away. They must have been married for more than sixty years and had been so close and loved each other so dearly I think it broke her heart. They'd gone everywhere together, done everything together, and I had never once heard them argue or say a cross word to each other. If my grandmother went down to the shops he would always come to meet her, either on foot or by bike, and they'd walk home together.

What I remember most clearly is the two of them laughing. On washday she would always take the wet sheets up the garden to squeeze them in the mangle. She would put them in and my grandfather would turn the handle. One day, when I was watching from the house, he must have said something to her that made her laugh – I don't know what, but she laughed so much she couldn't get the sheets into the rollers.

I was just thirteen when he died. He was eighty and had lived and worked in Great Massingham all his life. He had been a popular man and St Mary's Church, where the funeral was held, was packed, but among the familiar faces were a family of strangers sitting at the back. When the service was over, they came up to my grandmother and the man explained why they had come.

Many, many years earlier, he said, he and his sister, as children, had been starving hungry and my grandfather had taken a loaf of bread for each of them from the back of the baker's cart and told them to stuff it inside their jackets. The man no longer lived in the area but said he had never forgotten the kindness and had wanted to come and pay his last respects. My grandfather was buried in the churchyard under the shade of the horse-chestnut tree where I used to collect conkers.

His death changed everything. We had to leave the cottage, because it was tied to my grandfather's job; and, for some reason that was never explained to me, we split up as a family. My grandmother, who I looked upon as a mother, went to live on her own in a council house in Jubilee Terrace, nearer the centre of the village, where she was near her eldest son and his family, and my real mother and I went to a tiny new council-owned bungalow at the end of a cul-de-sac in Summerwood Estate. I was angry and I was grief-stricken. I felt as though I had lost everything. My mother had never been the one who cared for me or cooked for me, or the one who spent time with me, who'd taken me for walks or who'd taught me what I needed to get through life. It had been my grandparents who had done all that, and they were both gone. I didn't want to be with my mother and I blamed my grandfather for dying and leaving me when I needed him most. I was terrified; I didn't know how I was going to cope without him.

I felt the loss of my grandmother just as keenly and I was convinced until just last year that my grandmother had died of a broken heart within months of my grandfather, but it turns out I was wrong. Incredible as it might seem, I discovered just recently, when I went back at the age of forty-four and looked at the headstone on my grandfather's grave, that my grandmother had not died soon after him at all. She had lived for another thirteen years after his death yet I have no memory of seeing her again after we moved. All I remember was feeling bereft and abandoned and the need to get away from anything that reminded me of what I'd lost. Could I really not have been to visit her? The houses were only a mile or two apart. And did she never come to visit us? Or have I just blotted out those years when I was so lost and unhappy? I can't explain it any more than I can explain why the three of us didn't all move to the same house after my grandfather died. I was so engulfed by my own misery I couldn't think about anyone but myself. My poor grandmother must have felt she'd had a double bereavement

Those years must also have been very difficult for my mother. I took out my anger and my grief on her. I was at secondary school in Litcham by then, which was about seven miles from Great Massingham, and she was out at work every day, as usual, working long hours. I became very independent and shut her out of my life. I travelled back and forth on the school bus, which was a big blue double-decker run by Carter's of Litcham. It was the oldest bus in the company's fleet and the only double-decker. The kids from all the other villages came on single-deckers, and whenever there was snow, which could be five feet deep or more, there was just one bus that managed to struggle through – bypassing stranded cars and lorries along the way. To our annoyance, it was ours.

I seldom saw my mother. When I came home from school and at weekends, if there was work going, I went harvesting, baling, driving tractors, plucking turkeys, castrating pigs, helping cows give birth – anything and everything. And if there was no work I would go off with Whiskey, my dog. Sometimes I would go off for days, sleeping in barns – not thinking about how worried my mother might be. I became a bit of a recluse, a bit feral, wandering in the woods, being at one with the wildlife in a different world: a world where, increasingly, I felt I belonged – and the only place where I was able to cry.

Chapter Four

A MISSPENT
YOUTH

Apart from playing in the school sports teams, which I loved, my time at Litcham Secondary School was undistinguished. I had friends, but my best friend, Paul Battson, died of an asthma attack. I remember the headmaster calling the whole class together one morning and breaking the news. I felt at that moment as though I was destined to lose everything.

I was a regular visitor to the headmaster's office, so it was unsurprising that I left school with no qualifications as soon as I legally could, when I was barely sixteen. I needed to get out and earn a living, and I wanted to get away from home. I was still angry and hurting and wanting to forget. That was probably why, rather than looking for jobs on the land, where I'd been so happy with my grandfather, I ended up joining a roofing company called Western and Bolton Roofing. It was hard work, carrying tiles and running up and down ladders all day, but it made me strong and fit and it took me to building sites all over the county. Sometimes we would be on a job for weeks if not months and I'd stay in bed and breakfast accommodation or in hostels, only going back at weekends. Even then I wouldn't necessarily go home but often stayed with friends. I gave no thought to my mother's feelings. It must have been very hurtful for her.

It was through work that I began to make my first friends and develop a social life, which largely revolved around pubs. There were a lot of good pubs in the area and once every three months, on a Saturday night, there was a disco in the little Community Centre in Fakenham. It was *the* place to go. All the top DJs in Norfolk played there and people came from miles around to hear them. There was great music, drink, pretty girls that we'd take outside and kiss against the wall, and plenty of fights – all the good things in life. Then we'd make our way haphazardly home.

I remember one night the fog was so thick you could scarcely see your hand in front of your face, but one of my mates said he knew the road so well, he could do it blindfold. We all followed him on our little 150cc motorbikes – I was on the back of one, as I usually was – and he missed a bend. He drove straight into a deep ditch and we all followed him in there one after another, no one noticing until we were up to our axles in water.

Fakenham was the fashion capital of Norfolk. On disco days, we would go into town in the morning and buy all the gear we needed, have a few pints, go home, play football for a couple of hours, change into the new clothes, go back to Fakenham, have some fish and chips in the early evening, then move on to the Crown for some beers, then to the Rampant Horse, which was as rough as hell – any time you wanted a fight, you'd go there – before hitting the disco later.

One of my best friends was a tiler called Benny Elson who lived in Weasenham, a neighbouring village, and through him I met my first girlfriend, Michelle Pearce. Benny was older than me, like most of the guys I worked with, and Michelle was his wife Jac's niece. She lived in Weasenham too and one day when Benny and I were getting ready to go out she was visiting their house and asked who I was.

I started frequenting the Fox and Hounds in Weasenham, and Michelle would come in after school and hide behind the bar, whereupon Skiffy the landlord would signal to me and we'd go off into the woods together and sit and talk for hours. We wrote each other little notes and I used to walk her dogs for her. She said all the things I needed to hear; life didn't get much better. Her father was the one of the Queen's pigeon keepers – I built him a pigeon loft in their garden – and I remember arriving at their house one day to collect Michelle and finding everyone in a state of great excitement because the Queen had just been to visit.

I fell madly in love with her, but she was too pretty for me, and in the end she left me for someone else and broke my heart. We were both very young, but there was definitely something there and I often wonder how things might have been if I'd pushed a little harder or been less of an awkward prat.

Skiffy's real name was Freddy Scarf and he was a character. He didn't turn a hair when I celebrated my eighteenth birthday in the pub, after years of illegal under-age drinking there, but then he had been regularly paying me in beer for the game on his menu – game which I and a couple of mates had brought in through the back door in sacks! I had been taught to poach by Pete, someone I knew from working on the land. He was married with a family, but I never really knew much about him except that he was an expert on pheasants and how to get them illegally, which he had learnt from his grandfather.

Pete had a brother and the three of us used to go out with an old 4-10 double-barrelled shotgun. It was a genuine poacher's gun – it came to pieces, for easy concealment – which had been handed down in his family from one generation to another. It went off with a terrible crack and smoked like mad, so the safest night of the year was November the fifth, bonfire night, when everyone was letting off fireworks.

Pete tried to make a silencer for the gun but the first prototype, made out of copper pipe and baffling, made it too heavy to lift. The modified version was much more successful until one day Pete was shooting a bird directly above him. The silencer must have become misaligned as we climbed through a hedge and ended up right in the line of fire. So when Pete pulled the trigger flames shot out of the barrel, and the burning silencer sailed into the air and came straight down on his forehead, almost knocking him out.

It was dangerous business, and not just because of flying silencers. If we had been caught we could have gone to prison – and we came close time and time again. One night I felt a massive hand in the small of my back push me down into the hedge. I knew better than to yell. Pete and his brother were lying flat on the ground beside me, face down, and I lay there not moving a muscle for several minutes. There was not a sound to be heard; then I saw the outline of two pairs of water boots walk past on the track less than five feet from my face – gamekeepers patrolling their patch. My heart was pounding; I was convinced they'd hear it. It must have been four or five minutes before we dared move again. I asked how on earth they had known the gamekeepers were coming. They knew all the tricks; Pete's brother had smelt the men's cigarette smoke.

We always tried to avoid the areas where the birds were released, because that was where the gamekeepers expected you; they put down traps and they patrolled. And Pete taught me never to shoot a white pheasant, although they were obviously easier to see in the dark. Gamekeepers bred them specially, he said, because they were easy to count and if one was missing they'd know a poacher was in the area and would intensify their patrols.

So we walked for miles across fields, heading for pits, then we'd crawl through the undergrowth to the bottom, which was usually filled with water, and lie there out of sight. You could look up through the trees above you, where roosting pheasants were perfectly silhouetted against the sky and shoot them straight off the branches. As the youngest, it was my job to pick them up from wherever they fell, which was usually in the water, and put them into the bag. Pete did the shooting and his brother held the torch and did the spotting.

I was enjoying my new life. It was good to be one of the lads and I liked getting dressed up to go out and having a good time – they used to say I looked like George Michael in my white jeans – but I never lost the need to go off on my own with the dog and roam the countryside, watching foxes, spotting birds, looking for signs of other wildlife. There was always a part of me that remained separate from my mates. Life was good, but there was something missing.

One day I took the bus and went to visit the local zoo, just outside Thetford. I saw animals I had never seen before. I felt as excited as a child, and then I came to the wolf enclosure and there, standing less than ten feet away, were the creatures that had filled me with such terror night after night.

There was one in particular, a beautiful creamy-coloured male, with lovely golden-yellow eyes which immediately locked on to mine. We stared at each other, and in those few seconds I felt that he touched my soul. I felt as though this magnificent creature understood everything about me, knew my secrets, could read my deepest thoughts and fears, and could see all the hurt and pain. I felt he had the power to heal those wounds and make me whole again. It was an extraordinary connection, and I knew that what I was looking for in life was right there in front of me.

He probably looked at every member of the public in that way in the hope that they might throw him a piece of food, but I don't imagine that everyone would have felt what I felt, or seen what I saw. Maybe it was all those years spent with dogs and with foxes, living with one foot in their world, always being slightly at odds with the human world. Or maybe it was something deeper. Whatever it was, it was the beginning of a lifelong contract. I knew that everything I had been told about this creature was a lie, and that he and I had a lot in common and were both living out of our time.

I felt I needed to get back to the land, so I gave up the roofing business and applied for a part-time job as a gamekeeper's assistant on an estate that ran a big commercial shoot. It was good to be back among the hedgerows, but the work flew in the face of everything my grandfather had taught me. He had ingrained in me the principle that you kill to eat, you don't kill for fun. On this estate, so many birds were reared that you could scarcely put your foot on the ground without treading on a chick; and when it came to the shoots, there was no skill involved – it was slaughter. It was harder *not* to hit a bird than to hit one. They didn't even want to fly; you practically had to throw them in the air to get them to go anywhere.

I stuck it out for about sixteen months, but when I heard on the grapevine that Morton's farm estate, a much smaller enterprise, was looking for an assistant gamekeeper, I went there. It was one of the farms in the village, where I'd worked many times over the years, and the job came with a little one-room cottage, which was perfect. Monty, the head gamekeeper, was a craftsman of the old school, and I knew I would learn a lot from him. He trained me up and was very good to me; he also put a lot of trust in me, which to my shame I abused. But I was in the wrong job.

He wanted me to kill the foxes to stop them taking the young birds. Instead, I killed pheasants and the rabbits and fed them to the foxes. There was a particular vixen I had watched over several months as she built a den on a tree line and raised a litter there. I then watched her move the entire litter to another den she built on another tree line in a different field, across a road about five hundred yards away. For some reason she must have decided they were no longer safe at the first site, and so carried them one by one, holding them by the scruff of the neck in her mouth, across the fields under cover of darkness.

It was four months before I was caught. Monty had noticed that the number of pheasants had dropped and one day he found the evidence and confronted me. He had found the remains around the den site and the birds had buckshot in them. There was an awkward scene and I knew I had let him down badly. He was disappointed rather than angry which made it even worse. When I told the story to Pete, my poacher friend, he said, 'You can't run with the fox and hunt with the hounds.' He was right; and the episode did nothing to improve my popularity with the locals. To them, foxes were vermin, and I was despised for my views.

I was out of a job and a house, but I was in love – or, at least, so I thought. I had met a very pretty local girl called Sue and after a few months together we married in the church at Great Massingham. I very quickly found work in the building trade again and we rented a little cottage in the village. Sue was great and I was very fond of her, but looking back I don't think it was a passionate love affair for either of us. At the time all our friends seemed to be getting married and having babies, and it felt like the right thing to do, but in retrospect it was a mistake; we were too young. The one good thing about it all was that we did have a beautiful little girl together, called Gemma.

During that time I started studying foxes in earnest. I knew I wanted to work with animals, not bricks and tiles, but I couldn't see how I was going to do it, and the labouring jobs paid the rent. So I read books and went into the forest at night and out at weekends.

One evening there was a knock at the door and I discovered that not everyone in the village was against me. A woman stood there with a young fox kit hidden under her coat that she presented to me. The kit can't have been more than two weeks old and she had found him starving, cold and close to death. His mother had presumably been killed. I told her I would keep him until he was old enough to fend for himself and then release him into the wild.

I named him Barney and made a little den for him in the barn out of a large drainage pipe lined with straw and set about teaching him what I'd observed vixens teaching their young. I taught him to fend for himself and to avoid dogs, cars and more importantly people. When he was old enough for solid food, I fed him on rats, mice and rabbits, and showed him how these animals moved, how to catch each of them and some of the dangers he would face having to make a kill. I skinned and minced the kill, trying to make it like the meat his mother would have regurgitated, and gradually introduced him to fur and whole animals. I then showed him how to defend his food – I opened my mouth wide and made a fast cacking sound, which is what I had seen wild foxes do. He picked it up quickly and was soon defending his food from me. I played with him as I had seen so many kits do with each other – chasing him, rolling him over and having mock fights.

Eventually I decided he was ready to be released, but first I took him into the woods in a portable crate and spent several nights out there with him so he could listen to the sounds and get his bearings before I left him to fend for himself. When the moment came to release him, I had no idea whether my training would be of any use to him. He made a dash for the trees, turned for an instant to look back at me, and was gone.

Imagine my joy when I spotted him again many times in the next few years and knew that all those hours I'd spent as a child sitting, listening, watching and learning had saved this young creature's life.

Chapter Five

FOR QUEEN
AND COUNTRY

Looking back, it seems that everything about my early life was preparing me for my future with wolves, though at the time there didn't seem to be the slightest connection. Not long afterwards, I was in King's Lynn with three mates. One of them needed some money in a hurry, so we were in a back street stealing car radios – not something I am hugely proud of – when someone spotted a couple of policemen heading our way. We ran off into the High Street with two policemen in pursuit, desperately looking for a busy shop to disappear into. It must have been early-closing day because nothing was open except for the Army Recruitment Office, which had a welcoming light inside. We dived in, breathless and panting, and announced that we had come to sign up. I don't imagine they had seen so many people all week; they welcomed us with open arms and ushered us swiftly into a back room to see a video about life in the army. Perfect.

We were all impressed by what we saw, and it became my life for the next seven years. We signed up that afternoon, but in the end I was the only one who went the whole way. I had never considered joining the army – and had I not been dodging the police, probably never would have done – but the more I learnt about it the more it seemed the perfect career for me.

It hadn't taken long for Sue and me to realise that our relationship was going nowhere and the chance that the army presented me to escape into a new world was overwhelming. I was not built for domesticity; I was too wild, too angry, too disconnected. I was twenty-two and I wanted to get away from Norfolk; I loved my daughter but, apart from her, I didn't feel there was anything left for me there. I liked the outdoor life, I enjoyed physical exertion, I had been used to discipline from an early age and I was good at taking orders without question. These were all qualities I had learnt from my grandfather and were all essential components of a successful soldier. In one of the interviews I was asked why I wanted to join the army and told them about the stereos. I think they probably thought I was joking.

I was sent for about eight weeks' basic training at the Woolwich Arsenal, where two of the three trainers were from 29 Commando Regiment of the Royal Artillery. The one in charge was a man called John Morgan who had been through the Special Forces selection but had been injured on the last lap. He was a strong man, fair and balanced, never ruffled, able to deal with whatever life threw at him, but he was also someone you didn't mess with. If I had to name the role models in my life, and the men I've looked up to – heroes in the mould of my grandfather – he would be one of them.

His colleagues were 'Lugsy' Williams – so called because of his big ears – and a very short man called Corbet, known as 'Ronnie', after the comedian. He was a human dynamo. The man never stopped – I'm sure he did cartwheels and press-ups in his sleep. They used to take it in turns to take us out on what we called 'Bergen runs' of four, five or six miles, wearing boots and all the gear, carrying anything up to sixty pounds in a backpack. These were in addition to the normal training, designed to get our fitness up. It was crippling and I used to pray for John Morgan's turn because he was as slow and steady as I was. The others ran us all into the ground.

I did sufficiently well in my written tests to be given a choice of which service I joined, and having seen photographs of people abseiling out of helicopters and walking through snow and skiing, and having spoken to John Morgan and Lugsy Williams, I opted for 29 Commando Regiment of the Royal Artillery. It was based at that time at HMS Drake, naval barracks on the south coast about three miles south of Plymouth. The regiment's usual home was in the Royal Citadel, a beautiful seventeenth-century building in the centre of Plymouth. With its daunting seventy-foot walls, it was designed to fend off an invasion by the Dutch and had been one of England's most important defences for the following hundred years. When I arrived in 1986 the building was being renovated, and all 29 personnel had moved to this more modern facility (built in the 1880s) down the road.

29 Commando was a Close Support Artillery Regiment – part of the heavy weapons division – that supported 3 Commando Brigade Royal Marines. In laymen's terms, when the Marines took the beaches, we were there to draw fire; but it felt as though we lived in no-man's-land, between two worlds. We weren't quite the navy and we weren't quite the army, and neither seemed particularly fond of us. We went anywhere and everywhere the Marines went, and since 3 Commando specialised in operating in extreme temperatures and conditions, in frozen wastes, jungle and deserts, those were the places and conditions in which we trained.

The initial training took place at the Commando Training Centre Royal Marines, near Lympstone in Devon. It was the toughest thing I had experienced – and this from someone who had spent years as a roofer, running up and down ladders carrying stacks of tiles. We didn't stop; we were running or doing press-ups, sit-ups or pull-ups – strength and stamina training – all day long. It made runs with Lugsy and Ronnie feel like child's play.

It was relentless; day after day after day our bodies were pushed to the limit. We had tests sometimes as often as three times a day. We were worn down, exhausted, in fact beyond exhaustion physically and mentally. I would get into a bath at night and feel as though I'd never be able to walk again. Tomorrow couldn't come slowly enough; but it was all done with a purpose. As commandos, we not only needed the physical fitness to get through hostile terrain, we also had to have the mental stamina to be able to fight and defend ourselves once we got there. If we weren't up to it, we were no use to the unit.

And when we weren't pushing our bodies to the limit we were map-reading, learning to take bearings, doing survival training in extreme weather conditions, taking military tactical awareness courses, learning how to look after our kit and how to prepare for being dropped into an enemy zone at night 'by sea, by air and by land' – the force's motto.

During the training we were known as 'hats', which was short for 'crap hats', because we wore undistinguished black berets. The final test you had to pass to win the coveted green beret was a thirty-mile trek across Dartmoor that had to be completed in eight hours. It was a combination of running and walking in full gear. The drop-out rate at this stage was between forty and forty-five per cent. It was as tough as anything we had done, but our team came in on time. There was no heroes' fanfare, no ceremony. The instructors were at the finishing point waiting for us, and as we limped in on the verge of collapse, they flung our green berets at us. I can still remember the feel of the material, the excitement of holding it tightly in my hands, as we returned to base in the back of an open truck, tired and freezing cold; and the feeling of incredible pride. It was a sense of achievement unlike any I had ever had.

There was no resting on our laurels. That was just the beginning. We were away from base for eight and a half to nine months a year, and the training we were given in that time and the places we went to were phenomenal. I had thought I knew about outdoor living, but being out in the wild in Norfolk was a far cry from the frozen wastes of Norway in midwinter, when the temperature can drop to minus twenty degrees centigrade. That place will kill you if you don't know how to take care of yourself. I learnt all about survival. I learnt how to keep myself warm, how to be healthy and eat the sort of food that the body could use rather than food that simply satisfied hunger or was comforting. I learnt how and where to cross frozen lakes, and how to use the environment you were in to your advantage. In those conditions you could go from sub-zero temperatures to plus two degrees by doing something as simple as digging yourself a hole in the snow. I learnt where and how to make these holes, in the quickest time using the minimum amount of energy.

If we were travelling long distances on foot in those temperatures and that terrain, the leading person would never break trail for very long. He would lead for about five hundred metres, then taper off and go to the back and the next person in line would lead for another five hundred metres, and so it would go on. The logic was that forging a path through deep snow is more tiring than following in someone else's footprints, and on the presumption we would have to fight once we had arrived at our destination, every soldier needed to be as fit as the next.

I always used to wonder how people discovered this – until I was out on the mountains with wild wolves in central Idaho years later and I noticed they used exactly the same technique in snow. After a while the leader would break off and join the back of the line, ensuring that when they came to make the kill, every animal had conserved enough energy to be effective. My guess is that the Inuit, the indigenous people, learnt from the wolves, and passed on their techniques to our specialised troops when they arrived to train in those countries.

There was nothing I learnt during my time in the army that wasn't invaluable in my work with wolves, and many of the survival techniques were ones that wolves also used. In combat I was taught to go for the element of surprise, to fight your enemy in an environment *you* know, where the odds are in *your* favour, and to try and keep control. One person alone against twelve on enemy turf doesn't stand a chance, but by taking on those twelve in your own environment, your chances of survival go up considerably.

Wolves, I discovered, do exactly this. They will always make sure they change the environment to bring the odds into their favour before taking on an opponent. I've seen three wolves successfully take on a seven to eight-hundred-pound bear and remain in control throughout just by waiting until it was pitch dark for the final assault. Being nocturnal animals, the wolves could still see clearly and the bear, which is a fundamentally a day-time creature, was at a disadvantage.

My unit didn't go to Afghanistan or Iraq; the only active duties we did were in Northern Ireland, but we did a number of 'hearts and minds tours' with the United Nations. I remember in particular being in Cyprus where the UN was maintaining a buffer zone between the Greek and Turkish parts of the island. I was sent to the Turkish side one day to deliver food. I was the driver and I had a mate with me, but once we arrived, we were redundant. Local henchmen stepped in and started handing out the food – and violence if there was any trouble. I felt cynical about the whole exercise; it seemed to me that all we were doing was helping the rich get richer and the poor get poorer.

As I was standing around waiting, I noticed an old lady, struggling to wheel a wooden cart down a cobbled alleyway towards the lorry.

She had a lined and weathered face and was dressed in black, as so many of the women were. The henchmen didn't seem to be paying her any attention, so I quietly loaded her cart with food and while she followed, muttering, I pushed it back up the hill to her cottage, which must have been six or seven hundred metres away. I didn't speak a word of Turkish and she didn't speak a word of English, but when we reached her door she thanked me by holding my hand in hers. Then she did the most incredible thing: she reached into the cart and took out a precious apple which she insisted I take. I tried to explain that I didn't need it, I had plenty of food, but she wouldn't hear of it. I was so moved. This old woman had nothing. I had three square meals a day. Her generosity of spirit was humbling. Her culture and upbringing made it impossible for her not to repay an act of kindness, and much as I admire the billionaires who give millions to charity, there's nothing quite like the gesture of someone giving away a piece of fruit that to them could mean the difference between life and death.

There were many reasons why I loved the Forces – and moments like that were certainly one of them. Having been a solitary child, another thing I enjoyed was the sense of camaraderie. I loved the outdoor, Action Man lifestyle and I thought at that time that I believed in everything that the military stood for. It suited me down to the ground. I felt secure in the routine and discipline. I felt a sense of family among my colleagues in the ranks and enjoyed being part of a team. I imagined I would be there for a very long stint. I even tried to get into the notoriously difficult Special Air Services and the Special Boat Services.

Normally you could only apply for the SAS if you were in the army, and the SBS if you were in the navy, but the government was trialling a scheme to allow a crossover. I volunteered to take part in the trial. The SBS training was in and around Poole Harbour and presented no problems. Then I went up to Wales for the SAS training and that was carnage. I got through the first stage but I didn't get to Hereford, where the unit is based. It was disappointing but I was comforted to have made it past the first day. Out of the one hundred and fifty people that started, forty had fallen by the wayside before nightfall. Their exhausted bodies were lying over the Brecon Beacons like sheep dung.

I obviously wasn't destined to join the Special Services, but it turned out that I was not destined to make a long-term career of the army either. Instead, it proved to be a valuable apprenticeship for the real job I was going to do in life.

Chapter Six

UP CLOSE
AND PERSONAL

Ever since my extraordinary encounter with that big cream wolf in the zoo near Thetford four or five years earlier, I had wanted to see and get to know more about these creatures that had so preyed on my imagination as a child. I began reading natural history books and it seemed to me that a lot of what I had learnt about foxes from years of watching them were applicable to what I was reading about wolves. Foxes were being cruelly and systematically persecuted because of a reputation I knew they didn't deserve; with wolves mankind had gone one step further and exterminated them from most parts of the world. I began to wonder whether all the negative stories I had heard about wolves as I was growing up were any more reliable than the falsehoods I had been told about their small red cousins.

Wolves, I discovered, used to be everywhere. Once upon a time they were second only to humans in the breadth of their distribution across the globe – and when humans were hunter-gatherers they hunted the same prey as wolves and the species lived successfully alongside each other, to mutual benefit. Wolves were respected as powerful fellow hunters and given mystical and magical properties. Native Americans still believe that the spirits of their ancestors live on in the guise of wolves. They won't sign a treaty unless a wolf, or these days a dog, is present. There were countless legends through the centuries about wolves suckling human children. Romulus and Remus, the twins who founded Rome, were supposedly rescued and nursed by a she-wolf who found them in a basket floating down the river Tiber.

However, when man evolved from hunter-gatherer to farmer and wolves started preying on the livestock he farmed, the wolf swiftly turned from hero to villain. They were demonised, persecuted and hunted, in many places to extinction. Despite being endangered, they are still hunted in some parts of the world today and still widely feared as savage creatures which hunt by the light of the moon, snatch babies from cradles and leap on Russian peasants, tearing them from the backs of sleighs.

I had felt such intense and curious empathy with that wolf in the zoo that, on the basis of nothing more than instinct, and a habit of identifying with the underdog, I felt an overwhelming need to find out the truth and to do whatever I could to help and stand up for these creatures.

It quickly became an obsession. I discovered The Dartmoor Wildlife Park in the village of Sparkwell, near Plymouth, which had a pack of wolves, and at the first opportunity I made my way there and got chatting to the keepers. I went there repeatedly on any free days I had from the regiment, and offered to lend a hand at times when they were short-staffed. I came to know the owner of the park, Ellis Daw, who lived in an imposing house in the middle of it, and was soon volunteering to help look after the animals over Christmas and during other holiday periods when the regular keepers wanted time off. There was a flat in one wing of the house that the keepers lived in, and I was able to stay there. Whenever we had leave, and my friends and colleagues went off home to see their families, I went to Sparkwell. I didn't go back to Norfolk for over ten years. I felt the wolves were my family.

The park, about thirty acres in all, was on a hillside backing on to Dartmoor National Park, and the wolf enclosure was at the top of the hill, running alongside the perimeter fence. It was a small enclosure, not much more than an acre for six wolves, and fenced with heavy-duty six-foot-high link wire with a double gate to prevent a wolf accidentally escaping when the keepers came and went. Although the area was small, it was quite heavily wooded, and there was a bank towards the back under the shade of the densest trees where the wolves had dug an underground den. Otherwise there was a low rectangular hut by the gate that looked like an air-raid shelter and another smaller structure with a flat roof that the wolves seemed to enjoy lying on during the day. The keepers took carcasses in to the animals every few days. Otherwise, the only human contact was if one of the animals needed veterinary attention. The keepers certainly didn't make a habit of being on the wrong side of the wire for any length of time, and no one ever went near the wolves at night. The park closed before dusk and the keepers all went off duty.

It was common practice for everyone going into the enclosure to arm themselves with a broom handle, as they did with all of the big predators, just in case anything went wrong, but the wolves were never threatening. On the contrary, they seemed to feel threatened by us. They panicked when anyone went near them; they tore off to the far end of the enclosure or disappeared underground and only came to their food when we were well away. These didn't look to me like vicious creatures that would attack as soon as look at you.

Curiosity soon got the better of me. I wanted to get close to these animals and to know more about them, and so I started sitting quietly inside the enclosure. I sat there for hour after hour, for several weeks, hoping that the wolves might start to take an interest, as the foxes had done, and come and investigate me. They didn't. Then I realised what I was doing wrong. I was invading their territory in daylight, when *I* felt comfortable. What would happen, I wondered, if I switched the odds and approached them, as I had the foxes, at night when they had the upper hand? Might I then get a truer understanding of what these creatures were really about? I applied the psychology I had learnt in the army in reverse. I wanted the wolves to feel that *they* had the advantage and not me. My colleagues had been astonished by my desire to sit in the enclosure during the day, but when I told them that I wanted to go in at night they thought I was certifiable. To his credit, Ellis Daw, the owner, whom I had come to know quite well by then, allowed me to experiment.

Even now I have no idea what I wanted from these creatures or why I felt so compelled to get to know them in this way. Maybe it was a voyage of self-discovery, to lay the ghosts of my childhood to rest. Maybe it was because they reminded me of the dogs I grew up with and I was hoping that I would find with the wolves some of the comfort and security that I had felt with the dogs – and had not experienced fully since my grandfather died. Or maybe I was just plain nuts. What I do know is this: it upset me that these beautiful creatures found contact with humans so stressful, and I hoped that if they got to know me, I might in some way be able to make their lives in captivity a little better.

One night, when there was a new moon in the sky, I put on an old tracksuit and, taking my courage in both hands, went into the enclosure and locked the doors behind me. I was terrified, absolutely terrified; to the best of my knowledge, no one had ever done this before – and there had been plenty of accidents with captive wolves. There was no way of knowing how these wolves might react, whether they would hide away or tear me to pieces. But I had to know. Enveloped by darkness and stumbling over fallen branches and protruding tree roots, I made my way to the bank at the top, where I sat down and waited for I wasn't sure what. It was hard to see and the night was full of strange noises as the nocturnal animals in the park limbered up. But I soon began to relax. The wolves remained hidden in the shadows and gave me no cause for concern. I began to feel comforted by the darkness. As a child I had loved the dark and the noises of the forest; they had made me feel safe as I lay in my bed under the coarse black blanket in Norfolk, and they began to make me feel safe here too.

For several hours every night for a week and a half I went into the enclosure. I wore the same clothes each time, knowing from my experience of the wild the importance of scent. What I didn't know, at that time, was that diet was also important. I was eating normal human food, which, as I learnt more about wolves, I discovered was something I had to change. For the first three nights I sat in the same spot and although the wolves kept their distance, I could see that they were beginning to be a little curious. The next night I got up and moved to another part of the enclosure during the night. They immediately scattered, as though frightened, but I could see that a couple of the wolves went over to where I had been sitting to investigate my smell and urinate, or scent, over it. They then resettled a safe distance away, but I was aware that they were watching me. That went on for a few more nights. They were interested but they just didn't have the courage to come up and face me.

The next night the wolf we called Reuben, the one I now know to have been the beta animal, the bruiser of the pack, walked boldly up to me and started to sniff me all over and sniff the air. He didn't touch, he was just checking me out; and he did this for a couple of nights. The next night I was sitting up on the bank at the highest point in the enclosure with my legs out in front of me, knees in the air. This same wolf came over to me and did exactly what he had done the previous two nights; sniffed me, sniffed the air, sniffed down my legs;

and then suddenly without warning he lunged forward and in a split second his incisors had taken a hard very painful nip out of the fleshy bit of my knee.

I sat frozen to the spot. I didn't know what to do. If I got up and ran, would he run after me with the pack and bring me down? If I lashed out at him, would I make him more aggressive? So, out of sheer ignorance, I sat there thinking, Christ, this is it; game over.

But he backed off and stood looking at me, quizzically, as if gauging my reaction. Then he turned and disappeared into the darkness and I didn't see him again until the following night, when he came and did exactly the same thing. He repeated the behaviour every night for about two weeks, by which time my knees were black and blue. He might bite a different knee or nip my shin instead, but it was always the same procedure; he would come close, sniff, then lash out and disappear into the night. Sometimes he did it two or three times a night.

I had no idea what he was doing, but I knew that he can't have meant me any real harm because he never followed it up with any sign of aggression and he never called another wolf over to join him – and with jaws that are capable of exerting fifteen hundred pounds of pressure per square inch, he could have had my kneecap off in seconds. But he chose not to and that's what kept me going back for more. All I had to show for his assaults were thin lines of bruising on my knees and legs, like little wolf love-bites. I didn't react on any occasion, which I later discovered is what saved me.

The first thing a wolf will do, I came to realise, is find out whether a newcomer is trustworthy, and the way he does that is by seeing how the stranger reacts to a bite. The incoming wolf immediately exposes his vulnerable throat area to signify that he has come in peace and the established wolf will dominate him until he is satisfied there is no threat. If I had pulled away or screamed, it could have been all over very quickly.

After two weeks of nips, Reuben started rolling his scent over me. He started with my feet, rubbing them with the side of his face, his teeth, the back of his ears, his hackles and his tail. He then did the same to my legs, never biting, just rolling on me. If I got up and moved during this process he'd nip me, back off, and if I didn't react – which I didn't – he'd come and start rolling on me again. What he was doing, I realised, was testing me. That is the beta's role in the pack: to protect the others and to act like a bouncer on the door, making sure that no undesirable or threatening individual gets through. I must have satisfied him that I was acceptable, because after four or five weeks he started bringing other members of the pack over.

I later discovered that this is the process that happens in the wild when a lone wolf attempts to join an established pack. The ones that came to meet me were all high ranking and they didn't touch me initially; they just stood behind Reuben and watched and sniffed, as he moved slowly round my body, nipping. He nipped the back of my head, not quite as roughly as he'd bitten other parts, but enough to produce blood spots which turned into scabs. Once or twice I tried moving back to try and rub against him, but any movement whether subtle or sudden got me another nip. He was biting me to keep me in place – and establishing that I could cope with their world, in which nips and bites are an important part of their communication.

I knew scent was important but I discovered that if I put on different clothes or washed or ate different food, this beta male would start nipping me again until he was satisfied that the new smell didn't mean I was going to react differently to his approach or that my mood had changed. The other high-ranking wolves did the same thing, but he didn't involve every wolf in the enclosure. The lower-ranking members of the pack, I was to learn, don't question what the higher-ranking members decide; they are foot-soldiers – they have an important job to do but it is not to think for themselves.

Chapter Seven

A QUESTION
OF MORALITY

I felt deeply flattered to have these creatures trust me so much that they were prepared to rub themselves against me, and an incredible sense of achievement to be tolerated in this way. This may sound weird but it meant more to me than any human relationship I had established. I found myself looking forward to the end of the day when I could go and be with them again. It was such a privilege to be allowed to sit among this family group and to feel that in some small way I was becoming a part of it. I was beginning to need these creatures that I had been frightened of for so long; I wanted to be with them. But I wondered what they thought of me. What did they think I was? They were always curious when I arrived but what did they think when I left them? Did they miss me? Of course I was attributing to them human values and human emotions, which I came to understand are not part of their world. I had to learn to turn off my own.

After a while, they started greeting me when I went into the enclosure during the daytime and testing me in the same way as they did at night – a sure sign that they recognised and accepted me. There would be some nips and a bit of interaction which the other keepers began to notice. It felt good to watch their reaction, to notice the surprise on their faces, and to see them revising their view about these creatures that they fended off with broom handles. Little by little the days and nights merged and I found that a week had gone by and the only times that I had been away from the wolves was when I'd slipped out for some food. I once took a sleeping bag in with me, but that was a mistake. The wolves tore it to shreds. They accepted my clothing but nothing else; and the truth was I needed nothing else. When I lay down to sleep, they settled down with me and the warmth of their bodies kept me warm. My excitement at what I had achieved with them was hard to contain.

I never allowed myself to feel complacent, however. I knew that anything could happen and there was no guarantee that because my last interaction had been good, the next one would be too. Every time I went into the enclosure I was full of apprehension, wondering what would happen next. I watched the way they behaved with each other – the way they wrestled and played, and snarled and snapped – and knew that if they started to treat me the same way, I wasn't going to be able to cope. My skin wasn't as tough as theirs, I wasn't covered in thick fur, and if they were as rough with me as I'd seen them be with each other it was not only going to hurt, I was going to sustain real injuries. Would they recognise that my body was completely different from theirs? Their necks and throats, two of the areas they used most frequently to communicate, were also the best protected parts of their bodies. My throat was one of the most vulnerable. One bite like the ones I had seen them give their fellow wolves would have been it for me.

But that sense of danger was as appealing as it was appalling. It was like watching a horror movie from behind a cushion, not wanting to see, not wanting to turn it off, and not being able to resist peeping. The excitement and the pleasure I derived from being with them outweighed the danger. I felt comfortable with these wolves; I admired the respectful way they interacted with one another, the hierarchy that obviously governed the pack, the discipline they meted out to members who stepped out of line or pushed in to feed before their elders and betters had eaten. I wasn't able to articulate it at the time but what I felt most of all was a sense of belonging. Here was a group of some of the most feared and revered creatures on earth, and they had accepted me into that group. I had taken a rigorous entry exam and been tested within an inch of my life but, by a mixture of luck and intuition, I had passed.

But I wasn't allowed to bask in self-satisfaction for long. I went into the enclosure one evening, exhausted after a long day, and fell asleep. I was lying flat out, snoring my head off, and without warning Reuben ran over and bounced on to my chest, landing on all four feet. More than one hundred and twenty pounds of wolf on your chest is quite a wake-up call. As soon as he'd landed, he bounced off again and stood looking at me quizzically before setting off around the boundary, scent marking. He kept looking back, as if wanting me to follow – and I made the mistake of ignoring him and going back to sleep. What I didn't realise until it was too late, was that he was trying to teach me to identify his scent and it was an important lesson because his job was to look after the alpha pair, which included disciplining around the kill. Any food that had his scent on it was reserved for them.

The alphas are the most important pack members, because they are the decision-makers, and without them the pack is leaderless. So their survival is paramount. If food is scarce, they will eat first – they may be the only ones who do eat. Other members of the pack will go hungry, even the pups, and starve if necessary. And the rest of the pack knows better than to touch something that has the beta's scent on it. As it was, I learnt the hard way.

It was customary for the local shoot to drop off birds during the season and one day they delivered three ducks to the enclosure. At that time I didn't know much about the different foods they ate or the value the wolves placed on them – and during the winter months when it's cold and there's snow on the ground, fatty, greasy ducks were a valuable food source for the high-ranking animals. The alpha pair took the first two ducks and although I didn't want to eat it, I thought I had better protect my share, so I picked up the third. What I hadn't noticed was that Reuben, the beta wolf, had not only laid an arc of scent around it but had been watching me closely.

Within a split second I was on the ground. Reuben had come at me from about ten metres away with such force that I felt as if I'd been hit by a train. The duck went up in the air, I fell on to my back and lay there, completely winded, while he took my face in his jaws and squeezed. He was growling the while, a deep menacing growl, and saliva was collecting around his lips. I could feel the bones in my cheeks bending under the pressure. It sounded like a handful of dry twigs being crushed. I thought, this is it. No question – he's going to kill me. I fleetingly wondered what I could do, but I was being pinned to the ground with such force that my options were limited. So I decided to do what he'd already taught me: to show him respect and trust – knowing that if he had wanted to kill me, with the amount of weaponry he had, I'd have been dead by now. He was teaching me a lesson. So I tried to tilt my head to display my throat, which I'd been taught was the vulnerable trust area, and as I did so he moved his grip from my face to my throat, still growling. He held me in a vice-like grip for a few seconds longer and then he let go and backed off, still growling, his teeth bared.

If I had properly read the signs he gave me before he knocked me to the ground, and known what to look for, I would never have taken that duck in the first place. He must have been warning me off, and if I'd been paying attention I would have noticed the progression in his behaviour to that high-energy snapping and snarling which should have drawn my attention to his weaponry, as it's designed to do, and I would have seen his ear posture telling me that he was protecting the duck from afar. His ears would have gone out flat from his head like aeroplane wings, to indicate that he was covering something that belonged to him.

It was an experience that changed my entire perspective. I came out of that enclosure wondering just who the monsters on our planet really are. Humans have branded wolves as ruthless killers, but real strength comes in having the weaponry and not using it. How many humans, with that kind of killing power at their disposal, would have had the restraint not to use it?

By now I had spent seven years in the army, being a part of man's brutality to man and becoming increasingly sickened by it. If I had been a religious man I might have turned to the Church for forgiveness for my sins and for the sins of my species – as many army veterans do. Instead I looked to these creatures and I felt what I can only describe as a spiritual bond with them. That wolf in the zoo had looked into my soul and seen the grief that had marked my childhood. These wolves seemed to sense my anguish and my shame, and in some way I felt they were the key to my redemption.

There were so many things I loved about the army. It had taken me all over the world. I loved the challenges, loved being part of a crack team, and it was exciting to be in control of heavy weaponry. However, modern warfare is so removed from reality that much of the time soldiers don't know what they are fighting for. I became more and more disillusioned. I had been brought up to kill for the right reason and to respect the animal I killed and to respect its place in the world. As a soldier I was part of an organisation that, it seemed to me, often killed for greed and money and I didn't have an appetite for that.

The final straw for me was in Northern Ireland, where I did several tours of duty. The province was like a war zone, and I remember walking down a street one day in uniform and having to defend myself from a group of children, no more than six or seven years old. They were screaming abuse and hurling broken bricks and anything else they could get hold of. I am sure they were only doing it was because they had seen their parents and grandparents do the same, but there was so much hatred in their eyes. Those children should have been at home playing with Lego, dressing dolls or watching *Sesame Street*; they should have been anywhere but out there on those streets, because today's bricks will be tomorrow's bombs.

I don't know whether I killed people in Northern Ireland. I fired in the course of battle and people died, but I'll never know whether it was my bullets that killed them, and I don't want to know. It was sickening enough to have been part of it. It was not the right battle to have been fighting and I found that very difficult to cope with. Even those who wanted the army there didn't appreciate us, and the people who didn't want us, hated us with such passion that all we did was fuel the problem. There had to be a better way and in the end, years later, they found it; they talked.

In the short time I had spent watching wolves I could see such a stark difference between their aggression and ours – and I suspect that at one time, hundreds of years ago, there would have been very little difference. Wolves have the power to kill and threaten to use that power all the time, but they only use it when they must. They will fight to the death to save their family and to preserve the food sources that will get their family through the winter – and they will be archrivals with other wolf packs, but they also respect their rivals and value them for what they do. We don't value our enemies; in modern warfare, we don't even have to see our enemies – we can kill them at the push of a button; and most of us who are engaged in the fighting don't even know why they are our enemies. It went against everything that I had been taught as a child and I felt I had had enough.

Chapter Eight

A TICKET TO
A NEW LIFE

Wolves had got under my skin and my mind was in turmoil.
I felt nothing but contempt for my fellow man and nothing but admiration for these creatures which had admitted me into
their world. Theirs was the world I wanted to stay in. It was safer
than mine; it was more disciplined, and I had a greater sense of
belonging.

I had to work out my contract, but shortly after I left the army I
found myself on a plane to America. It was insanity by any standards.
I was going to meet a man I had never met, to work on a programme
for which I was not qualified, in a country where I knew no one, and
I had sold every possession I owned to buy the ticket. The man was
a Native American Indian I had heard about, a member of the Nez
Perce tribe called Levi Holt. He ran the Wolf Education and Research
Center on tribal lands near Winchester in Idaho, with a captive pack
designed to teach people about wolves and give tribal members a
chance to connect with their culture. He was also managing a controversial reintroduction programme of wild wolves into the Rocky

Mountains. It was run by a team of highly qualified biologists and I didn't have so much as an O level in woodwork.

It all began when I saw a documentary on television called *Living with Wolves*, which featured an American couple called Jim and Jamie Dutcher. They spent six years living with a captive pack in Idaho. The film was riveting; this couple had done everything I had done and had drawn all the same conclusions about pack structure, hierarchy and the importance of family to these creatures. It was as though we had been living parallel lives. Now, after six years, their permit to house the animals had expired and they needed to find a new home for them, and it was the Nez Perce tribe and, in particular, Levi Holt who had come to their rescue and taken the wolves in.

I had never met Levi, but I had spoken to him on the telephone and told him I would like to come across to Idaho and study. He said that was fine – but since it was a scientific programme and I had no qualifications, I would have to do an internship so that they could be sure I would know how to record data correctly and be able to support the biologists in the field. Then he told me what it would cost and mentioned a figure that audibly took my breath away. It was several thousands of dollars and he picked up my reaction down the line.

'What's the matter?' he asked.

'I've sold everything,' I said, 'I barely have enough money for the air fare.' Looking back it was probably a crazy thing to do, but I did crazy things in those days.

'So what are you going to do?'

'I hear you have a captive pack that you use as ambassadors to teach people about wolves. I've worked in wildlife parks with captive wolves and maybe I could help out with them and that would pay my way through the internship.'

'There are only so many hours in the day,' he said. 'How are you going to do it?'

'How about if I work all day and study at night?'

'Hang on a second,' he said. 'Let me get this right. You want to come over here and work all day and study all night for your internship?

'Yes.'

The phone went dead for what felt like hours while he went away to consult with colleagues.

'OK,' he said. 'Buy your ticket, come over and we'll see what we can do.' It wasn't until later that I discovered how much they'd laughed at this mad Brit who was prepared to come over on a wing and a prayer and on the promise of nothing but a tent to sleep in; but my idiocy had appealed to them.

A week later I was on the plane, and I admit I was terrified. I didn't know what I had let myself in for. I had sold my car, my trinkets, my knives that I'd had since I was a child, most of my equipment and clothes, and had scraped together the money for the fare. If it all went wrong I had nothing to return to. The army had been my home for the last seven years and there was no way I could have gone back to Norfolk.

I flew into Boise, the capital of Idaho, which lies in the south-west of the state. There I was met by a tall Texan cowboy named Rick, who was married to Cathy, a volunteer at the Center with Levi. I was to spend the night with them and the following morning she would drive me up to Winchester. After a very pleasant meal and a comfortable night at their home, Cathy and I, plus a friend she took along for company for the return journey, set off at first light for the reservation. Rick stayed behind to look after their young child. It was a drive of about two hundred and fifty miles, and the slight flurry of snow we left in soon became a more serious storm. We stopped several times along the way to put snow chains on and take them off again when the road was clear, but by the time we hit the Rocky Mountains we were into deep snow and the chains were on permanently. We were now into wolf country – a rocky terrain, with lodgepole pine forests and snow-capped mountains – and most of the traffic on the road was associated with the logging industry; huge lorries driving back and forth moving timber. We were in the car for most of the day, and as we drove Cathy explained the work that was being done at the Center and how the release programme worked.

This programme had been a political hot potato for many years, ever since the US Fish and Wildlife Service, which was responsible for protecting endangered species, proposed a recovery plan for the wolf in 1980. The wolf was officially classified as endangered in forty-eight states in America in 1978. The plan was to reintroduce wolves in north-western Montana, central Idaho and Yellowstone National Park in Wyoming, but it had been thwarted again and again with writs and injunctions, largely by the farming community, who were afraid that wolves roaming wild would kill their livestock. Finally in 1994, after much argument, the Secretary of the Interior signed the release plan – which called for the state agencies to manage the wolves once they had been released – but all three states declined to cooperate. Finally the Nez Perce came up with a management programme for Idaho and in January 1995 – after fifteen years of debate – fifteen Canadian Grey wolves were released into about thirteen million acres of national forest in the Rockies. Two years later they released another twenty, and they were doing so well that the biologists were already predicting that it would be no more than seven years before they could be taken off the endangered species list.

We arrived at the Center just as it was getting dark and everyone came out to welcome us. I think they were keen to take a look at this madman who had travelled all the way from England. The Center was about half an hour's drive out of the town of Winchester up a windy mountain track. The whole area was breathtakingly beautiful with mountain trails through forests of giant Ponderosa pines and Douglas firs. The main attraction was a big lake that brought tourists to the area – as well as eagles and fish-eating birds. In summer the lake offered canoeing and water sports and, in winter, ice-skating and ice-fishing. The population of Winchester was less than three hundred people, and the facilities amounted to a canteen, a pub, a grocery store and a gas station, and this little town was where we went each week to stock up on supplies and to have a shower and launder clothes.

There was no running water in the camp and no electricity; drinking water had to be carried in and cooking was all done on propane gas appliances. One of the biologists showed me round. The accommodation comprised a cluster of individual tepees, one smaller one which was the toilet, and one larger tent, set apart from the main living quarters, which was the kitchen and canteen, where there was always a big pot of coffee on the go. It was set apart because bears frequently came out of the forest in search of food and would follow their noses. Any food had to be either buried or hung up out of reach to prevent them from taking it. The tepees were allocated in order of seniority; those at the heart of the camp being the most prestigious. There was one, I noticed, that couldn't have been further away. It was right on the edge of the forest; it had a hole in the roof, moss growing up the sides of the canvas and a door that was hanging off. Pity the poor devil that has to live in that one, I thought to myself. And yes, I was that poor devil.

The tepees were semi-permanent. Each one had a wooden floor, a wooden platform bed about three feet off the ground and a little wood-burning stove, which was essential in those temperatures. That night I sat in my tent listening to the wolves that I would meet in the morning, and stoked the fire with logs. I was broke, and I had none of the right equipment because I'd had to spend everything I had on the air fare. I had borrowed a friend's sleeping bag, which was far too short, I had no pillow and none of the creature comforts that adorned the other tepees, but by the time I put my head down my nerves had dissolved and I had a very good feeling in the pit of my stomach. I felt that this could be what I had been searching for.

The next morning I was awake before anyone else, too excited and too uncomfortable to sleep. I pulled on my army boots, put on fewer layers than I would have liked, and stepped outside into the cold of first light: it must have been about minus fifteen degrees. I thought that I could compensate for poor-quality clothing by my knowledge of survival, and the golden rule is to be aware of your body temperature; to resist the temptation to put on every garment you have, because you will warm up and if you sweat everything becomes wet, then icy cold.

As the sun started to rise over the Sawtooth Mountains I could see the full beauty of my surroundings. The snow was two to three feet deep, crisp underfoot and lay heavily on the tops of the trees – the most magnificent trees with huge trunks that rose more than a hundred feet above my head, and smelt faintly of vanilla. It was so silent you could have heard a pin drop; I had arrived in paradise.

The wolf enclosure was near the visitor centre, where members of the public came to see the wolves and learn about them and the history and culture of the Nez Perce. It was one of the main tourist attractions of the area, but also very useful as a way of countering the fear and prejudice that these creatures aroused in so many people. They had eleven grey Timber wolves in captivity living in forty-eight acres of forest, and the area was double-fenced with a strip between the two fences. It became my job to walk around the perimeter between the fences in the early morning looking for breaches or for frozen drifts of snow that could raise the ground level enough for the wolves to escape over the top.

Once back from my dawn patrol I would go into the cooking tent and fill in the log book, noting any unusual findings. Then I'd pour myself a mug of hot black coffee or, if no one else was up, I would brew the first pot of the morning. Coffee was the only thing that was provided. Everyone bought and cooked their own food but there was coffee on the go throughout the day, and for the first three weeks I lived on black coffee and JuJuBes, a sugar jelly sweet that I discovered I could buy very cheaply in the grocery store in Winchester. I used to go down there – the walk took about two hours – and buy three pounds at a time, which only cost a few cents, and which saw me through the coming week. They were stacked full of sugar, of course, which gave me an instant high followed by a terrible low. It wasn't an ideal diet for anyone working eighteen-hour days in sub-zero temperatures, but I didn't have enough money for anything else and I knew that it was only a matter of time before I wouldn't even be able to afford the JuJuBes.

There were about twelve of us in all, mostly tribespeople. There was a permanent animal manager, a couple of Center managers, two or three biologists and about five or six students at any one time. They were graduates or people needing to complete coursework before graduating, and stayed for about three months. Academically I was way behind everyone and I knew I had been given the opportunity of a lifetime. I lived in fear that they would send me packing at any moment and I was desperate to learn as much as I could before that happened. There was so much to learn; it was an incredible privilege to be among these Native American Indians who had lived alongside wolves for centuries and viewed them not as an enemy or a lower life form, but as brothers, sisters and teachers.

Once I had patrolled the perimeter, checked the fences and had breakfast, other tasks for the day included collecting wood for the camp stoves, driving out to pick up carcasses from farms or road kill that people had reported, feeding it to the captive wolves and looking after their welfare, preparing tepees for the arrival of new students, clearing snow from tracks and doing general maintenance around the camp. When the visitor centre was open I might have to take groups on tours of the site and give talks and presentations or man the shop selling souvenirs and booklets.

Sometimes I would go much further afield, accompanying the biologists who were monitoring the movements of the wild wolves. They were electronically tagged so we could find them in that vast area and study their behaviour – and also warn farmers if they seemed to be heading too close to livestock. We would often camp out on these trips, and it was always in the dead of night, when the temperatures plummeted, that I wished I had come to Idaho equipped with the right gear and a warmer pair of socks. I was lucky to have my army survival training to fall back on.

Once my daytime duties were over my night-time studies began. The internship covered everything from the welfare and security of captive wolves, to wolf behaviour and communication, as well as field biology which involved data collection and record keeping. I read books, studied maps and listened to talks given by tribal elders. I would go and sit between the two fences or walk around the perimeter, getting to know the animals inside and listening to the sounds they made, watching their communication and behaviour. I was learning from everything I smelt, heard and saw; getting to know the individual pack members and building up their confidence in me.

Levi Holt was everything I could have hoped for. He was hard to age but must have been in his fifties and looked like an archetypal Native American chief. His face was creased and lined and framed by jet-black hair which hung in two long plaits down to his waist. He had the air of one who knew everything and gave away nothing. Every now and again for special occasions he would get dressed up in the full tribal costume, but day to day he wore jeans, T-shirts, jumpers and anoraks like the rest of us. Any romantic illusions that I might have nursed about how the Nez Perce would be living on the reservation – based on cowboy films I'd seen – were quickly shattered. There were no painted tepees, Appaloosa horses or loin cloths, no buffalo grazing in the background. *We* lived in tepees at the Center, but these were a very poor people and elsewhere on the reservation they were living in desperately poor housing, dressing in cheap American clothes, driving beaten-up cars and scratching a living in any way they could. They were a shadow of their former selves but they still had great respect for the earth, the rivers and the environment because they had never lost touch with the elements that sustained them. They drank from the rivers and took their food from the land and the creatures that roamed on it.

I have never met people who, even in extreme adversity, were so ready to laugh. With them, every day begins and ends with a miracle, and to be part of that even for a brief period was amazing. They were so connected to their families, to their ancestors and to the natural world around them. They couldn't understand the way the white man has mistreated the earth, poisoning it with intensive farming and crop spraying, polluting rivers, destroying forests and upsetting the delicate balance of nature. They wanted to own the land so that they could purify it and show future generations how to live on it, with it and for it. I remember one night in the town we watched a documentary made by a Frenchman in which one of the neighbouring farmers was asked whether he thought the Nez Perce should have their tribal lands returned to them. His attitude, which they felt the Government shared, was no: the Nez Perce lost the war, they lost the land, they have to live with it.

I asked what could be done, what help anyone could offer, and Levi's brother said, 'What we really need is another messiah who would speak up for the Nez Perce. The problem with us is we have too many chiefs and not enough Indians.' They all fell about laughing.

One day the elders invited me to a powwow at which they asked for my advice. They were expecting a visit from a young member of Congress. There was an important Bill going through the House, I don't know exactly which, and they rightly guessed he was hoping to secure support for it from the Nez Perce. It was a great honour to be consulted and after some hesitation I told them I didn't trust politicians: they speak in half truths and promise the earth but seldom deliver. They sat round the fire, smoking and warming their hands, nodding from time to time as I spoke, not looking as though they were very interested in what I had to say. And why should they have listened to me? I went away feeling rather low and dejected, and when the Congressman arrived my fears seemed to be confirmed. They appeared to be taken in by his demeanour, to be sucking up to him; they were feeling his suit and admiring his shoes and patting him on the shoulder. It was like something out of a novel – the poor barefoot savage overwhelmingly impressed by the white man. They invited him to see all the most important areas and introduced him to all the most important people. The icing on the cake was when they gave him a tribal name, which was the biggest honour they can bestow on an outsider. They called him Walking Eagle, which seemed to me to be about as noble as a name could get until I discovered that it meant he was so full of shit he couldn't fly. Far from being taken in, they had seen right through this man and played him at his own game.

They would always complain that we Western people were too serious – we should look for coyote medicine. The coyote is the trickster, the spirit guide that walks the path of the dead and the living to embarrass us and make us laugh. They told me a story about a white man who came to the reservation once. He was there on a voyage of self-discovery, hoping he might find some answers from the wise Indi-ans, to help lift his depression. He was an earnest young man and wore the weight of the world on his shoulders. One of the tribal elders told him he must go off into the forest for three days to find scats – drop-pings from deer, bears, mountain lions, coyotes, foxes and wolves. He returned with a great collection that the elder then said he must mix with water and make into a paste. That took him a further two days. It was now day five and in the summer heat the smell and the flies were appalling. Next, said the elder, with a stick he must inscribe a circle around himself in the sand and pour the paste he had made into the groove made by the stick. Finally the elder told him to sit inside the circle for as long as it took for the coyote to come and tell him what to do next. It was several hours before it dawned on the white man just what he'd done. He'd spent three days gathering other people's crap and was sitting right in the middle of it – and finally realised the irony of his situation. He sat there roaring with laughter, released from the worries of the world.

It would be wrong to say the Nez Perce lived as their ancestors did, because they blatantly didn't, but they hadn't lost all the old ways. The Shaman was still an important part of the spiritual well-being of the community, as were the sweat lodges where people went several times a week to pray and connect with the Creator and the spirit world and be healed and cleansed of impurities. The Shaman led the ceremony, summoning visions of past tribal members or creatures to guide him. No drugs or hallucinogens were used, but the heat was so intense that I found it had much the same effect.

These sweat lodges were dome-shaped, usually made of willow – the wood of love, which bends but doesn't break – and covered with animal skins and blankets. Inside there was a fire pit, in which red-hot stones were placed, set slightly off-centre to represent the heart, and now and again it was sprinkled with herbal water to intensify the heat. It was the dry heat of a sauna that made you sweat profusely. They were not tall enough to stand in and, with eleven or twelve people inside, very cramped and claustrophobic. They were supposed to resemble the womb, dark and warm with a small entrance facing either east or west depending on where you wanted the prayers to be heard. You went into it naked and backwards to symbolise re-entering the womb, and you might stay in there for five hours or more, talking, offering prayers and giving thanks to the spirits, the elements and the sacred powers. When you finally emerged you were reborn, both physically and spiritually.

It was the most amazing experience. I remember sitting there aware that the tribal elders were talking about important issues and knowing that I should be concentrating but feeling so spaced out I couldn't focus; but it was almost as though the information skipped the usual route and went straight into my long-term memory. That night I would dream about the conversation and wake up the next morning able to remember everything.

Chapter Nine

FOUND OUT

About three weeks after my arrival at the Education Center I went into the cooking tent for yet another cup of black coffee to insulate me against the cold, and one of the biologists, who was busy cooking, turned to me and said, 'Don't you ever eat?'

'Of course I eat,' I lied. 'I just do it at different times from everyone else.'

As I turned away I saw Levi, that all-knowing Indian, standing in the doorway, arms folded, with a look on his face that said, 'I hear what you're telling me, but it isn't the truth.'

I thought no more about it until I was in the grocery store in Winchester a couple of weeks later buying my supply of JuJuBes. As I turned, clutching my three pounds in a brown paper bag, there was Levi again, standing some feet away, arms folded as before, with the same look on his face.

'We eat at different times, do we?'

Oh God, I thought, he's found me out, he's going to put me on the first plane home.

'When you get back up to the camp,' he said, 'I want to see you in the office.'

I had a long climb back up the mountain track, plenty of time to think about my fate, and when I reached the top I had come to the conclusion that I would have to hold my hands up and say I was sorry. I would pack my bag and go without any argument, asking for no more than a lift to the local airfield at Lewiston. What awaited me in England would be anyone's guess. But I had had nearly four weeks of the best time of my life and, given that I wasn't qualified and I wasn't paying my way, it was four weeks longer than I'd expected.

Levi stopped me in full flood. 'I've had a word with the biologists,' he said, 'and they like what you're doing around the wolves; they find it very helpful. So I'm going to give you a small wage, but I'm not going to give you the money; I'm going to credit it to the shop, so that every week you can go down to the town and buy yourself some proper food that you can store in the tent and eat like everyone else.'

I was so happy. In the time it took him to say those magic words, my fortunes were completely reversed. I had an income, however small, I had somewhere to live, among people I respected, doing work I loved, and I would be able to eat properly again. It was more than I could have hoped for and I stayed for a further five months. Looking back, I think the fact that I was prepared to struggle and live off jelly beans in order to live and learn alongside these people went a long way to cement my relationship with Levi and the biologists at the Center. I heard them on more than one occasion say to students who arrived clutching every last comfort, 'Look at that guy down there. He doesn't have anything; he lives off the bare minimum and he works all day and studies all night.' But I was used to hardship – I was used to sleeping on the barn floor as a child – and, if anything, living the way I was in Idaho, out of a Bergen day sack, with no spare clothes, no pillow and no furnishings, took me back to those happy days

70

which I had tried so hard in the past to re-create. To me this felt comfortable, this felt like home.

After the small enclosure at Sparkwell it was good to see wolves with so much space to roam, although on subsequent visits I realised that even these wolves could suffer from the behavioural problems that I had seen in small enclosures and had always attributed to the cramped conditions. On the face of it, these animals had everything that nature intended and yet they began to have difficulty living with each other. It was a valuable lesson that space was not the most important factor. What was missing, I came to realise, was a rival pack. Just as human beings pull together in the face of a common threat or enemy, so do wolves. If life is too easy for them, food is plentiful and there is no immediate danger, they start to turn on each other.

These captive wolves had been brought up in a very sociable environment and were well used to humans – they were ambassadors for their species – and it was no great challenge to go into the enclosure with them. The biologists did it frequently, albeit during the day. When they went in, however, it was in a dominant role, and that was how they told me to behave around the wolves. They said I must never interact with them, I must never look them in the eye, never get my body lower than theirs, and I should only ever touch them, if absolutely necessary, in the area around the shoulder and neck. They said that if ever I showed any sign of weakness the animals would take over.

After my third week in the camp I was going into the enclosure during the day and doing everything the biologists said and demonstrating to them that I could be trusted to be around the animals without causing problems to them or me. But I didn't get the sense that these were wolves at all. They were like the shadows of wolves – too domesticated and being bossed around and intimidated by humans.

What would happen, I wondered, if I went in with them at night as a low-ranking member – as I had at Sparkwell – and allowed them to behave like real wolves and dominate me?

After six weeks I persuaded the managers to let me experiment, and one night I unlocked the big iron gates and let myself into the enclosure. Everyone thought I was crazy; it was unheard-of to try and join a wolf pack as a low-ranking member – it was a reversal of everything they believed – but the truth was I wanted the wolves to teach me about their world, not vice versa; I wanted to become one of them, and if I tried to dominate them that would never happen. The biologists would never have understood that. They studied wolves as an academic exercise and they did it from afar. They watched the animals' behaviour through the lenses of high-powered binoculars and presumed to interpret what they saw on the basis of their understanding of human behaviour.

From the limited time I had already spent with captive wolves, I knew that things were seldom as they seemed and that if you really wanted to understand wolf behaviour you had to live among them. Only then – if you were able to think as a wolf – might it be possible to help prevent wild wolves going beyond the park boundaries and raiding livestock, which is what everyone, including the biologists, feared one day might happen.

I was nervous – although I didn't let anyone know just how nervous; I had no idea how these wolves would react to me on their territory at their time of the day. I was going against my entire commando training. There were eleven of them, one of me, and my human eyes were useless in the dark; I was at a serious disadvantage. Being in the enclosure that first night was scary – although there were much scarier moments yet to come. I was stumbling around, crashing into rocks, falling into water, tripping over in the snow, not knowing where I was or where the wolves were or how to communicate with these creatures. It was like being set down in the middle of Red Square in Russia and being surrounded by people who didn't speak a word of English with everyone looking at me expectantly.

But then the panic subsided. The mist cleared for me and I stopped thinking these wolves were going to harm me. The following night I went in again and there was a moon and a thousand twinkling stars. The reflection of the snow made it almost light and I was able to make out trees and paths, so this time I was able to move about the enclosure without too many bumps or falls. The animals stayed away and I sat and listened to the noises of the night. I could hear a grey owl hooting, a lone coyote and the grunting of a grizzly bear somewhere too close for comfort. But having regularly fallen happily asleep as a child with the noises of the forest, these noises, although different, were strangely comforting.

I went in night after night, and the pattern was similar to the one I had experienced in the UK. They were curious about me but kept their distance at first, gradually coming closer and finally giving me testing bites. They would mouth my hands and arms and then take themselves off to the back of the enclosure for long periods. Sometimes I'd follow, discovering that the more familiar the paths became, the easier it was to move about in the dark. Memory played a big part not just in my navigation but in theirs too. If something unfamiliar was added, or a tree fell across a track, they wouldn't always see it; and I definitely wouldn't.

This was a big pack, but they were healthy animals in good condition, and among the eleven there was every rank and no indication that any one of them needed to be dispersed. A pack is only a pack, or a family, because they need one another – they stay together as a matter of need, not choice. If you had wolves in a captive environment where food was scarce, with no rivals threatening their territory, the pack might well reduce to one breeding pair. That pair would be genetically programmed to survive and the rest would be seen as rivals for the limited food supply. The two would start picking on the other animals, fighting with them and excluding them from the food, and in a natural environment those animals would disperse and go and join another pack where they were needed. In captivity they are dependent on their keepers removing them or they would eventually die.

I had the feeling, as the months went by, that they accepted me as part of the family and were trying to teach me about their world. It was as if they were saying, 'If you're going to be around, we'll teach you the different sounds that we make, the different smells of our family members, and about the territorial boundary that we lay down every single night that keeps us safe. This is where you sleep, this is where I sleep; if you have any problems you go to him, you don't come to me; you certainly don't interact with her. I'll tell you when you can come over here. You can approach him whenever you want, you can groom him and you can bite and nip the scabs off his body where he's been play-fighting, but if you come and do that to me, I'm going to let you know very quickly by biting you on the face that you can't do that.' The body language they used to articulate these rules gradually became clearer and I started making fewer mistakes, but when I made a mistake I was disciplined as they disciplined their own.

I would have been happy to stay up there in the mountains with the wolves and the Nez Perce for ever, but after about nine months I felt the time had come to tear myself away. I had completed my internship and I needed to earn a living. Levi was paying for my food but I had no source of income and a seriously depleted bank account. I had no alternative but to go back to the UK. I was very sad to leave what I firmly thought of as home, and the people – and wolves – that I regarded as family, but I knew I would be back.

I now had a clear vision of what I wanted to do with my life: the wolves had taught me about their world, and I knew how precarious it was. Unless someone could teach the wolves about our world and act as a go-between, their release into the wild would be short-lived. I would be that someone.

Chapter Ten

EARNING
A CRUST

I arrived at Heathrow Airport and headed straight down to Plymouth to see if I could pick up the pieces of a relationship that had begun just before I went to Idaho. Janet Williams and I had met in a pub while I was in the army. Her friend had been going out with a friend of mine at Plymouth and we had been good mates for several years before we got together as a couple. Almost immediately after getting together, I went off to America, but Jan had been very understanding and it was wonderful to see her again.

From there I went to the Dartmoor Wildlife Park at Sparkwell. I was hoping that Ellis might give me a paid job and also give me the opportunity to put some of what I had learnt in Idaho to good use with my wolf family there. Ellis seemed pleased to see me and was very interested in what I'd been doing since we last met. It was coming to the end of the season but he had been short-staffed during the summer and needed someone to look after the big carnivores. These included lions and tigers as well as the wolves, and the job came with board and lodging. I had a room in the wing of the house where I'd been before, along with the other keepers, and meals were included.

It was a perfect arrangement except that Ellis could never afford to pay any of his keepers during the winter months when there were no visitors. So although I had a roof over my head and I was working with the wolves I loved, I had virtually no spending money. But every cloud has a silver lining and the upside of that was that when the summer came around I was owed a lot of back pay. Ellis was very good to me and I have a great deal of respect for him; he cared deeply about the animals in his care and despised the bureaucracy that went with owning a wildlife park.

He had had the park since the early sixties and was irritated by the new rules and regulations and health and safety restrictions that dictated how he behaved. His methods were unorthodox but he'd looked after the animals his way successfully for years. He had an old bison, for example, as mean as hell, that he'd ride into the shed it lived in at night. He wasn't afraid of any animal and was infuriated by any busybody who tried to tell him what to do. Whenever inspectors were due to visit, as they did from time to time, Ellis would have to be kept well out of the way, lest he give them a piece of his mind.

Admire him though I did, his methods of moving the tigers would have made even the most liberal zookeeper's hair stand on end. The tigers had two enclosures, one for the day, where they exercised, and one for the night, and the two were some three hundred metres apart, across the middle of the zoo, past the monkeys, the wolves and the racoons. Now tigers are very fond of food, and so the way we moved them from one enclosure to the other was thus: one handler would attach a length of chain to the collar of the tiger and attempt to hold it while another handler ran at full tilt from the night enclosure to the exercise area, carrying a big chunk of meat. The object was to reach the gate to the day enclosure before the tiger, so you could shut him safely inside. Meanwhile the handler holding the chain would be bumping along the ground behind the tiger like an amateur water-skier in an effort to slow him down, and the operation's success depended on the weight and strength of the handler on the end of the chain. If the tiger reached the handler carrying the food before that handler reached the enclosure it would leap on him – all nine hundred pounds of it – bringing him to the ground, and sit on him while consuming the meat. On occasions, I was that handler. Once the tiger had eaten, it had no interest in going into the exercise run when there were so many interesting places to visit in the park and we were sunk.

That was bad enough, but when Ellis and his grandson went out and bought a whole lot of used riot shields from the police that he wanted us to hide behind while we moved the tigers, we said enough was enough.

The wolf pack was sadly diminished when I arrived back. When I had lived with them before there had been six wolves but they were all of much the same age – a common problem with captive packs at that time – and they were reaching the end of their lives. Now there were only three – Zac, an alpha male, and Lucky and Dakota, both females. Dakota was there on loan and, shortly after I arrived, went back to where she had come from; and then Lucky died. I was with Lucky all the time for the last week and a half of her life, trying desperately to keep her alive. She lay with her head on my lap and I dropped tiny amounts of water into her mouth, but in the end she quietly slipped away.

Zac was then on his own and so I moved in with him to keep him company and stayed for about six months until some other wolves were found. By day I did my usual work and at night I went into his enclosure and slept there. Every time I went in he would go through the ritual of rubbing himself against my feet and legs and then work his way up to my head and if I wasn't careful and allowed him to get behind me he would nip the back of my head, often drawing blood. He was testing me – demonstrating that if *he* could sneak up behind me and bite the back of my head, then so could an enemy, which meant I was not up to the job of protecting the pack.

Before Dakota left, she starred in a television programme made in the park. It was called *Talking with Animals* and presented by Charlotte Uhlenbroek. As part of the title sequence Charlotte howled and a wolf, which was Dakota, apparently howled in reply. It was all superimposed, of course, but as her keeper it was my task to get Dakota to perform and she refused to answer Charlotte's howl. The only thing that would induce her to open her mouth was if a lion roared. So I had to run across to the lion enclosure to stir up the lions and get one to roar so that Dakota would howl. That was my introduction to television.

It was also my introduction to the wolves at Longleat Safari Park, which came to play a big part in my life a few years later. It was where the bulk of the programme was made. I knew Longleat as a great wildlife park and I had been there as a visitor many times, but this was my first visit as a professional. Their wolves were in captivity but far wilder than the wolves at Sparkwell because they didn't come into contact with humans at all. Visitors saw the wolves from their cars and the keepers largely managed them from vehicles too. I hoped that one day I would be back.

During that time at Sparkwell I took a few months off in the winter, when the park was quiet, to visit Canada. I had been there once before during my time in the forces, when we were stationed outside Wainwright in Alberta. I had hoped to see coyote during that time but only glimpsed one very briefly. They are notoriously shy. This time I was part of a study to try and map out coyote migration routes. There had been attacks on poultry, and there were fears that this was because their traditional corridors had been blocked by human expansion. Our task, as volunteers, was to sit out for twelve-night stints in various locations to establish where they were and what routes they were taking. I was there for three months and sat night after night, watching and listening, eager to see this creature that the Native Americans call the trickster. But in three months the only coyote I saw were three dead ones that had been killed on the road. There wasn't a living specimen to be seen.

But the irony of it was that they had seen me. At the end of one of these fruitless sessions, a Native American took me, and the other volunteer I had been on watch with, around to the other side of the rocky outcrop where we'd spent our cold and fruitless vigil. There in the dirt, not more than fifteen metres from where we had been sitting, were a collection of neat little paw prints. Wile E. Coyote and his friends had been watching us all the time – no doubt laughing their heads off. My friends on the reservation would have enjoyed this story.

This trip to Canada made me nostalgic for Idaho, and as the year went on I felt an overwhelming desire to see my Native American brothers again. I telephoned Levi and asked if I could come over. I knew he wouldn't be able to pay me but that didn't matter. I just needed to be there. Thanks to Ellis's erratic payment system, when he did finally pay me I had nearly a year's salary that I hadn't touched. I had also done a few bouncing jobs here and there at nightclubs in Plymouth. I had enough for another trip.

This time I flew into Lewiston, the local airfield, so there were no long journeys through the snow. It was fantastic to be back; to the feeling of space, to the big skies, the giant trees of the forests, the lakes, the mountains, and the squeak of hard, deep snow under my boots. I revelled in the smell of the clear, crisp mountain air and the sounds of the creatures that shared this magical wonderland. It was even good to be back in my old and tattered tepee.

Levi seemed delighted to see me, although he was always hard to read, but apart from him and a couple of the biologists, there was no one in the confines of the camp I recognised. It was a shame because I had always been teased about the English drinking strong beer, so this time I'd arrived with a bottle of English beer, but it went down well with the new guys and it wasn't long before I had friends among the new intake. The work, though, was unchanged and I quickly settled back into the old routine. It was a true homecoming, to a place where I felt I fitted completely and could be myself. There was something so special about the Native Americans and I felt that a part of me had stayed here at the foot of the Sawtooth Mountains while I was back in the UK. It was a joy to sit listening to the elders tell their stories again and to go into the stifling heat of the sweat lodge and sit for hours feeling at perfect peace with the world.

The only real change was in the wolves – the last place I had expected it. They had been so well balanced when I was last there, but this time there were a lot of niggling fights breaking out over food. The hierarchy had changed and the pack was less disciplined than it had been. I didn't expect them to remember me and I am sure they didn't, but they allowed me to join them again. I went through the ritual that I did every time I went into a wolf enclosure – even among wolves that I'd left just a few hours before, paying the high-ranking members respect, allowing them to scent roll around me and test me. It is what all wolves do when they've been away from the pack; they greet each other and in that greeting and lowering of the body establish their rank within the pack.

I was given the title of assistant field biologist and, as well as looking after the captive pack, my job was to go out on trips with the biologists to monitor the movements of the wild wolves. Levi had a theory that there had been wild wolves in the Rockies long before the fifteen Canadian wolves were released as part of the reintroduction programme in 1995. He believed that wild wolves had come back into the area using the old migratory corridors than run between Canada, Montana and Idaho, and we were trying to establish whether this was true or not. All indications were that it was true. The incoming wolves had been electronically tagged before leaving Canada but they had then been given a 'hard release', meaning that a cage was set down and the door opened with no further human involvement. They had arrived in pairs but had immediately to set off in opposite directions, suggesting that they knew there were other wolves in the locality with which they might breed.

Thirty-five wolves were released in all, but the whole programme was fraught with controversy. The farmers and livestock owners took legal action at the last minute to try and prevent it, fearing that the wolves would prey on their stock, but the judge turned down their request for an injunction and the release went ahead. The local schoolchildren had wanted to name the wolves, but that met with furious opposition too. Parents were afraid that if the wolves had names the children would think they were friendly, and be tempted to approach them if they saw one. So they were given numbers such as B2M, B3F, B4F and B5M – the M and F denoted male and female. By 1998, the number of wolves in the area had increased to one hundred and twenty-one, suggesting again that Levi was right and the original number was more than fifteen.

The best time to track the wolves was in the winter, when there was snow on the ground and their movements were easy to follow, and wolves, like most animals tend to keep to an area they have marked out as their territory and move about within it. So, having established the various packs' territories in the snow, we had little difficulty finding them at other times. Once again my army training kept me alive on those trips in the snow – knowing how to find food, how to keep warm, how to avoid overheating or dehydrating. In freezing temperatures more people die of heat-related conditions than of cold.

The seasons were spectacular and more clearly defined than anywhere I had been before. They took me back to my childhood in Norfolk, where I had so loved the different times of year and the changes in the hedgerows and the daylight and the temperature that each season brought. Here in the Rockies the colours were in a different league; they were sensational: deep rich reds, oranges and gold that made the forests look as if they were on fire. Levi once told me a story about how the leaves came to be such a vivid colour in autumn. He was reminded of the story when we were deep in the forest one day. We would often walk together, just as I had done with my grandfather, and he would stop every now and again and drop to his knees to examine a scat or a footprint.

As he was squatting down I spotted an enormous bear less than forty metres away from us. 'Bear!' I exclaimed.

'I've seen it,' he said calmly. 'It's been watching us for the last twenty minutes.'

I couldn't disguise the panic in my voice. 'But it's a bear, and we don't have a vehicle to jump into and we're on our own.'

Bears can run at the speed of a horse and climb most trees. 'Relax,' said Levi. 'My people have made peace with the bear; we have nothing to fear.' I didn't want to get hung up on a technicality, but would this bear know I was English? 'Long ago,' he went on (while I began looking feverishly for escape routes), 'a bear was being chased by three hunters. Wounded in the back, it ran up a mountain to the highest, most inaccessible place it could find, but the hunters followed. With nowhere left to run, the bear jumped off the mountain and carried on running in the sky – and the hunters followed. They can be seen to this day, in the constellation known as Ursa Major, the Great Bear

– and every autumn when darkness falls, the bear is said to run upside down, and the blood that spills from the wound in its back falls to earth and turns the leaves crimson.'

This was one occasion when I can't say Levi had my full attention. Trust him though I did, I couldn't help wondering whether this particular bear was aware that Levi's people had made peace with his forebears – or whether their pact would extend to me. While Levi walked nonchalantly on, I kept looking feverishly behind me. Just in case.

The forest was full of potentially dangerous animals. One of the students that year kept herself fit by jogging twice a day. Morning and night she would run down the track in the direction of the town, a distance of three or four miles. One day I had been out collecting food for the wolves with one of the biologists and noticed the girl's tracks in the new-fallen snow. After about a mile, her tracks were joined by the tracks of a big cat. It was a mountain lion that had obviously noticed her routine and, unbeknown to her, had followed her to within a hundred and fifty metres of the camp. It had probably followed her before – these cats can watch their prey for days before they strike. She had been taking the same route for three weeks – but she didn't go jogging again.

The dangers were not exclusively from the wild. Every week we used to go into Winchester for a shower and a pint or two, and one night there was a karaoke contest in the pub. Thinking karaoke was a bit of fun, as it is in England – something you did when you'd had a skinful of beer, and got better at the more beer you drank – I volunteered to have a go. What I didn't realise was that they took their karaoke very seriously in Idaho; the singers were semi-professional and these were the regional championships. So when I went up to the microphone and sang my own version of the Beatles' song 'Yesterday', re-titled 'Leprosy' ('… I'm only half the man I used to be …'), which used to go down a storm among the lads in the squadron, I was practically lynched and had to run for my life.

I was never a very heavy drinker, but one of the handlers at the Center was, and he would often wend his way back from the pub on those nights very much the worse for wear. His tepee was near the wolf enclosure and his route took him right alongside the perimeter fence. We started to notice that when he came past the wolves on Saturday nights, reeking of alcohol and staggering as he walked, the wolves went wild. They knew this man well and yet they were prey driving – leaping at the fence and bouncing off it and running back and forth in a feeding frenzy. We thought it must be the smell of alcohol on his breath that was confusing them, because they were never normally aggressive towards people and certainly not towards the people who handled them.

We ran some experiments. We covered him in alcohol and got him to walk in a straight line past the wolves, and they didn't turn a hair. Then we made him do it staggering, as if drunk, when he was in fact stone cold sober, with no trace of alcohol anywhere, and they went crazy. We videoed him to see if we could work out what was going on, and then one of the biologists produced a video he had made of wolves hunting among a herd of bison. One of the bison calves was injured, and when we played the footage of the calf on a television screen alongside the footage of the handler staggering, we realised that the pattern of their movement was exactly the same. The wolves were not reacting to the alcohol; they were seeing him as prey, and the chances are they would have taken him if they had been able to get at him. It left a serious question mark about whether he would be able to continue working with that pack.

Chapter Eleven

THE CALL OF
THE WILD

These wolves had been born in captivity but they had not lost any of their instincts. Being in with them was always challenging and unpredictable and I never felt I could let down my guard for an instant. But I started to wonder how different wild wolves would be and whether I could be accepted by a pack that had never encountered humans. That would be the ultimate experiment. I was also keen to discover whether Levi's theory was right and there had been wolves already in the area that had used some ancient route – and what that route might be.

The biologists at the camp were quite forcefully opposed to my plan; some were downright hostile. They thought my theories and beliefs were misguided and apart from any scientific objections, they thought it would be a suicide mission. To them I was a maverick from a foreign country with no qualifications – and it was hard to argue against that. What I wanted to do went against every scientific principle; as biologists they observed but they didn't touch, and they followed well-defined methodology. But I wasn't a scientist; I didn't have a reputation to lose, as they did. I didn't have a fear of not succeeding; from a scientific point of view I had nothing to lose and everything to gain.

They had other concerns too. They were afraid that I might change the wolves in some way, stop them being fearful of humans and encourage them to approach people and therefore farms and communities. This was less easy to dismiss, but my hope was that I might be able to teach them something about humans before they met a mother taking her young child to school and their first experience became a disaster.

There was no certainty I would even find wolves, let alone get close to them, and there was a strong possibility I might be killed in the attempt, but I was determined to try. The final decision, however, was Levi's, and being the sort of man he was he didn't stop me. I think that secretly some of the Indians – maybe even Levi – felt slightly envious of what I was doing. They too might have liked to take off into the forest, but they had families and jobs and responsibilities.

I had prepared myself as best I could. I was physically fit; I had been running, walking and lifting weights for months. I had studied maps, read books and talked to the tribal elders about the wolves. And before I left England I had gathered together some good kit. I had been to a shop that catered for extreme sports and explained what I needed, and they had given me a number of items to trial for them, free of charge. I had three pairs of socks, for example, that were supposed to breathe and not need washing, and a kind of second skin that I wore in place of underwear that was warm in the cold and cool in the heat. The rest I had bought: good walking boots and an all-in-one, supposedly waterproof quilted jumpsuit with ventilation panels under the arms. Other than that I had jeans and a couple of layers on my top, gloves and a hat.

I didn't take a sleeping bag or any kind of shelter and I didn't intend to do any cooking. I wanted to be as much like a lone wolf as I could, so a fire was out of the question and a sleeping bag would just have been a nuisance. I took a day sack containing a water bottle, purification tablets, a knife, some wire and some string to make snare traps, a signal flare in case I needed to alert anyone to my position, a compass, a map, a notebook and pen and some very salty beef jerky in case I had difficulty finding food.

I set out from the camp as soon as the sun was up one autumn morning and took the old trail that followed the Salmon River. It was the path along which the legendary Chief Joseph took the Nez Perce to escape the US cavalry in 1877. Although that journey ended in his surrender in Montana, it was acknowledged as one of the most brilliant military retreats in American history. With a band of about seven hundred Indians, fewer than two hundred of whom were warriors, he fought two thousand US soldiers, and to this day he is honoured among the tribe as a humanitarian and a peacemaker. The elders would talk at length about Chief Joseph and the history of the tribe and how their lands were systematically taken from them by the white man. Joseph had promised his dying father than he would never sign a treaty selling the land that held the bones of his father and mother. 'A man who would not defend his father's grave is worse than a wild animal,' he allegedly said, but in the end he decided that breaking the promise to his father was better than further bloodshed.

It was a track that tourists used during the summer months; the scenery was spectacular, with glorious colours, but I knew it was not as benign as it looked. I would need all the survival skills I could muster to stay alive in this terrain – and a great deal of luck too. The Rockies were beautiful but hostile and they covered a vast area. I was stepping into the unknown, against all advice, and I wasn't sure if, or for how long, I would be able to cope. At that altitude the temperatures dropped to dangerous levels at night, and if the cold didn't kill me – or the wolves – there was always the possibility of an angry bear or some other predator. I had had rudimentary lessons on how to deal with bears, but they still terrified me. The biologists had talked about taking guns and radios and telephones and arranging rendezvous every twelve hours, but it wouldn't have worked; it would have involved too much contact with humans which would have frightened the wolves away. I wanted to give myself the best chance of success and that meant taking risks that maybe others wouldn't have taken. I was going against every safety code known to man, but then I'd always gone my own way, trodden a different path from the herd.

I would like to say that my apprehension soon disappeared, the training kicked and I was rapidly focused on staying alive. But that would be a lie. I was in shock for the first two to three weeks – convinced that if I managed to get out of there alive after any longer than that I'd be very lucky. I barely moved in that time, rather like an animal tentatively exploring a new environment. I stayed close to safety, to what I thought of as my 'get out of jail free' card. I had agreed a rendezvous point with Levi where I would leave my day sack – my bag – and he or someone from the camp would drive to it every couple of days to check that I was OK. Any time I wanted to come home I simply had to wait there; and we both used the notebook as a means of leaving each other messages. The track would have been impassable when the snows came, but there were search and rescue helicopters available if it became necessary and the team at the camp knew what they were doing. If I had been attacked by a bear, of course, or any other animal, no amount of contingency plans would have helped.

Those first few weeks I walked no further from the bag area than fifteen or twenty miles. It was a battle between my determination to find wolves and the very human side of me that was scared stiff and didn't want to commit suicide. I was so frightened of predators that

I didn't dare move after dark, and for the first four nights I slept in a tree, although sleeping was hardly the word. I was listening for every sound and occasionally nodding off briefly, and it was only when I fell out of the tree on the fifth night that I started sleeping on the ground. I didn't fall far; not more than fifteen feet, but I realised that if it happened again and I injured myself, I would probably die anyway, either from the cold or starvation. The Native Americans would always say that every warrior wants an honourable death, and I didn't relish the idea of being known as the only person who worked with wolves to have killed himself falling out of a tree.

Gradually I became more confident and began to venture out by day. I analysed scats and tracks on the ground to establish what sort of animals I was sharing this untouched wilderness with. Then I plucked up the courage to stay up at night. I changed my sleeping pattern – although I still wasn't doing a whole lot of sleeping. I started cat-napping and dozing mostly during the day. I thought it was important not to establish any patterns that might attract the attention of a predator. I made rudimentary snare traps with wire and string and a bendy stick, set them in runs where I could see animals followed the same paths day after day, and caught my first rabbit before my rations of jerky ran out. I skinned and gutted it but only ate the legs. I had eaten rabbit raw before, a strong, gamey meat, but I had to be really hungry, which I was later, to eat the rest of the animal – and starving to eat the stomach content. I also caught birds, rodents and other small mammals such as squirrels. I didn't go for anything larger than a rabbit because being on my own I couldn't risk being gored by antlers or injured in any way. That would have stopped me hunting, and without food I would have died.

Killing wasn't hard for me. I had been killing for the pot since I was a child, and even before I was old enough to do the job myself I had seen my grandfather do it so often that it had never crossed my mind to be squeamish. But I realised during my commando training that most people were. One day we were each given a soft, fluffy rabbit to look after for the afternoon. Four or five hours later we were told to kill the rabbits; they were our next meal. My rough, tough fellow recruits couldn't do it; they were horrified, so I had to dispatch the whole lot myself. The only problem here in the wild was the likelihood of other predators finding the kill before I did. I was eating a diet, like the wolf's, that provided quality not quantity, and one meal of raw meat gave me enough slow-release energy to keep going for a day and a half to two days. Sometimes I would supplement it with nuts and berries but I always did a poison test, a survival trick I had learnt in the army, before eating too much of anything.

As the weeks went by I established a routine and found an area in which I felt comfortable. I could hear deer, badgers and owls, and a wolf or coyote gave a brief call, but I didn't see a living thing for four weeks. I was in my element – alone with nature and living on my wits – surrounded by the most breathtaking scenery and on the track of wolves. It was like being a learner driver passing my test and suddenly having the freedom to take the car out by myself. I was feeling positively cocky, invincible and as though I could have stayed there for ever.

Then I experienced my first reality check. The weather changed and for four days the most horrendous storm raged around me. Nothing moved, the animals sat tight and my food source dried up. I realised that when bad weather hits, nature just closes down and sits it out. I had no alternative but to do the same; I sheltered under a collection of evergreen trees and became bored and depressed. My routine was what had been keeping me happy. Now I was hungry and my mind and body were beginning to shut down. Then the training kicked in and I remembered what I'd been taught in the military about how vital it is to keep thinking positively. No matter what situation you find yourself in, no matter how hopeless it appears, you have to quickly look for your options: how are you going to feed yourself, and what can you use to protect yourself, or to patch up your wounds? You have to keep your spirits up – or you are dead. Wolves are the same; they never give up, never feel sorry for themselves, and even if they are mortally wounded they keep running. And above all things I wanted to be like a wolf. Most human beings want to make the animals they love be more like them; I had always wanted to be more like the animals I loved.

It was two and a half months before I found the first trace of a wolf. I was beginning to despair when I came across a small water hole with a bank of soft mud around it, and in the mud was the print of one large male wolf. It was the most exciting moment but also unnerving. Seeing no evidence of any other animals, I guessed he must have been a lone wolf. I decided to stay there that night and when the light faded I howled. It was ridiculously brave – or foolish – because it immediately made my position known to any predator. And all for nothing; there was no response. I was disappointed but not really surprised. That night I didn't even doze; I lay under a tree and listened to all the creatures of the forest grunting, hooting and calling, aware that I had recklessly put myself in danger.

I saw and heard nothing for the next three weeks. I became very depressed and began to wonder what on earth I was doing here. I longed for some comfort and normality; to be able to relax and enjoy a full night's sleep without having to worry because I'd heard a twig snap. I hadn't had that luxury in more than three months.

And then in the middle of the night I heard the first sound. It was a low tone, so probably a male, and I guessed it was a wolf of beta rank and probably one that was away from his pack rather than a lone wolf. It was coming from the tree line but it was hard to gauge distance. I reckoned he might have been about three-quarters of a mile away. I was tempted to howl back but thought better of it. If I had howled I would have had to move – I wasn't going to be a sitting duck like the last time – and I didn't want to have to stumble around in the dark.

Another three weeks went by with nothing – not a paw print, not a sound – and then suddenly as I was walking down a track in the middle of the afternoon, a big black wolf crossed the track about one hundred and fifty metres in front of me. It stopped fleetingly and looked straight at me with piercing yellow eyes before disappearing into the forest. I didn't have time to see whether it was male or female, or whether it matched the description of any of the wolves that had been released. It was gone in a flash and I was left wondering whether I had really seen it or it had been a figment of my imagination.

I was so excited. The doubts I had been turning over in my mind about the trip vanished. The depression was gone. All I thought about from that moment onwards was how close I might be able to get to this creature. Was this the wolf I had heard howl? Was it the one whose footprint I had seen in mud? I had seen no evidence of more than one animal in the area. And what if I discovered it was a genuine wild wolf, born and bred in the area with no interference from man whatsoever? I hardly dared consider the possibility. Given its response to me, it was obviously not used to humans or comfortable around them. How would I do it? I considered leaving some food around, but then realised that although that might attract the wolf it might also bring other predators into the area. Should I take my courage in both hands and try to communicate with it? If it was a lone wolf it might respond on the grounds that even though it wouldn't be a pair bonding it is always safer to be two than one, but it would be alerting others to my whereabouts. I weighed up the pros and cons of all my options.

I had to take a risk; that was what I had come here for and what the last four months had been all about. If I did take it to the next stage – and it was a completely different stage to take it to – then my routine would have to change; I would have to step right outside my comfort zone. I wasn't going to be able to sit tight at night; I would have to sleep through the day and move around in the dark, which was a prospect I didn't fancy at all.

To do anything in that environment, whether it's for survival, recreation or charity, takes courage. It means exposing yourself to everything we humans fear most – the dark, the forest, the wolf, the bear and all the dangers of nature. The Indians had the right idea. They used to send their children, at the age of eight or nine, on to the mountain alone for five days. Some of them still do it today. It was a kind of baptism that exorcised the childish terror that the rest of us feel even as adults; they made peace with the natural world in the way that Levi had made peace with the bear. He didn't fear it, and it didn't fear him.

Fitness is the key to every creature's survival. No predator will risk taking down another predator that is fit, because there's a chance it might get injured in the attempt, and the minute any animal has an injury or shows weakness of any kind it might as well be dead.

That first night was terrifying. I knew what I was doing was dangerous, more dangerous than any of the nights I had spent with captive packs. My eyes were not designed to see in the dark and if I stumbled or fell a predator could have me in seconds. It was like swimming with sharks: they had all the advantages and I had none. I didn't go far; no more than six or seven miles, stopping after every step and listening, knowing that however quiet I tried to be, with every step I was giving away my position. There was no moon and I was surprised by how much I could see without it, but everything appeared in shades of grey. I scanned my surroundings for movement; that was the key. Every sense I possessed was heightened. I took deep breaths of air to catch smells; I used the wind to bring sound and scent of the creatures around me, something I'd never done before. I could hear every stretch and sigh and, at times, I swear I could hear my own heartbeat, it was thumping so loudly.

Bears were my greatest fear because they were so unpredictable. Since man's interaction with them, their patterns of behaviour had changed and they were just as likely to be wandering through the forest at night as in the day. Because of their experience of picnickers and campers they had come to regard man as a supplier of food and would follow humans in the expectation of being given something to eat. That is why they were around the Education Center so much. They were fast and agile, and if you inadvertently surprised a bear or came between a mother and her cubs it could be game over very quickly. It took a long time for me to conquer my fear of them, and I think even today my immediate reaction to bears is one of fear not respect.

The night – which I had thought might be my last – passed without incident. Dawn brought the first light of a new day and I was alive and unscathed and ready to welcome it with open arms. I felt elated. I may have flunked every exam at school and been a failure in so many ways, but suddenly none of that mattered. I had achieved more in this one night in the wilds of the Rocky Mountains among some of the most dangerous mammals on the planet than I had achieved in thirty years living among my own kind. The excitement I felt that morning was hard to contain. It was good to be alive – and never again would I be made to feel inadequate.

Chapter Twelve

A WAITING
GAME

It was, however, just one night. I tried to rest the following day but I was too excited for that and the next night I wasn't up to it, so I stayed put and went out again on the third night. What I would have done if the wolf had howled, I wasn't sure. Would I have howled in return and let every predator in the forest know where I was? I told myself that I was waiting for him or her to call me, but I think it was just an excuse. I was still very afraid.

I had established a resting place where I felt safe and comfortable, about eighteen miles away from the track where I'd seen the wolf. It was in a clearing. I had a big rock behind me and a good view of the immediate area in front of me, and although I never allowed myself the luxury of sleeping for hours at a stretch, I could sleep in short bursts and feel reasonably secure. It was from there that I went out each night in search of the wolf. A wolf's territory is generally egg-shaped, so I walked in egg-shaped circles, growing more confident as time passed and I continued to find myself alive at first light. My senses were improving. My eyesight was never going to be good in

the dark, but everything else made up for it: I could hear a pine nee-
dle drop, and I could smell the different animals that observed me as
I crept through their world without needing to see them move.

The one animal I neither saw nor heard nor smelt was the wolf. He
or she seemed to have vanished and after a while I decided to go back
to the bag area, where I had left my day sack, to see if there was any
news for me and to let Levi and the others know what was going on.
I felt a huge sense of despair. Having been so elated after the sighting
and surviving my first night in the forest, I was now as low as I had
ever been. I was on an emotional roller-coaster and quite unable to
control it. I had come so close and yet was still so far. I still didn't know
whether this wolf was truly wild or whether I would ever see him or
her again. I began to have all the nagging doubts over again about the
whole mission. There was no note for me at the bag, but from the
footprints on the ground around it I knew that Levi or someone from
the camp had been there. So I wrote a note myself, telling them about
the sighting, took more of the jerky, putting what I didn't eat into my
pocket, and set off back to where I had just come from.

It must have been a good four weeks before I saw another wolf –
or maybe it was the same wolf. It was early evening and I was resting
under a tree in a clearing with the wind towards me. That was the
way I preferred to be, so that I could smell any creature before it came
into my line of vision. I was becoming more like a wild animal with
every day that passed – and probably smelling more like one too. I
hadn't changed my clothes in five or six months or done more than
every now and again splash water from the river over my face, my
crotch and under my arms. My hair was uncombed and my beard
unshaven.

This wolf was big and black and came out of the tree line heading
directly towards me. It stopped, looked at me quite calmly for thirty
or forty seconds and then turned to its right and disappeared back

into the forest. It didn't seem to be afraid of me, which made me suspect that it had been watching me for some time and for whatever reason had finally decided to put in an appearance.

For the next month I saw it intermittently every two or three days. It would appear when I was least expecting it and in every situation. I would be walking through the forest and, after stopping to rest, be sitting listening to the life around me, and suddenly there it would be in the clearing; or I'd be setting a trap, eating or collecting water from the river and I would look round and see two big amber eyes watching me. I got the feeling it was following me around and seeing far more of me than I ever saw of it. I never spoke – I didn't want the wolf to think of me as human or to teach it to think that humans were harmless. The plan I had in my head was to frighten the wolf when I left the forest so the lasting impression it would have of man would be negative. But that was for later. Right now I wanted it to trust me, so every time I saw it I dropped down low, or lay propped up on an elbow to let it know I was no threat.

After another couple of weeks our courtship moved to a new stage. It was early morning and I was half awake, half asleep when I heard the magical sound of a howl. This time it sounded more like an enquiry than any of the previous howls I had heard. What should I do? Answer and expose my whereabouts or play safe and stay silent? I weighed up the options. I now knew this area well and the only tracks I had seen were deer; I hadn't come across any evidence of predators – although that didn't mean they weren't there. I decided to go for it. I cupped my hands around my mouth and gave the response I hoped this wolf was wanting. I waited with bated breath, my heart in my mouth. Minutes passed, which felt like hours, and then the silence was broken by a long mellifluous howl that made the hairs on the back of my neck stand up. I had a reply. I could hardly believe it; it was a miracle. He or she had called back to me. I still hadn't seen this creature for long enough to know for sure what sex it was, but guessed by its size that it was a male, although black females also tended to be large animals.

That exchange was the turning point in our relationship. Over the next two weeks scarcely a day went by when I didn't see this wolf – and it was a young male. He didn't come much closer but I would see him standing watching me, and when our eyes met he would look, linger for a moment or two and then disappear into the trees. At night we howled back and forth to each other, and the distance between us would have been no more than two or three hundred metres.

And then I made the most amazing discovery. This was not a lone wolf. He was part of a pack of five and my guess was that either he had been curious about me and had taken it upon himself to investigate or, more likely, he had been sent to check me out by the alpha female.

I was in a clearing late one afternoon, sitting with my back to a rock, when he appeared out of the tree line as he had now done so many times before. As I looked at him, wondering whether we would ever get any closer, a second wolf appeared and then a third, fourth and fifth. One by one they wove in and out of the forest, giving me just the briefest glimpse of each. There were three males in the pack and two females, and seeing them together I realised that the male that had been communicating with me was possibly a pup from last year or the previous year and one of the females was his sister. The others were all fully-grown adults and not one of them matched the descriptions that I had of the wolves that had been released; these were not B2, B3, B4 or B5. Unless I was much mistaken, these wolves were truly wild.

I was so excited. I could scarcely believe it. This was the most incredible sighting. I had seen what others had only dreamt of, and I'd seen them because they chose to make themselves known to me.

This was so much better than anything I could have hoped for. I was on a complete high. And then as swiftly as my spirits had soared, I was brought back down to earth. The wolves disappeared. I searched for them. On the assumption that they had been watching me for weeks if not months before they let me see them, I repeated my pattern of behaviour. I stayed in the area and I called, but nothing came back. I started to worry that the young male had been chastised for getting too close to me, that he'd made a mistake and they had punished him by moving away. All sorts of crazy ideas went through my head as I went through the motions of my daily life. Yet I somehow couldn't believe them; I kept coming back to my conviction that the adults had been using him to investigate me.

A month later I was once again sitting in a clearing with my back against a rock when the pack reappeared as suddenly and as silently as they had vanished. They had lost a member; one of the older males was missing, and they seemed to be more flighty than they had been when I had first seen them. Even the young male seemed apprehensive and wary. Despite this, they settled down to spend the afternoon resting and playing by the tree line about a hundred metres away from me. The young ones were wrestling with each other, growling and whimpering, breaking away and then pouncing, and they would squeak when the play became too rough. The older ones growled from time to time in a grumpy sort of way, and when the pups had exhausted themselves with their mock fighting they lay flat out and slept while their elders kept watch.

That night I heard the pack howling, presumably for the fifth animal. I wondered where he was and what had happened to him. He could have been lost or killed during the month they had been away or he could have been right here, in the area, patrolling around the back of me, preparing to catch me off guard. I was not foolish enough to think, because they had come back and allowed me to watch them relax, that they necessarily thought of me as a good thing. I wondered what they *did* think of me; or if they had any idea that they were the highlight of my day – or how incredibly proud I felt to have made such progress with them.

The progress continued. I saw them most days. I had my sleeping area still, but every day I walked the ten or eleven miles to the clearing where I had first seen them. That was where I continued to see them, and although they still kept their distance, they seemed to be a lot more comfortable and relaxed in front of me. For the next three or four nights they howled. I assumed it was still for their lost family member but he never responded. One night I plucked up the courage to respond instead – as a lone wolf might have done, when he sensed there was a vacancy – and the whole pack howled back to me. It was another memorable moment and I realised I was losing my fear. I was taking comfort in their presence, feeling as though in some way I was coming under their protection in this hostile environment that I'd battled by myself to survive in for so many months. I didn't feel so alone any more. I realised I was beginning to need them.

I hoped and expected the distance they kept from me would steadily diminish, but what actually happened took me by surprise. The brother and sister were playing about fifty metres from me, and the adult female was about a hundred metres away. I hadn't seen the other male – or given it any thought. Suddenly I heard a twig snap just behind me. I quickly turned and there was the male, a big powerful animal, standing less than ten metres from me. I was sitting, defenceless; he could have been on me in a flash, and I realised once again just how vulnerable and inadequate I was in their world. His presence wasn't threatening though. He didn't even look at me. He looked over my shoulder at the young ones playing and I felt as though he was including me in the family group, just as the foxes had done in that field in Norfolk. Previously I had been an outsider observing a life that didn't involve me; now, rightly or wrongly, I felt a great surge of belonging.

Things moved rapidly after that. One day I was squatting on a low rock watching them interact in their usual way when the same big male broke away from the others and came directly towards me, trotting at first then slowing to a walk. I was expecting him to turn away at any moment but he kept on coming until he was within about seven metres. His tail went up, and I wondered what he was planning. I was not in a good position to defend myself. My bottom was lower than my knees and if I needed to get up in a hurry it would be difficult; but if I moved now I might destroy everything we had been building up to. He eased forward slowly, then crouched down and stretched his head until it was about twelve inches from my legs – as though not wanting to get his body any closer than absolutely necessary. Next he began to sniff my knees and then my walking boots and he seemed particularly interested in the instep. My heart was in my mouth. Where was this going to end? As purposefully as he had arrived he turned and walked back to the others, moving his tail from side to side as he went, and they greeted him as though he had been away for weeks, frantically licking his mouth and muzzle area. In the midst of this frenzy he turned on the young female, growling and snapping at her, and she quickly dropped down on to her back and displayed her submissive underside for a moment. Then she was on her feet again and they all disappeared into the forest.

I heard nothing from them that night and was disappointed. I spent the night trying to figure out why he had broken the pattern and done what he did so suddenly. What was his next move going to be, and how should I prepare? Should I go to the clearing in the dark? I decided against it. That would have been giving them all the advantages. These animals were built for the dark, I wasn't, and if the big male had come at me in the dark as he had done in daylight, my reaction might have been very different because I would have felt less confident and that might have had unfortunate consequences. I decided to keep to my routine and return at first light – fully expecting that to be the day when I would meet and greet the whole pack.

Chapter Thirteen

WORTH
THE WAIT

There was no sign of them; and no sign again on the second day. It wasn't until the afternoon of the third day that they appeared, while I was dozing. Their energy levels seemed to have changed and they were more assured than before and more purposeful, as though they had some kind of agenda. I was relieved to see them and watched while they interacted with one another. Then the big male broke away from the others and made a beeline for me, as he had done before but more confidently. He didn't crouch down this time, he remained standing while he sniffed, and then without warning he lunged forward and nipped the flesh beneath my knee with his incisors. It was exactly what the beta male at Sparkwell had done before accepting me into the pack at the wildlife park. He immediately pulled back and looked at me, quizzically. It was painful and he drew blood but it didn't feel dangerous. I wanted to grin from ear to ear but I didn't react. He lunged forward again and nipped the same place, three times in all, stepping back and looking at me after each bite, and then he turned, walked back to the rest of the pack and lay down with them. The temptation to go and join them was practically irresistible, but I didn't want to do anything that would spoil the magic of what had just happened. An hour later they were gone.

Two days after that we had a repeat performance. Again it was the big male, but this time the two youngsters came with him and stood either side of him watching. Occasionally he snapped and growled at them as if to keep them in order. He sniffed my knees and feet, checking for any new smells or danger that I might be bringing to him and the pups. Again he nipped my knee several times, and then he brushed and rubbed himself along my sides, as a dog might do, and sniffed round the back of my head. I could feel his fangs on my neck. I was frozen to the spot, waiting for his jaws to clamp around my throat, which would bring either instant death or acceptance, but it didn't happen. At that moment, the young male gave me a much gentler nip on my knee while the older male knocked me off my perch on the rock. As I fell I put a hand out to steady myself and found it resting on the pup's shoulder. He didn't pull away; he felt like no wolf I had ever touched, and in that split second I was overcome by an incredible surge of love for this creature and his family and an overpowering need to be part of it.

I knew there and then that when those wolves went back to the dominant female I was going to go with them. It was now or never and I had to satisfy this incredible urge to be accepted. I followed them. I was on all fours, which was clumsy and cumbersome, but they looked back several times and saw me behind them and seemed unfazed, so I kept going. I was confident I had made the right decision until I reached the matriarch. She was hostile, not ready to tolerate me coming any closer than twenty or thirty metres and was clearly extremely nervous. She barked and growled and the others immediately looked as though they realised they had done something wrong. The young ones sprang to her side and stood glaring at me. I got the impression that the older male was trying to act as go-between to diffuse the situation, but at the end of the day his loyalty was to his leader. She got to her feet, flattened her ears, lifted her lips over bared her teeth and let out low barking noises which warned me to stay away. She then took the young pups and ran into the forest. The big male lingered; the young male reappeared and stood next to him for a second or two, then they both turned and were gone.

I felt huge depression – and loss – but then I reminded myself of just what I had achieved that day. Three of them had accepted me; the female hadn't and her decision had been final, but I had still made great strides. I went back to my night-time resting place as darkness fell. If the female had accepted me I might have been tempted to follow the pack and make a bid to join it that evening, but since she hadn't I didn't feel safe staying in that area in the dark. I thought she could be dangerous.

That was the last I saw of them for a week and a half. I decided it was time to go back to the bag area; I had lost track of how long I had been gone by this time, but it must have been nine or ten months and I thought I should leave a note to tell Levi what was going on. It was a journey of two and a half days from my overnight spot and during that time I mulled over in my mind what had happened. On the one hand I was elated; on the other I was profoundly depressed. I had no idea where the pack went when they disappeared and I was entirely dependent upon them coming back and finding me. Now that I had upset the dominant female, however, maybe she would never bring them back again.

I reached the day sack, wrote a note and spent a couple of nights there chilling and catching up on some real sleep – something I hadn't had in months – before retracing my footsteps. I had enjoyed having a full night's sleep and I was tempted by the idea of a shower, some human company and a hot meal, but I was too excited and too close to give up now. I had a chance to go further towards infiltrating a wild wolf pack than anyone, so far as I knew, had ever gone before. I had to go back.

I arrived back at my sleeping site two and a half days later and the next morning made my way to the clearing in the forest where all our interaction had taken place. No one came. I repeated the process every day for a week before the four wolves reappeared. There were no calls; they just suddenly came out of the tree line and were there. Wherever they had been, they looked well fed.

I was sitting on my rock, as usual, and the big male and the pups immediately came towards me. They seemed more confident than before. The female stayed back and I respected her distance. That evening they went into the forest and I went to my resting site and the next day we met again. And so it went on for two weeks, if not a month. Every time I attempted to get any closer to the female she laid her ears back, growled and ran off, but slowly, bit by bit, I managed to get closer before she ran away, and eventually she stood her ground and just growled. Sometimes the big male would push me away.

I continued during that time to interact with the other three members of the pack, however, and the bond with them quietly intensified. In some ways they were like the captive wolves I had known and in other ways not. The language they used was similar but these wolves were stronger and they were constantly on guard, alert to every sound and scent and change in the air. One of them was always on lookout and even the pups would stop in the midst of their play every now and again and listen. Their play-fights and games were far more intense than those of captive wolves. Their bites were more painful and they didn't pull their punches; they played as hard and roughly with me as they played with each other. I was covered in cuts and bruises but it was manageable. My all-in-one suit was quilted but it didn't protect me from the bone-crushing strength of their jaws, and it was still scary when they held me down with their full weight on top of me.

When the pain was too intense, I had to give a shrill, high-pitched yelp before they would release me, which seemed to get the female to her feet. She didn't come and help me but she seemed interested in what was going on. She still wouldn't let me near her. Whenever I came close she would growl and lift her lips at me. It was never going to be a friendship made in heaven. The only consolation was that she was as intolerant with the pups as she was with me.

I felt we had reached a bit of a stalemate. I was almost a member of the pack but not quite. They would still go off into the forest every now and again for days if not weeks and leave me behind. They would call from afar but they were locating calls, not rallying. They weren't inviting me to join them and I still had no idea where they went when they left.

Early one morning I was in the clearing when the four of them appeared after a long absence. As usual, I lowered my body as they came towards me – this time even the female came as if to greet me. She stopped within about ten metres of me and sat and watched as the big male made contact. I could tell that their mood had changed; they were more boisterous, the energy levels were up. He barged at me and covered me with his powerful body; I crumpled to the ground under his weight. I wasn't particularly worried; he had done this kind of thing in the past, but before I realised what was happening the female had changed places with him and the snarling and growling that she had been doing at thirty metres she was now doing three inches from my face. I could feel the warmth of her breath, her lips were lifted right back from her teeth; I thought this was going to be the end. The male tried to muscle in. I didn't know whether he was trying to save me or join the kill, but she snapped and bit his muzzle and he retreated. I lay there helpless. I had no choice but to take whatever was coming to me.

She was on me for the longest two or three minutes of my life but she didn't harm so much as a hair on my head. When she finally let me go she loped back to the others; my disciplining was over. The incident didn't seem to change her attitude towards me but it radically changed my attitude towards her. I knew she could have killed me easily but had chosen not to and that made a big difference. Up to that point I had believed she was dangerous. Now I thought of her as an intolerant aunt; a creature that was incredibly knowledgeable, rightly respected and very much in charge but one of those characters who were always bad-tempered. We would learn to tolerate each other.

Every night I battled with my better judgement over leaving the wolves. I had begun to feel safer with them than away from them, but my routine had been to leave them as darkness fell and be back again by first light. One evening tensions were low, they had all had a good feed and even Miss Grumpy seemed relaxed. I decided to stay and see what happened. It was a massive anti-climax. I didn't sleep a wink – kept awake by a mixture of fear and excitement – but they all slept soundly until morning. The male pup came and lay alongside me, which was warming even though we weren't touching. It was strangely comforting to have another creature sleeping alongside me after all these months on my own. I could hear his breathing and I felt his every twitch. When morning broke I was walking on air. I had done nothing more than spend the night with these wolves, but it meant I had been accepted. I couldn't have felt a greater sense of achievement if I'd run a triple marathon.

The next stage was to try and stay with them when they went off into the forest. Like every step I took with these wolves it was fraught with danger. If I managed to keep up, which was a big if, and they took me somewhere completely unfamiliar, I might not be able to get back. And if they began to hunt, I knew I wouldn't have a hope of following. I would then be on my own in an area I didn't know with all the vulnerability of being alone. The situation didn't arise.

For the next day and night they were restless and in the early hours of the second day they took off. I was right behind them and did my best to follow, but as soon as we were among the trees they were invisible in the darkness and they were gone. Dejected and disappointed, I had no alternative but to go back to the clearing and wait and hope for them to return.

It was a long wait but one morning, I'd lost count of how many weeks later, they not only reappeared, the young female had brought me food. It was the leg of a red deer. She played with it for a bit then dropped it purposefully by my side. I started to eat it and she sat and watched – so I was obviously doing the right thing. I was hungry and after months of nothing bigger than rabbit, it tasted fantastic. For the next few weeks this became the pattern. They would go off hunting and leave me – even in the daylight I found it impossible to follow – but they would always bring me something on their return. It seemed clear to me that they didn't want me to hunt but were happy to have me around and to feed me.

When they were gone I would howl and sometimes, if they were near enough for my ears to pick up the sound, I heard them call back. And they always seemed to call when they were on their way back. Their voices were familiar and comforting and gave me a very warm feeling. I realised how attached I had become to these wolves and how dependent I'd become on their being around. I would worry that one of them might not come back. It might have an accident or be injured or, worse, killed – as I assumed the fifth member of the pack must have been – and I would hold my breath until I counted them all safely into the clearing. I was even pleased to see the grumpy female. It was like the agony of waiting for loved ones who are late coming home. Then there would be a great greeting ceremony. They licked me furiously around my face and mouth, exactly as they greeted each other, and I was so excited to see them I did the same, running round to each of them like a little pup, frantically licking and nuzzling and vying for their attention. The only exception was the female, who still wouldn't let me anywhere near her – but she wouldn't tolerate the others either.

Sometimes it would suddenly strike me: if anyone had suggested a year or more ago that I would one day be happy eating nothing for three days and then be so thrilled to see a pack of wild wolves that I'd go around licking their jaws, I would have laughed at the absurdity of the idea. But right now, these wolves were the most important thing in my life; they were my family and I loved each and every one of them. But I knew I had to let them go.

Chapter Fourteen

THE PATTER
OF TINY FEET

Abattle had been raging in my head for a long time; I had been in
the wild for about eighteen months. I wanted to stay with these
wolves and be a part of their world more than anything I had ever
wanted, but in my heart of hearts I knew it was time to leave. It was
one of the hardest decisions I'd ever made but I had no doubt it was
the right thing to do. I had always had the biologists' concerns in the
back of my head, and the relationship had now moved on to a different level. I had done what I set out to do and I was worried that if
I stayed any longer they might well get a false sense of security about
human beings and that could be very dangerous for them.

I had taken great pains not to display any human traits, and I
behaved in every respect like a low-ranking wolf, but there was no getting away from the fact that I was human.

I didn't know exactly how long I had been living like this. Spring
was approaching once again and with it the breeding season; what
would my role be then? Would they ask me to leave the pack, or would
they want me as nanny to look after the pups? That would have been

a huge responsibility that I wasn't sure I was up to. And would my being human seal their fate in the future? Would they learn to trust humans as much as they did their own kind, with disastrous consequences? And so very quietly under my breath I said 'Goodbye and good luck, guys' and set off for the bag.

I walked for two days and two nights, crying most of the way, able at last to display the emotion that, with the wolves, I had kept bottled up, and able at last to use my human voice. I felt utterly bereft and although I knew the arguments about why I needed to leave and rehearsed them over and over again to myself as I walked, often out loud, I couldn't stop thinking I was making a big mistake. I had come so far, jumped through so many hoops – and had the scars to prove it. I had been on a mental and physical roller-coaster for months – living with fear and danger twenty-four hours a day – but I had come through that. I was now part of the pack, the wolves accepted me, protected me, fed me.

No one had ever done this before. There were stories about children being adopted by wolves and walking out of the forest on all fours unable to speak, but no one had gone into the forest as I had done and become part of a wolf family. By the time I reached the rendezvous point I realised I could no more leave those wolves than fly to the moon. I wrote Levi a note telling him what I was doing and turned round and retraced my footsteps.

In the time I had been away the weather had broken. Winter was on its way and the first snows arrived a few weeks later. That would change everything. It would make getting about more difficult but, on the plus side, the snow would enable me to follow the wolves at my own pace. At last I would be able to find out where it was they went to when they were away for so long. But I still had the dilemma of how far to follow them. I could get back to civilisation in just over two days from the clearing – I had just done it; I knew the terrain well enough to walk it in the pitch dark and I knew the animals that lived in the area. If I followed the wolves for another two or three days I would be completely out of my comfort zone and too far away to have a realistic chance of making it back to the bag area if I broke a leg or found myself with some other kind of injury. But had I really come this far only to turn back now because it seemed too risky?

The day the wolves left, I followed. Their pace was slower than on the occasions I had tried to follow them in the past and they seemed to be waiting for me. Even the grumpy female stopped every now and again and looked back to make sure I was keeping up. We must have covered ten or fifteen miles, heading towards the north-west, and the terrain was getting steeper and more rugged by the mile. The bag, my security, as I was acutely aware, was south-east, so we were travelling in the diametrically opposite direction. I had imagined they might take me to their hunting ground, but I was wrong. We came instead to a steep hillside, heavily forested with a river running along the valley about six hundred metres below.

We arrived there before the snow and the ground was thick with pine needles; and the smell, like so much of the forest, was pleasantly aromatic. There was also a strong scent of wolf, and from the way the animals relaxed when we arrived I guessed they came here often. It was possibly where they lived during the winter, or it might have been where the youngsters had been born. Whatever it was, they made every indication that we were here to stay.

They never let me follow them to the hunting ground. The big male growled and went for me if ever I tried – it was his way of disciplining me – but I was never without food. It came thick and fast and I was always presented with as much as I could eat. I was eating much better quality meat with them than I had ever managed by myself, and good clear water was just a short walk away down the track into the valley. On occasions when I was left alone I took the opportunity to wash in the stream, and although it was still nothing more than splashing icy water over me, it helped dislodge some of the mud that was caked to me and made me feel slightly fresher. It was hard to feel entirely fresh when I was wearing clothes that I had been in day and night for the best part of eighteen months. They were beginning to fall apart in places, and the one-piece suit had taken a bit of a battering from teeth and claws during fights and romps with the wolves but it was all holding together, and even if it was no longer entirely waterproof, on many occasions I was thankful to have had such a sturdy and warm outfit.

We were entering the breeding season, and suddenly everyone's blood was up. The energy levels of the males went through the roof as they began their courtship and my role turned into resident punch-bag. They were in deadly competition with each other, each desperate to convince the dominant female that he was the one she should choose as her mate – the one who could defend her most effectively – and they were ready to see off any other passing males that might have fancied their chances too. They prowled about looking for trouble, nipping each other repeatedly on the flank hoping to provoke a response, which for me, without the layer of fur they had, was very painful. They simply wanted to get their pheromone and adrenalin levels up to make themselves more attractive to the female, and the harder and more aggressively they fought, the higher the levels rose. So they would pick fights and take their frustration out on the lowest-ranking member of the pack, which was me.

These fights were infinitely more intense than anything I'd experienced with them before. My all-in-one suit had ventilation patches under the arms, and their incisors took great chunks of flesh out of me, the size of 10p pieces, that hurt like hell. With hormone levels now soaring, they would go and scratch the ground, roll and scent, leaving a powerful message for the female about their prowess. And while they spent all their time trying to impress her, she was busy trying to suppress the lower-ranking female.

Most of the cuts and bruises I had from these encounters were comparatively superficial. If you live with a pack of wolves you have to expect to get hurt, but they could also be gentle and they would look after me as they looked after each other. They would lick my wounds, which is probably what stopped them from becoming infected. The biggest danger was not the cuts, though, it was the blows to the head that would knock me out briefly, and sometimes they thumped my body or knocked me to the ground with such force that my urine had blood in it for several days afterwards.

I was also beginning to question my diet. I had eaten nothing but protein and a few nuts and berries for a very long time. For the first year or more I had felt fitter and healthier than ever before, but now that I needed extra energy to try and hold my own with these testosterone-charged wolves I realised I had no reserves.

The males were not just pushing and nipping and fighting, they were also trying to mount me, along with every other wolf in the pack. This was a whole new experience – a hundred and thirty pounds of growling wolf on my back with his teeth in my neck and his front legs and claws locked around it. I was powerless; there was nothing I could do but wait for him to get off. Sometimes he came at me from the back, sometimes the side, sometimes the head, and he'd be growling and snapping at the younger male all the while. He was displaying his right to be the breeding male, and if I tried to move or get him off me he just tightened his grip.

This courtship behaviour went on repeatedly for two or three weeks and it was relentless. They were the toughest weeks of my life – and I had been through commando training and an SAS course. I was up day and night, sleeping on my feet, and it was wearing me down. I was becoming a different person; instead of enjoying the calm

Holding a five-day-old wolf pup. *Roger Cooke*

With Helen and Cheyenne at eight months of age. *Linda Cowen*

With Cheyenne and Nataa at eighteen months. *Linda Cowen*

Inside the main wolf enclosure at Combe Martin giving the daily wolf talk. *Roger Cooke*

Zarnesti, the European wolf injured as a pup who connected so movingly with the disabled child. *Roger Cooke*

Elu at the age of ten, the matriarch of the wolf packs and the mother of Yana, Tamaska and Matsi in 2004, and of Cheyenne, Nanoose, Nataa and Tejas. *Roger Cooke*

The wolf pack during feeding. *Roger Cooke*

Matsi displaying defensive behaviour during a pack feed. The position of the ears warns others to stay away. *Roger Cooke*

Cheyenne keeps a watchful eye. *Roger Cooke*

With three-week-old pups. *Roger Cooke*

In the omega role during a moment of tension between two adult wolves. *Roger Cooke*

Matsi, Tamaska and Yana – captive but far from tame. *Roger Cooke*

Shadow, who died unexpectedly in January 2009. *Roger Cooke*

With Levi Holt,
my Native American
brother. *Bernard Walton*

With Tejas. *Roger Cooke*

A traditional wolf greeting from Tamaska, while Yana holds Matsi's muzzle. *Simon Frazier*

A greeting from Matsi. *Simon Frazier*

and balance of their world I found myself getting angry at the way they were treating me. Every time I moved there was a wolf on me or nipping me and I was tired and sore. I had gone beyond exhaustion. I had finally found my limit.

Just as I was on the verge of collapse the pack disappeared and left me alone for a week and a half. I was so relieved I broke down and wept. I couldn't have gone on with that level of brutality for a moment longer; I was shattered physically and emotionally. Where they went is a mystery, but I assume that while they were gone one or other of the males, or maybe both, mated with the dominant female. I certainly saw no evidence of actual mating when they were on the hillside site, and when they returned their mood had changed. It was as though someone had turned off the pressure. They were like a different pack – calm and relaxed; even Miss Grumpy was tolerant, her mind presumably on other things. She would come and stand beside me without growling and snarling. It was as though she was aware that she was going to need her family around her in the coming months. It was so refreshing and such a relief. If they had been the same creatures they were the previous week I would have had to leave them.

Life returned more or less to normal. There seemed to be an abundance of food being brought home. I was always given my fair share but they would take some of it and hide it in caches round and about, mostly in the riverbank. The mud was a natural preservative and I assumed they were doing this because they expected lean times ahead. Possibly they knew they would be going to lose their hunter, the female, as she reached the later stages of her pregnancy. The other development was that sometimes when the others went off hunting they left the young male on the hillside with me.

The gestation period for a wolf is sixty-three days, and as she neared the end of the second month it became clear that she was carrying pups. She became lethargic, the hunting trips were far shorter than they had been, and she began to look swollen and pregnant. That was the point at which she started making a den and a birthing bowl for herself. She took herself up on to a high ridge about four hundred metres above us on the tree line and began digging beneath a small rock formation. She was at it for over a week, and each time she came down for a rest and some food, her coat and paws were covered in mud. I was longing to see how she was doing but it was a very private affair – the others were quickly seen off if they tried to go near her, so I didn't even attempt it. I contemplated instead what my role would be when the pups were born. They didn't make any attempt to get rid of me, and I wondered whether they might have been using me, a human in a world that was naturally fearful of humans, as a means of defence.

And then one day she went into the den and didn't come out for a week and a half. The mood among the rest of us was very flat; the males didn't leave the resting site. The only one that moved was the young female, who went off by herself every now and again, for short periods, no longer than twenty-four hours, sometimes returning with small bits of food, sometimes not. If the fathers were tense, they weren't showing it, but it was obvious that everyone knew what was happening underground.

When she finally emerged, thin and clearly lactating, she was triumphant. She was a changed character; flirty around the males and even the female, she went running from one of us to the next, nipping our mouths, frantic for food. Then she ran down to the river and found two or three food caches and ate ravenously. The only inkling that this was the same wolf was when the older male went too close while she was eating and she went for him. After no more than an hour she ran back up the hill and disappeared underground.

There was no knowing how many pups she had given birth to or if any of them were alive. It looked as though pups had been suckling, but there was always the possibility that she might have rolled on them and squashed them after a few days or rejected them. It was another five weeks before we knew the answer. During that time our routine continued. The males lay around, the female brought back food – not much, but what there was we shared.

She would come out of the den, and as soon as she had eaten and had a drink from the stream she would go straight back. At five weeks she came out looking purposeful and back to her old self, snarling and growling at everyone. She then took the big male and the female and disappeared for the day, leaving me and the younger male to guard the den. They came back full, with their bellies distended, and each one carried a piece of meat in its mouth from what was obviously a big deer that they had brought down. Her priority was to feed the pups, and that was the moment when we knew for sure that this had not been a phantom pregnancy. She raced up to the den and called them, and we could hear them squeaking as they scrambled out of the den into the evening light for the first time. We couldn't see them, because the area was too well hidden, but it sounded as though there was more than one. She would have regurgitated food for them, then taken them all back into the safety of the den for the night while the rest of us ate the first real meal we had had in weeks. I was incredibly hungry and it tasted so good.

She repeated this process for the next week or so, and then one day she called the big male up to the den after making him regurgitate food for her by nipping him around the lips. From the bottom we could hear a lot of squeaking, and then he came back down the hill, leaving her with the pups. This happened morning and night until one magical morning she came out of the den and tumbling down the hill behind her were two small bundles of black fur.

The excitement among the wolves was unbelievable. They scrambled and fell over one another to get to the pups, to sniff them, poke at them and generally investigate, and the pups were completely unfazed. They rolled over and exposed their little pale tummies – something their mother had taught them in the den – then wriggled to their feet and went scavenging for food. They didn't even mind me, although I looked nothing like their mother, and in less than two minutes they were nipping at my mouth with their needle-sharp little teeth. Their education had begun underground weeks ago, when they were still blind, and they already knew who they could trust and how they should greet their elders. Their mother had introduced them to my scent and the scent of every other wolf in the pack. Every time she had come out she had rubbed herself against us one by one and taken that smell back into the den, so these pups already knew every member of their family and knew without doubt that these individuals were trustworthy.

I realised as I watched that extraordinary scene of nature and nurture just how privileged I had been over the last two years or so to have been accepted by this remarkable family. And just now, with these baby bundles of fur nibbling my face – a human face – begging me to regurgitate food, I had been witness to a miracle.

Chapter Fifteen

A NARROW
ESCAPE

What I had always loved about wolves was how important the family unit was to them, but it wasn't until I was with these wolves that I fully understood the social structure and different ranks and the jobs they did within that family. I knew there was one who was more aggressive than the others and I knew there was one that everyone listened to, and there was a lookout, but having only had captive wolves to go on, it wasn't entirely clear. Less clear was what value they put on me, but it seemed that what this pack wanted me to do was interact with the youngsters, and to inform them about our world.

They were particularly curious about how I moved. They used me as a plaything. They would see how fast I ran and would trip me up by nipping at my ankles from behind to see what happened, as if trying to assess my strengths and weaknesses. Given the distance they could travel and the length of time they were often away, I had to assume that they might well have gone on to the perimeter of farms and ranches and even towns. Humans were encroaching on their world so rapidly that the two were always in danger of coming into contact, and it was as if they wanted to know how to read us; how we would react to an encounter and whether we were dangerous.

I will never forget something that happened when the pups were about nine weeks old and their mother and the big male had gone off hunting. They had been gone for a couple of days and there was no knowing when they would be back. As usual, the young male and I were guarding the den area and, unusually, the young female was prowling around on the ridge acting as lookout.

I had not been feeling particularly well. The weather had changed, spring was here and it was very hot in the sun. I had been feeling sweaty and very light-headed, almost faint, and was experiencing tremendous thirst. I think my body was in revolt about what I had put it through in the last two years. The stream, fortunately, was not more than six hundred metres away, and I had been wearing a path to it as I went every hour or so for a drink.

It was late afternoon and yet again I felt an overwhelming desire for water. I got to my feet and started down the usual track in the direction of the valley. As I did so, the young male flew at me from the other side of the den area and knocked me to the ground. He was a big, strong wolf and I felt as if I had been rugby tackled by three players at once. I lay there, shocked and winded and unable to move. This was completely out of character but he meant business. He was standing over me growling and snarling, his eyes blazing, his ears flat against his head, hackles raised, his tail in the air and his teeth bared. I wouldn't have argued with him, however I had been feeling, but under the circumstances I didn't have the strength for it.

Looking as though he might rip my throat out, he backed me into the blackened hollow of a tree that had obviously been struck by lightning some years before. I crouched, imprisoned, in this bowl of charcoal while he stood over me, and every time I tried to move he growled

and snapped the air with his jaws. I knew those jaws could have broken every bone in my body. I had never seen him behave like this. In
all our time together, even during the mating season, when he had
been so dominant and forceful, I had never thought he wanted to kill
me. Now I did and I began to fear for my life. For the next three-
quarters of an hour he held me in suspense.

I couldn't work out what was going on, or what I had done to make
him so hostile. I began to think that maybe he was planning to wait
for the rest of the pack to come back before he killed me. My life
flashed before me and I realised I had brought it on myself by being
so pig-headed. Everyone had told me it was insanity to try and infiltrate a pack of wild wolves, and they were about to be proved right.
They clearly were different from captive wolves and, however much
I thought I'd been accepted, I had been kidding myself. They would
obviously put up with humans for so long but turn on them when
they were no longer useful. As the minutes ticked by I became increasingly terrified. I had no means of defending myself; I was on my own,
miles from anywhere. I even began to wish the grumpy female would
come back; as the leader of the pack she might have saved me. Now
no one would ever find me – they wouldn't even know where to begin
to look.

Suddenly, as dusk began to fall, his mood changed. The aggression
vanished and he was balanced and calm once more. He looked at me
with soft eyes and blinked. I didn't trust him. I thought, here we go,
he's giving me a false sense of security, but he began to lick my face
and all around my mouth, as though he were apologising to me. This
was no longer a wolf that wanted to kill me; this was the brother I had
known and loved all this time.

Shaking, I ventured out of the hollowed tree and he made no
attempt to stop me. He then started to walk down the track towards
the valley that I had tried to take earlier. After a few steps he stopped

and looked back, which I knew meant he wanted me to follow him. So I went after him and the pups came too. About seventy or eighty metres from the den area, he stopped and scented a scratch mark on the ground, and I looked down and there was the biggest pile of bear droppings that looked and smelt different from any I'd ever seen. There were deep scores on the ground and gouges in the bark of the surrounding trees, where a huge grizzly had scraped his claws and left his calling card. What I later learnt from the Native Americans was that a bear will indicate his intentions by what he leaves on the ground, and this bear was out to kill a predator.

Suddenly it all became clear. This wolf hadn't wanted to hurt me. On the contrary; if I had walked down that track three-quarters of an hour earlier the bear would have had me. The wolf had saved me from certain death. I owed him my life.

About three weeks later I was kneeling at the stream splashing water on to my face when I happened to catch sight of my reflection. I hadn't seen myself in months and I literally didn't recognise the face that looked back at me. It was thin and gaunt with sunken, darkened eyes, long matted hair and a bushy beard. I looked nothing like the fresh-faced youth that left the Education Center two years before. I looked like a wild man and it shocked me to the core. I had lost a huge amount of weight and my health was definitely beginning to deteriorate. The pups meanwhile were doing well. They didn't need me and unless I was prepared to die in this wilderness, I needed to go home and soon.

I left in the early morning with no ceremony. In this state I didn't know how long it would take me to get back to the bag. A week, maybe more. I was drained; I had no energy to do anything other than place one foot in front of the other. I didn't even have the energy to cry. None of the wolves had tried to stop me, but then how were they to know we would never meet again? I looked back just once to see if any of them were following, but they weren't. They were making their way up to the den area and the pups for the start of a new day. Life was already going on without me.

I had stashed some pieces of meat from the last kill in my pockets and stopped every now and again to rest, eat and drink. My walking was slow. I kept to the stream when I was uncertain of the route, but most of the tracks I took were familiar and at night I stopped and slept soundly. I was so tired that I didn't even worry about predators; didn't even care perhaps. It was a full week before I reached the rendezvous point, and my old day-sack was still hanging in the tree where I had left it, looking a little weather-beaten. I pulled it down and sat with my back against the tree to wait for someone to find me, and finally, and for a very long time, I cried. The pain and the grief for all that I had left behind cascaded over me, and I cried and sobbed until I had no more tears.

I didn't know whether Levi still sent a vehicle out every two days, as we had arranged. It was months since I had left my last note and he knew how dangerous my plans had been. Maybe he thought I was dead and had stopped coming so regularly.

While I waited, I contemplated just how dangerous what I had done had been – and I scared myself with the realisation of how close I had come to death. By rights, no human should have survived what I had been through. The environment and the weather conditions alone were enough to kill me, not to mention the lack of food and the diet I had been eating. Add to that the wolves – the strength and size of the creatures, the battering they gave my body and the intimidation. Yet it was the wolves that had kept me alive. They had fed me, kept me warm and kept me safe. I would not be writing this today if the young male had not protected me that afternoon and stopped me walking down to the stream as I intended. The bear would have killed me; there was no question about it. The only thing the wolves hadn't been able to do was make my body tolerate their diet. It had obviously been able to put up with raw meat for so long but not indefinitely. And now, as I sat and thought about returning to civilisation and all that that might bring, I had a real craving for honey.

It was twenty-four hours before I heard the drone of an engine making its way up the track. It was a 4x4 from the camp but the driver was someone I didn't recognise. In two years there had been a turnover of staff, so my appearance was not as shocking to this guy as it might have been. My smell would have been quite another matter, but he was too polite to say anything. I didn't speak much on the way back to the Center. There was too much – and yet nothing – to say. I hadn't spoken to another human being in two years and I was feeling strange and disoriented.

When Levi saw me his usually inscrutable face looked horrified. I wasn't prepared for the strength of his reaction, but it told me that the change he saw in me went further than my appearance, as indeed it did, and when he held out his arms to embrace me I broke down. These two years had changed me in every way and the enormity of what I'd experienced was beginning to dawn. I had survived but I had said goodbye to everything that I loved and to a world that I could never recapture. I felt weak and faint and emotionally confused. Not many of the guys had known me when I left but those that had looked as shocked by the sight of me as Levi. They could scarcely believe that I was the same man. He asked me if there was anything I needed. I said 'Honey', which someone quickly brought, and watched by Levi and the others who had crowded round, I ate my way through half a jar.

The events that followed became a bit of a blur, but I remember being driven down to Winchester for a shower and the incredible sensation of warm water on my body and thinking this was what civilisation was all about. It was a terrible shower, in a wooden shed and with abysmal pressure, but it felt like the Ritz. I was a very strange sight with my clothes off. My face and hands were heavily tanned and weather-beaten but my body was lily white, and when I shaved off my beard my face became two-tone. My body was so emaciated that I looked like cross between Man Friday and Albert Steptoe; I was skin and bone – I had lost three and a half stone – and although an incredible amount of dirt had come off in the shower, some of it wouldn't shift. I looked as though I was wearing someone else's head and hands – but a head that had a pure white band around it where the beard had been. I wondered what people would think of me when I travelled home to the UK.

Everyone wanted to hear my story. There was so much to tell that I adopted a kind of shorthand and kept strictly to the facts. The biologists wanted data: how many wolves there had been, what they were like, whether they had bred, how many pups, what location they had been in, where they hunted, where they went, what tracks they took. From everything I said they agreed that these didn't sound like any of the wolves involved in the reintroduction programme but were almost certainly wild wolves that had come into the area using the old corridors that Levi had spoken about. Everyone was excited to have Levi's theories confirmed; but there were still people in the camp – mostly the biologists – who strongly disapproved of what I had done. They were as interested as the others in how I survived in that environment, how I managed to get into the pack and how I kept my sanity – which at times I wondered myself – but they did not give me a hero's welcome. They were angry that I had put myself at risk and the wolves at risk – while others thought my achievement was amazing. And the Native Americans saw it as commendable but not that remarkable. Their people have been going out and living in the mountains alongside the creatures of the wild for hundreds of years.

I was tempted to get on a plane straight away. Now that I had irrevocably made the decision to leave the wolves I had a real desire to be home. I was tired of being judged and condemned for what I did or didn't do, but I was persuaded to stay at the camp for a couple of weeks, to let my health recover and to try and adjust to normal life. But it was not easy. I knew that mentally and emotionally I was in for the long haul, but I was surprised by how long it took even to get back to a normal diet, and how difficult it was. I longed to eat junk food – I was dying for pepperoni pizza and ice-cream – but my system couldn't take it. That kind of food went through me without touching the sides and made me feel very ill. My stomach had shrunk so drastically that I could only eat the smallest amounts of food – what I would eat as a plateful today would have done for three days – and for a good few weeks carbohydrates made me vomit or gave me diarrhoea.

But the hardest thing was adjusting to the human world. The world I had come from, and felt I belonged to, was so simple and balanced. There was no deception, no malice and no gratuitous cruelty. Everything was done for a reason that everyone understood, and although they could be rough and aggressive and fight for what was theirs, they also had a gentle, caring side to their nature and looked after their own with great tenderness, as I had seen and experienced. Keeping the family unit safe and fed was what mattered most to these animals, but they had respect for the creatures with which they shared their world. They killed to eat; never for fun and never more than they could use.

More than ever I was struck by the contrast between them and human beings, so many of whom took everything for granted. They were greedy and selfish and plundered the earth as though they were the only species that mattered. And so much of our world is dangerous and uncaring. At the airport waiting for my flight I watched parents arguing with their children and disciplining them for nothing. I wanted to say, 'Stop it. Enjoy your children; appreciate what you've got.'

Chapter Sixteen

ANOTHER WAY

The last few weeks had been an emotional seesaw and, now I was back, all I could think of was finding a way of helping improve the lives of wolves in captivity. I had learnt so much about them, far more than I would have learnt in a lifetime of watching them from a distance. So often their behaviour was misinterpreted and their needs were neglected, and I had a burning zeal to make a difference.

I headed straight down to Plymouth to see Jan. I was completely out of money and I needed a job that paid me a decent wage but also allowed me to work with animals – preferably canids. I asked around and made enquiries, and using my Forces connections I enrolled on a residential course in kennel management run by the army in Melton Mowbray in Leicestershire. I started with the basic handler's course, then went on to the baiter's course, where the dog learns to take the intruder's sleeve, and finally took the kennel handler's course. It was about three months in all and I learnt everything from feeding and looking after the animals to teaching them and their handlers to attack.

Dogs are used by the army for all sorts of tasks; they go into war zones to sniff out explosives, they patrol secure units and, like police dogs, are trained to arrest intruders by taking hold of the person's arm. But unlike the police dogs, these animals don't stay with their handlers in their homes and they don't have to differentiate between good guys and bad guys. Anyone who is inside the perimeter fence when they shouldn't be is an intruder, and the dog is trained to attack and arrest them.

It wasn't my style of training but I saw it as a means to an end. It was a way to an income and to work with the animals. This was a tough, military environment, where men and dogs alike obeyed commands without question. The man in charge was a tall, thin sergeant-major called Sid Gillam, whom we nicknamed Blakey after the authoritarian character in *On the Buses*, the 1970s television sit-com.

Blakey was rigid in the way he trained the dogs that came through his unit. The handlers were taught to dominate. This was not the place for my theories about allowing the creatures to dominate me. No one dared to challenge his methods – including me – although it was obvious to me that there was a kinder and a more effective way. Fear and intimidation had never seemed to me to be a good basis for a relationship, and these animals were so much stronger and faster than their handlers and their sensory perception was infinitely greater.

But I had learnt from the Native Americans that no man has the right to tell another what to do, so I kept my views to myself. My brothers in Idaho would tell me that it's good to have a dream, but unless the world is ready to receive it, the dream has no purpose. Blakey belonged to a generation that was bound by rules and regulations and didn't question accepted practice. He was not ready for change – he didn't even use food as a reward when training the dogs, which civilian trainers had been using for years. These dogs were trained by brute force.

Blakey took himself and his job very seriously and we used to love winding him up – and it was so easy. Every morning at breakfast I used to steal a sausage and put it in my pocket. As a result the dogs I was handling never left my side. They behaved immaculately – no force needed at all – and at the end of the training session they got their sausage. I came top of the class every time. Blakey guessed I was up to something but could never work it out.

Not long after I finished and had left Melton Mowbray he appeared in a television programme in which expert dog trainers were pared with celebrities to help them train their dogs. Blakey's partner was the camp comedian Julian Clary, who had a little lapdog. It was a brilliantly wicked piece of casting. The two men could not have been more different. Blakey trained large dogs to go into war zones and come out winners, and there he was on the nation's TV screens holding Julian's ball of fluff on a pink lead. The poor man never lived it down. The next time I saw him I asked how Julian was and he clipped me round the ear and told me never to dare mention that name again. But Blakey was a good man and I had a lot of respect for him. As well as running the training centre he was a veterinary inspector and as such went round the barracks every three months checking that the dogs were healthy. So I stayed in touch with him and, to give him his due, when he came to see what I was doing with the dogs in my care he was persuaded that his methods were not producing the right results. And years later he came to visit me in Devon to look at what I was doing with wolves. He was one of the few men I regard as having had a guiding influence in my life.

My first job after training was that of Assistant Kennel Manager at Headquarters Land Command just outside Wilton in Wiltshire. I was looking after about six dogs in the kennels at Erskine Barracks. The animals' job was to protect and guard the camp, and mine was to make sure that they remained in peak operational condition for twenty-four-hour duty. There were some wonderful characters among them but they were not pets by any stretch of the imagination; they were working dogs – German Shepherds – bred to go up against humans, and they were hard animals that needed a lot of careful handling. I felt very sorry for them. The dogs had six to eight weeks of training for this work; the handlers had just two, and in my view it should have been the other way round. Some of the handlers hadn't a clue what they were doing and the dogs ran rings around them.

There was a lovely young Brummy soldier we used to call Yim Yam because of his strong Birmingham accent. He so wanted to be a handler but he had no experience of dogs at all. Every time he let his animal off the leash, instead of running and apprehending the training target, it ran past him and weed up a lamp-post. But he adored the dog and every morning would come into the kennels and say good morning to him and then go from one kennel to the next greeting each of the dogs by name. One night I had been out drinking and decided to curl up in the kennels with one of the dogs rather than go all the way home. Early the next day, when it was barely light, this lad came in to say good morning to the dogs as usual, going from one kennel to the next – 'Morning Shadow, morning Dusty, morning Kelly' – and when he got to mine he couldn't see me in the dark of the kennel and in a very deep voice I said 'Morning Yim Yam'. The expression on his face was a picture. I think to this day he believes the dog was talking to him.

We had moments of good fun in the barracks. There was a sergeant-major called Tony Frangos, who was from the same commando unit I had been with; he was very fit but small and for some reason we were always playing practical jokes on him. I remember someone once put raspberry jam on his telephone receiver, and there was the occasion when we put his beret into the freezer the night before he had a big meeting with the regional sergeant-major and all the bigwigs from the parachute regiment. Frangie sat there with his beret quietly thawing and dripping icy water down his collar, unable to say a word. Most shameful of all our exploits: the base commander had discovered that brass fittings, handles, doorknobs and knockers and other valuable bits and pieces had been disappearing from a disused building in the barracks that was due for demolition. There was a suggestion that Frangie's men might have been responsible. He leapt to our defence with the ferocity of a mother tiger. There was no way his men would steal; this was an outrageous slur on his men's integrity; he could vouch for each and every one of us. 'Don't worry, lads,' he said after recounting the story; adding as an afterthought, 'You didn't take that stuff, did you?' We had to come clean. Our lockers were stuffed with brass.

The real problem with the dogs we were handling was that the army didn't understand the importance of the dog's natural rank, and they were asking animals to do jobs for which they were completely ill-equipped. You could not put an alpha animal into an attack role. It couldn't cope. The alpha is the decision maker and the most valuable animal in the pack. Its whole being would be telling it to stay out of danger and to hide round the back of its handler and let someone else do the dangerous job. No low-ranking animal could do the job either because they don't have the natural aggression. The perfect attack dog was the beta animal. He relished the task and was tenacious and fearless. By failing to appreciate the distinction, the army lost a lot of good dogs.

They were not much better at dog psychology. When a dog had the baiter's arm in its jaws, the handler would shout 'leave it', commanding it to let go, and be enraged if the dog disobeyed. What no one seemed to understand was that this was working against the animal's natural instinct. In the wild, the wolf will hang on and won't release its grip until its prey is dead. That's how it survives and how it feeds the pack. The dog was being instructed to let go when it knew the prey was still very much alive and kicking, so of course it was confused – and it would have heard the shouting as encouragement from the pack. But I had to tread carefully. I was a new boy on the block and couldn't hope to change the culture overnight. Furthermore, what I had at the moment were just theories. I needed to put them into practice.

One of the joys of the job at the barracks was that I worked abnormal hours. Because handlers were on duty twenty-four hours a day it wasn't unusual to be at the kennels in the middle of the night, and this was a good time to do some training with them without distractions. It also freed me up for a little moonlighting, and it wasn't long before I found myself in demand as a dog trainer for civilians working at the camp and in the local villages. It was all done by word of mouth but I found it very gratifying to see how receptive people were to the things I was telling them – and it brought in some extra money. The traditional dog training at that time, even for pets, was still very much based on force, and I turned that on its head. I used as motivation the animal's natural system of rewards, such as food and warmth, and as deterrents their own forms of punishment, namely deprivation and cold. I also insisted on dog owners bringing the whole family to training classes, because dogs see themselves as part of the family pack, even if there are just two people in the household, and training a dog to respond to just one member of that pack upsets its natural instincts. If small children are in the house any confusion in the dog is potentially dangerous.

When things go wrong, dogs are very seldom the problem. The problems are invariably the humans who have bought the wrong animal for their situation and have failed to train it in a language that the dog understands. People often try so hard to do the right thing but end up with the dog ruling and destroying their life.

I had a couple with the most beautiful Retriever that used to fetch balls and toys that the owners threw for it in the garden. As time went by the dog refused to give up the toys it retrieved and growled if anyone tried to take them away from him. No one dared challenge him, and by the time the dog was two years old he was the undisputed king of the castle. The owners had virtually been reduced to living in a cupboard under the stairs because the dog had gradually taken possession of the rest of the house. Every time they went into a room he growled so aggressively that they hardly dared move. It broke the owner's heart, but that dog had developed such a high level of possession that there was no alternative but to re-house him.

The problem is that we go against nature when we ask a dog to retrieve an object and give that object to us. In the wild what they retrieve is theirs – and the way they indicate to their fellow pack members that something belongs to them is by lowering their ears and covering the object. If the ears go sideways like aeroplane wings it means that others should stay away. But we have altered the looks of dogs so radically in our breeding that most dogs' ears now flop over and they can't use them to communicate. Instead they growl. If the dog is a high-ranking animal and growls when the owner tries to take the ball from it, and the owner backs off, then the dog quickly learns that that is the way to possess not just the ball but anything it wants. So we have to try and get rid of that instinctive behaviour, but it's as much a case of educating the owner as it is of educating the dog – and usually that is much harder.

I remember the receptionist from a local veterinary practice ringing me to see if I could help an old man, in his eighties, who was having problems with an eight-month-old Collie cross that he had re-housed. She said he couldn't cope; how much did I charge? I said £5.50, which barely covered my petrol, and still she beat me down. He was an old-age pensioner, she said. 'OK, I'll charge him four pounds.' It was agreed and as I drove into the village following the directions I'd been given, I came to a huge house. If this was his, I thought … but it wasn't. His was next door, and even bigger. What's more, he owned most of the village. I was doing some serious muttering under my breath, but the minute I met the man I had a change of heart. He loved the dog but he was a man who could barely walk without assistance and he had a dog that wanted to run for miles and herd sheep. They were a complete mismatch. But the man had a housekeeper, so I got him to take the dog on a lead into a paddock at the back of the house and I asked him to stand at one end of the field and his housekeeper at the other and gave them each a supply of food. Then I let the dog go and he raced from the old man to the housekeeper; each time he reached one, he or she gave him a bit of food and moved a little closer to the other, and the dog ran to the other and they did the same again. The dog tore back and forth, slowly shepherding them into the middle of the paddock. It fulfilled his natural herding instincts and it gave him the exercise he needed. When the man and the housekeeper had reached the centre of the field, the man put the dog on the lead again, and the three of them walked calmly back into the house.

In those days I was experimenting. People came to me with puppies to train and also with older dogs with behavioural problems, like the Collie cross and the Retriever, and I applied what I had learnt about wolf behaviour to them all. Of course it was still early days for me – there were many things I didn't know about wolves – so it was as much of a learning experience for me as it was for the owners, but what I was telling people seemed to strike a chord and many of them found their dogs were transformed. The timing couldn't have been better. There was a sudden and refreshing interest in dog psychology, and people were beginning to look to the wolf as a means of understanding why their dog behaved the way it did. It felt as though the world was ready – but while other behaviourists based their teaching on what they'd observed about wolf behaviour from afar, mine was based on a unique perspective. I had lived with wolves.

Chapter Seventeen

THE PROOF OF THE PUDDING...

The Native American Indians say that if you think of a captive animal as being in a cage, then so will the animal, but if you give that animal the impression that the cage is a means of keeping it safe and secure, and you enrich its life within it, then the animal will regard its cage not as a prison but as a haven. It seemed to me that most wolves in captivity felt they were in cages. Those that I had known bore little resemblance to their wild counterparts; they had had their spirit broken and most of them wouldn't have taken freedom even if you had left the gate to the enclosure wide open.

I was convinced that I could improve their lives by making it resemble life in the wild, but I needed credibility. I had experience of wolves that went way beyond what most biologists could claim, but I had no initials after my name, so I set up an organisation that I called Wolf Pack Management. It was just me at that time but I thought it sounded impressive. I desperately needed to put my theories to the test. I enjoyed my work with the dogs but my real mission was wolves, and as luck would have it, Wilton was within easy reach of Longleat Safari Park, which still had a thriving pack of Grey Timber wolves.

Longleat was, and still is, one of the most highly regarded wildlife parks in the world and I knew I couldn't find a better pack to study. The park is set in the grounds of a magnificent stately home belonging to the 7th Marquess of Bath. The house, which is Elizabethan, is an amazing attraction in itself, but it's surrounded by the most fabulous parkland, designed by the great eighteenth-century landscape gardener Capability Brown. This extends to nine hundred acres, with a further eight thousand acres of woodland, lakes and farmland – unspoilt countryside as far as the eye can see – and that's where the animals live. The wolf enclosure couldn't compete with the space the wolves had in Idaho, but the cramped enclosure at Sparkwell bore no comparison and it was refreshing to see captive wolves – along with lions, tigers and every sort of wild animal you can think of – in such good conditions in England.

I went to see the head warden, Keith Harris, and introduced myself. I told him what I had been doing and asked whether I could put some of my theories to the test with his wolves. Despite the quality of the conditions in which they were kept and the good health of the animals, Longleat had a problem. The wolves were not breeding. In the early days there was little understanding about pack management and the need to create four-year gaps between generations to ensure a successful breeding pattern. Like many other wildlife parks, they had brought together a number of wolves at the outset, taking them from other parks that had surplus animals, and the current pack were all of much the same age. They were getting too old to breed.

In the wild there would always be several generations in one pack and always young females coming through. They would breed to provide new pack members to defend territory, to hunt and to continue the line. In captivity, these wolves had a square meal as often as they needed it, of good-quality food, delivered to their door and there was no threat to their territory. There was no reason for them to increase pack numbers, and so they didn't. Wolves have an extraordinary ability to manage their own bodies and to decide whether or not to have young. Females will often have phantom pregnancies, or they will have genuine pregnancies which they can abort if they so choose. If a wolf decides the timing or circumstances are not right for her to give birth she halts the pregnancy and absorbs the pups into her body.

I was confident I could improve the lives of these wolves and, who knows, maybe even encourage them to breed, but it was hard to convince the management that they should pay me when their wolves were in every respect, apart from reproducing, healthy and happy animals. However, Keith Harris was interested in what I had been doing with the Nez Perce and agreed to let me work alongside their keepers, as long as it was on a voluntary basis. Since I already had an income from the army, I was happy with whatever terms they liked to set out; my primary interest was in helping the wolves, and and this was the ideal testing ground.

Visitors come into the park by car – hundreds of thousands of them every year. When it opened in 1966 it was the first drive-through safari park outside Africa, but because the animals are in the lush green English countryside rather than the African bush, and in enclosures of a few acres rather than a few hundred, they are highly visible and entirely unafraid of vehicles, so you can see the animals at very close quarters. Longleat became the model for many other zoological parks around the world.

The Wolf Wood was beyond the tigers and the lions, in an area of perhaps four or five acres. In the centre was a copse of mature trees, mostly oaks, with no thickets or ground cover. The whole area was grassed and in one corner near the boundary fence was a small man-made pool for drinking water. There were six or seven wolves in the pack at that time and I remember watching a young male wolf one day stalk a rook that was bathing in it. The wolf had been lying some distance away watching the pond and must have noticed that every time a bird came to bathe and splash about, it took longer than usual to get into the air afterwards; the water on its feathers interfered with its aerodynamics and made it fly less efficiently. He crept forward until he was about fifty metres away, and I thought what a silly wolf thinking he could catch a rook – but he got it.

The only building was a simple brick structure that was used by the vets if and when they were needed; and the whole area was securely fenced and gated, as every enclosure was. During opening hours, members of staff would sit in 4x4 vehicles, painted with black and white stripes to look like zebras, parked in each enclosure in case any visitor felt tempted to get out of their car. I used to feel sorry for the volunteers that worked in the park, having taken the jobs because they wanted to work with animals but spending their days as glorified car-park attendants.

Cars were part of their landscape; humans on foot were not, and docile as these animals might have looked from behind the wind-screen, in reality they were dangerous. Not even I was allowed inside the enclosure with the wolves – their insurance wouldn't cover me – so all my days off from the job at Wilton I spent parked in the enclosure studying the wolves and getting to know them from my vehicle, which was then a white Citroen van. The wolves came to recognise the van and whenever I drove in they would come and scent mark all over it. I didn't think anything of this until I noticed that the lions seemed to be taking a very close interest in my van. I would follow the keeper's vehicle out of the park in the evenings, and the lions paid the keeper's no attention at all, but mine they ran towards – particularly the females. One evening one of these females took a massive swipe at the back of it with her paw and with such force that the whole vehicle rocked. The only explanation I could come up with was that she objected to the scent of the wolves. The next night I tried hosing the van down before leaving the park and the lions didn't so much as look up when I drove through their enclosure.

At night, when I wasn't allowed in the enclosure, I took up semi-permanent residence across the valley from the wolves in a small copse, about five hundred metres away as the crow flies. It was a good vantage point from which to watch and listen, and I felt very much at home as I settled down night after night with torch, binoculars, sandwiches and a thermos of hot tea. I sat at the base of a big hollow oak tree that also housed a couple of owls, and enveloped by the darkness and the noises of the night, I might almost have been a child again, at home in Norfolk being lulled to sleep by the hooting of owls and the other nocturnal creatures going about their business. There was something quite magical about sitting there in the middle of one of the finest landscapes in the country howling to a pack of wolves and having them return my call.

Having watched the pack's behaviour for several weeks, I began what I call an 'enrichment programme'. I rigged up a sound system at a couple of vantage points outside the enclosure – one of which was the copse with my hollow tree – and at dusk and dawn, when these animals are most active, I played tape recordings of wolves howling that I had recorded in Idaho. The idea behind this was to fool the wolves into believing there was a rival pack across the valley, which I hoped might induce the alpha female to produce pups.

The knowledge that there is a stronger or bigger pack in the locality, which might attempt to take over their territory, brings a pack together, in exactly the same way as human communities are brought together by the threat of an enemy invasion. And the instinctive action of any species that thinks its future security might be in danger is to breed. Let that pack know that there is an alpha female out there, who might challenge the resident alpha female, and she will either rise to that challenge or roll over and admit that she is past her prime and surrender the role to another pack member better equipped for the job.

This, at least, was the theory on which I was working. What I didn't know was what would happen in practice with a pack of wolves that had never known the wild. I was relying on their genetically inherited memory.

My equipment was rather Heath Robinson. It needed to be easily portable because wolf packs obviously move around, so in order to be realistic, the sounds of their howling had to move around too. But it also had to receive and carry sound over long distances. I managed to beg a satellite dish from a small electrical shop in Wilton that suited my purpose perfectly. I rigged that up to a tape recorder and a loudspeaker. It didn't look very elegant but it was effective and I was able to take it to other locations within the park. But my base was always the hollow oak.

The tapes appeared to do the job, and after weeks of uncertainty Macha, the alpha female, was showing definite signs of being pregnant.

I've known a great many wolves over the years and lots of them have been wonderful characters, but one of the wolves at Longleat will be in my heart for ever. Her name was Daisy and she was the one that Macha chose to act as nanny to her cubs. She was a dominant female, a beautiful animal who always seemed destined to be the bridesmaid and never the bride. That spring at Longleat I remember watching her waiting patiently – as we all were – for her leader to give birth, and after sixty-three days of pregnancy, the moment arrived. Macha had taken herself underground into the birthing bowl she had excavated inside the den, and all the while Daisy lay nearby under the shade of a big oak tree waiting for the telltale squeaks that would signal all was well. The moment she heard those yelps and squeaks, she sprang to her feet and went eagerly to the mouth of the den where she stood for a few moments listening; two pups had been safely delivered and were suckling contentedly. Daisy was clearly desperate to get at them, but she had to wait for another five weeks before she could take charge and do her job.

Five weeks is the normal length of time the pups stay in the den after birth. During that period they see no one but their mother, who suckles them and keeps them warm, the two requirements most important to a wolf's wellbeing. No one is yet sure whether the pups are born to the rank they will hold as adults or acquire it during the first few weeks of life – i.e. whether it is nature or nurture – but where they suckle on the mother is certainly significant and the mother can influence that. The pups that take – or are allowed to take – the teat closest to the middle will do better than those that feed on the outside. The milk in the middle is of better quality, and they are kept warm by the closeness of their siblings suckling alongside them. These animals will hold higher ranks than the ones who are pushed to the edge and as a result they will have a richer scent. And what begins in the first five weeks of life continues into adulthood. The high-ranking animals eat the richest food, smell stronger and command the greatest respect.

What the pups also learn during those first five weeks in the den is who the various members of their family are, how the pack system works and how each member needs to be greeted when the moment to meet them arrives. Every time the mother emerges from the den to feed, smelling of her cubs, she rubs herself against other members of the pack and carries their scent back into the den for the pups to smell. If the wolf she rubbed against was a high-ranking member, the mother will take the pup's head or neck in her jaws and very gently turn it to expose the youngster's throat, which she will then lick all over, teaching the pup that when he finally meets that high-ranking animal he must roll over, exposing his tummy and throat, and be submissive. So entirely through scent she introduces the pups to the family and the family to the pups, and when they stumble out of the den, wobbly on their feet and still half blind, they know not only the character and social position of every member of the pack they meet but also how to behave.

At five weeks she starts the weaning process and they begin to move on to solids in the form of regurgitated meat. Initially it's their mother who regurgitates food for them, but then the nanny takes over and, as they grow, they can induce any member of the pack to regurgitate by nipping the adult's lips with their needle-sharp little teeth. While the mother is nursing, she can't go far from the den and so other members of the pack bring food for her. In the wild they will often carry a piece of meat from the kill up to forty miles to feed the alpha female, and they will do the same for the nanny when she takes over the care of the pups. Alternatively, one of the wolves will take over the task of looking after the pups for a short period while the nanny follows a trail deliberately left for her to the site of the kill.

Bringing up the next generation is a collective task. The mother leaves the cubs so that, as the alpha female, she can get on with her job of leading the pack, and the educating and nurturing of the young falls to the nanny and in time the wider family.

Looking at Daisy, who was so dedicated, so tolerant and such a wise creature, I found myself contemplating my own childhood; and seeing some parallels. I began to think that maybe deep down, I had felt that my mother had rejected me. Much as I had adored my grandparents, who were the most important people in my life, I realised that I had felt hurt and angry that my mother had abandoned me to their care. It wasn't what happened to anyone else. The central figures in other people's lives were their mothers and fathers, not grandparents;

but I didn't have a father, and my mother wasn't there. I didn't even know she'd lived with me for the first thirteen years of my life; I thought she had been forced to take me in when my grandfather died.

But watching how the wolf mother brought up her young made me see my life from a different perspective. So much about my childhood experience seemed similar to what I was witnessing here, and slowly it started to make sense. I hadn't been deprived; far from it. My childhood had been enriched by the patience and wisdom that comes with age – something many children never get, and something my mother, as a young woman on her own, could never have provided. She'd had to go out to work, to bring home food, just as the alpha female did, and she left the child-rearing to the member of the family that she deemed most qualified. I felt we were as one.

Chapter Eighteen

DIVIDED
LOYALTY

When I found the job at the kennels in Wilton I rented a small bungalow on a farm just outside Salisbury and Jan came to live with me there, plus two of her children from a previous relationship and a couple of Huskies that I'd rescued.

Moving into this little bungalow together was everything I thought I wanted, and Jan was a complete star. She had had no experience of dogs, let alone large, dangerous ones, yet she joined me working with the attack dogs at the barracks; and she immersed herself in wolves. She must have wondered many a time what she had taken on. It wasn't quite how she imagined life would be. She had envisaged a conventional future for herself, working in an office, driving a nice car, living in a neat semi-detached house and effortlessly paying off the mortgage. As she once said, her most exciting or dangerous decision before she met me would have been which brand of orange juice to buy. All of that changed, and many were the times she would come out with me on a winter's night and sit in the pitch dark and the pouring rain, helping operate the tape recorder to try and convince the wolves we were a rival pack across the valley.

I couldn't have asked for a better girlfriend. She never complained about the bizarre lifestyle or the fact that I spent most of my evenings and weekends at Longleat. She gave me all the space I needed to do my own thing, and when we had children, she was a fantastic mum. Jan already had three children, although only two of them lived with us, so when she went into labour with our first child, Kyra, she'd done it all before and was very relaxed. She calmly ran herself a bath and told me to stop panicking. Moments later she screamed 'It's coming!' and was suddenly as panic-stricken as I was. I bundled her into the car and set off at top speed for the hospital in Salisbury, phoning ahead as I drove to say she was about to give birth. I looked round at Jan lying across the back seat and I could see the baby's head. I thought I was going to have to deliver it in the car, but we screeched into the hospital entrance and two nurses were ready and waiting and practically caught Kyra seconds later, as she burst into the world kicking and screaming. It was one of the most exciting and joyful moments of my life.

After Kyra was born Jan had to stay at home and look after her, so our nights of sitting out under the stars – and the pouring rain – were limited. I was working day and night and becoming more and more obsessive about all the things I was doing. Even when I was at home I was busy logging my findings, listening to recordings, rationalising the information I'd been getting from this captive pack of wolves. I was fascinated by them and equally fascinated by what their behaviour told me about the attack dogs I was working with in the day job, and also the domestic dogs that people were bringing me for training. I could see that in our ignorance we humans were badly letting down our best friends and that we needed to change our thinking radically if we were to redeem ourselves.

I knew I had only scratched the surface and needed to learn much more if I was to be able to help them – and the place to learn was Idaho. I determined to go back to see my Native American family again and to be with wolves that I could study at close range. England was home and where my family – my blood relatives – were; I would always feel the draw to come back, but my spiritual home was in the American north-west. The tribespeople were my brothers, the wolves my adoptive family, and year after year I felt the need to sit at their feet and listen to their words of wisdom. Once I was there, the responsibilities of home and family seemed a million miles away.

My being away seemed to suit Jan. We became like a service family, much as we would have been if I had stayed in the army and been sent away for long tours of duty. Jan built herself a life around the children and her friends and family, who were based in Plymouth, where we eventually bought a house together. She was very independent and I think I disrupted the quiet order of her life on the occasions when I reappeared. She was probably happier without me and switched off so completely when I was gone that she found it hard to have me back.

I spoke to Blakey about going back to Idaho and asked if he would put in a word for me with the authorities, and he convinced them that further training among the Nez Perce would benefit the attack dogs. They allowed me to take extra leave which, added to my annual entitlement, gave me six weeks. It was long enough to make the cost of the journey worthwhile. I left not long after Macha's pups were born at Longleat, and while I longed to watch them grow and develop, I also longed to be among the mountains and the wild wolves once more.

Each time I went back to Idaho I imagined that my experience and seniority might earn me a better tepee. Yet time after time I was allocated the tatty one that was down by the edge of the forest away from the main body of the camp. To begin with I had thought it was because I was the newcomer. Then I thought that, because I was white, maybe I was being punished for the collective sins of the White Man who had persecuted the Native American tribes over hundreds of years. Finally, after the third or fourth year of being shown to this tent, I summoned the courage to ask Levi why I was always given the tent by the forest. In typical style he didn't give me a direct answer; he told me a story. It made little sense at the time but I came to understand what he was telling me.

One day, according to legend, a squaw was collecting firewood for the village when she came upon a young wolf cub that was cold, hungry and close to death. She looked around for its mother or other members of the cub's pack, but there were no signs of any. So, rather than leave it to certain death, she wrapped it in a blanket, put it into her basket and took it home to her tepee. There she looked after it, fed it on warm fresh milk and nursed it back to health. She raised it as she would her own child, she fed it meat from the hunt as it grew, and everywhere she went the young wolf trotted by her side. The two became inseparable; they went to collect firewood together and to fetch water from the river, where they would sit and watch their reflections in the early morning sun. In the cool of the evenings they ran and played together in the forest before going home to sleep curled up alongside one another.

One day when they went down to the river to collect water, they sat side by side, as usual, looking into the murky depths, but instead of seeing her own reflection staring back at her, the squaw saw the reflection of two wolves. Her own face had become that of a she-wolf. Greatly alarmed, she ran back to the village and sought out one of the elders of the tribe and explained what had happened, asking why she had been cursed in this way. The elder said, 'This isn't a curse; it's a gift in return for your kindness. You must pack up your belongings and take them to the edge of the forest, where you will live between the two worlds – the human world and the wolf world.'

What Levi was telling me was that I too had been given a special gift and it would be my role in life to live between the two worlds.

As I returned to camp one day I found a letter waiting for me from Jan. It had sad news. Soon after I'd left, Macha, the mother of the pups at Longleat, had died. I felt as though I had been told a close and dear friend had gone. I knew that the pack would have been howling for her, and I was gutted that I hadn't been able to howl with them and share their grief. Instead I went down to the enclosure with the captive wolves and cupped my hands around my mouth and howled alone and mournfully, hoping that somewhere, somehow, Macha might hear me and know that I was missing her. And as I lay in my bed that night, in that twilight zone between waking and sleeping, I imagined that I heard her familiar voice say one final farewell.

Wolves don't share our emotions and can't afford the sentimentality that we humans wallow in. The pack immediately restructured itself, and to my great joy Daisy took Macha's place as the alpha female and the following year it was she who was pregnant. I was again in Idaho on what had become an annual visit when she gave birth, and I heard that things had gone badly wrong. The keepers had found Daisy wandering around the enclosure with a dead pup stuck halfway out of the birth canal. She was in serious distress and needed emergency veterinary help. They darted her with tranquilliser and operated to remove the pup. One had been born but they found several more dead inside her. She was not a young animal and there was a strong possibility that, if she became pregnant, this might happen again, and so, reluctantly, the decision was taken to sterilise her.

I arrived home shortly afterwards to an impossible situation. The pack had an alpha female that couldn't breed. Somehow, she would have to be persuaded to surrender her role and allow a younger female to take the lead. The question was, could I persuade her by the use of tape recordings? If I was able to convince her and the rest of the pack that she was being challenged by a stronger, younger lone female looking for a vacancy, then I hoped she might step aside for one of her own pack members, a younger dominant female such as Zeva, who was one of Macha's early cubs.

With the help of Jan and one of the keepers I first of all played recordings of a full pack from a couple of locations, as I had done before, to give the impression that there were rival packs in the area, which would encourage the captive pack to pull together as a family. Then I played a recording of an alpha female from various points closer to the enclosure, to suggest that she was moving around in the buffer zones between the territories of the three packs. The howl of a wolf that can't breed sounds very different from that of a breeding animal, and I knew that when she returned the challenge from this lone female, the pack would notice the difference and put pressure on Daisy. My fear, however, was that if Daisy refused to relinquish her position, and the rest of the pack wanted her gone, they would push her out and she would have nowhere to go.

In the wild that situation is solved by dispersal. The wolf that is no longer wanted leaves the pack and goes off in search of another pack to join. In captivity that can't happen and the wolf that would have dispersed gets attacked. The other wolves bite it on the base of its tail where there are scent glands. If those glands are destroyed by the creation of an open wound, the animal loses its identity, and therefore all status, and as a result is kept away from food and very often dies or is killed.

Fortunately Daisy accepted demotion. However, since the lone wolf they had heard looking for a vacancy didn't exist, we then had to persuade the pack to promote from within. I started to intersperse the lone wolf with recordings of a full pack again, which I hoped would have the effect of bringing them together. I also made sure that at their next feed, the wolves were given a whole carcass instead of hunks of meat that had already been dissected. In the wild, the kill is very important as a means of defining which animal holds what rank within the pack. The individual lumps of meat that wolves often get in captivity blur the distinctions, and this pack needed to work out its hierarchy.

It was another five days before the voice of a new alpha female rang out in answer to the challenge. It had been a long and nail-biting wait, but during the early hours of the fifth morning, in reply to my challenge from the lone alpha female, Zeva's howl pierced the silence. Her voice had taken on a new authority and she was defending her position and her patch with vigour. She was backed up by the rest of the pack, their howls indicating that they were firmly behind her. Even Daisy's voice could be heard among them rooting for her new leader.

It was the most thrilling moment for me and made all those nights spent out in the wet and the cold worthwhile. Unless this had all been coincidence, which seemed highly improbable, we had just witnessed an incredible breakthrough. We had restructured this pack from the outside; with nothing more sophisticated than tape recordings, we had demonstrated that it was possible to influence and alter the behaviour and make-up of a pack of wolves, and that had to be good news for biologists and for farmers who struggled to keep wolves from taking their livestock. I felt that what we had achieved offered great hope for the future.

Ironically, Zeva chose Daisy to nanny her pups when they were born and she once again fell into the role she had performed many times before. She looked after them diligently, and when they were eighteen months old she lay down one day in the shade of her favourite tree and quietly passed away. She was a very special wolf who had touched me greatly and I was sorry to see her go.

Chapter Nineteen

FINDING
A HOME

News travels fast in the animal world and my success at Longleat was beginning to be recognised. I was approached by a number of other wildlife parks and zoos wanting help and advice about how to manage their wolf packs. I also started working with the public. As night fell Jan and I would take visitors to one of the copses near the wolf enclosure for a Howl-in. I would explain to them why wolves make that eerie, spine-chilling sound by the light of the moon that's in every horror movie. I would give a number of rallying howls, as if gathering my pack around me, then Jan would howl, as if joining her leader, and from across the park came the sound of the captive pack in full cry, defending their territory against us.

Humans have long believed that wolves howl because they are grieving for a lost a member of the pack. That's not true. It often is a mournful, grief-stricken sound, but they howl for all sorts of reasons and in different ways – with different intonations, just as we humans do when we speak – and there's a lot of information in a howl. It *can* be that they've lost a member of the pack and they are howling to see if they can call it home, but they also howl to defend territory, to tell individuals or other packs where they are and to rally the troops. If the howl is cut off short it means danger, stay where you are, stop doing what you're doing, I'm taking charge. If it goes on for a long time and tapers off it means quite the reverse: keep doing what you're doing. If it is low and deep it is defensive, warning rival packs to stay away. If they are under threat the whole pack will howl together and the mid-ranking wolves will even disguise their voices and use yips and yelps between howls to give the impression to the rivals that their pack is larger than it actually is.

Wolves whine and whimper when they are face to face. They howl to communicate from a distance, where we might use a mobile phone, and they can adjust the volume for short, medium and long range. If a pack member has gone hunting and failed to return, the pack howls to let the missing wolf know where the pack is in case he has lost his bearings. And if the missing wolf hears his pack calling he will reply to let them know he's on his way. Each animal's howl is as distinctive to that wolf as the way it looks, smells and walks; and once you start to study them and live among them, you quickly notice how different each wolf is. They are as unique as humans and their voices just as distinctive. Even in the dark I can tell which wolf is approaching by the sound of his footsteps and by his smell; and I can tell which animals within any pack are howling.

Each rank has its signature howl; the alpha's voice is deep and low and he or she howls intermittently: howling for five to ten seconds then pausing for the same amount of time before howling again. The pause is important because he is listening for a response. Depending upon what comes back he will get the others to add their voices or he'll move and call from a different location. The beta also has a low voice but he howls continuously for three or four times as long as the alpha. And so it goes throughout the pack: the mid ranks, the mid to high ranks, the low ranks and even the omega all have individual voices.

This is how a lone wolf, looking for a pack to join, knows where and when would be a good moment to try. If he hears the pack calling for a missing member several days running and hears no answering howl, which suggests that the missing wolf might be dead, he knows that there could be a vacancy. Wolves are not sentimental. Their prime concern is survival, and in the wild that means being able to feed and to defend their territory, and a pack that is missing a rank is vulnerable.

However, they won't take in a defective lone wolf and will turn on individuals that are not fit enough to do their job within the pack. I have seen wolves play terrible tricks, which amount to premeditated murder. The alphas have suppressed one rank in the pack from howling, giving the impression to the lone wolf that that rank was missing, and when he has turned up hoping to fill the vacancy the beta wolf has killed him. It's survival of the fittest.

I thoroughly enjoyed what I was doing at Longleat. It was fantastic to be given the opportunity to put my theories into practice and I enjoyed watching the faces of the public, particularly the children, light up when they heard the wolves howling. I am sure the park valued what I did, but the Howl-ins were the only thing I was ever paid for. This meant I had to work round the clock trying to fit in everything I did there with the army job and the private dog training that I had to do to support us.

After a couple of years at Wilton I moved to Warminster. I had landed a job at the Land Warfare Centre and Battlesbury Barracks, which was much closer to Longleat, and the Longleat Estate allowed me to rent one of their cottages in the village of Corsley Heath. There were more than twenty dogs in the kennels at Warminster as opposed to the six at Wilton, so it was a bigger job and there was more scope to make a difference. However, neither the day job nor the dog train-ing was particularly well paid, and since Jan was pregnant again, money was becoming an issue.

I couldn't see an immediate solution until one day the BBC arrived at Longleat to make a pilot programme about wolves. It was provi-sionally called *The Beast Within* and was presented by Philippa For-rester. It was designed to highlight the similarities between the wolf and the domestic dog. I was asked to take part – and television paid a lot better than anything else I had ever done. It was a subject that I knew like the back of my hand and we had a lot of fun doing it. We filmed in the park and I also went down to the BBC studios in Bris-tol. The programme was a great success; everyone seemed very pleased with the result and with my part in it. They talked enthusiastically about a series being commissioned on the strength of the pilot. I felt confident that a new career beckoned. But time passed and I heard nothing; then one evening the television was on – and there was Philippa Forrester presenting the first of a brand-new series about wolves. Without me.

I was gutted and rang the BBC to find out what had happened. I was told by someone in the production office that they had contacted Longleat to try and book me for the series and been told that I no longer worked at the park and that they had no idea where I had gone or how I might be contacted. I was furious. Longleat knew exactly where I was: I was in the middle of sorting their breeding programme. It was a critical time for them, and I can only think they must have been afraid they would lose me. I can understand why they were wor-ried – but I would have liked to have made the decision to refuse the job for myself.

It was the beginning of the end. I stayed on for a few more months but I knew the time had come for me to part company with Lon-gleat. Things rapidly went downhill; they wanted more of me and I wasn't prepared to give it. I had been there for four years and had always slightly resented the fact that they had benefited from my research and my expertise but never offered to reward me. They had provided me with the cottage, but it was very basic and I'd had to pay rent on it, and I had been scrimping and saving all that time. This was the final straw: they had deprived me of an opportunity to make some money and to make a bit of a name for myself. I told them I couldn't go on like this; they either had to put me on the payroll or I would have to go elsewhere. But by that stage I had virtually made up my mind to go.

If there was any lingering doubt in my mind, Jan removed it. She went into the dining room of our cottage one day, where Beth, our newborn baby, was sleeping in her cot, and found a large rat sitting on top of her cleaning its whiskers. Jan had put up with a lot and been heroic in helping me with the wolves, but she had had enough. She wanted to go back to Plymouth where her family lived and I couldn't argue. So we bought a house together not far from her parents and she took our two children, Kyra and Beth, straight there. Another child, Jack, was on the way. I told Longleat I was leaving and handed in my notice at the barracks.

It was no secret that my dream was to have my own wolves, and at around this time I was offered a couple of male Timber wolves by the Paradise Wildlife Park at Broxbourne, one of the places where I used to help out from time to time. They were nearly three months old and needed to be re-homed because their owner, a private collector in the West Midlands, had tried to socialise them but had left it too late and they would never be as tame as he wanted. They were perfect for me and I was dying to say I'd take them, but I had no land and so I couldn't commit. Then, in the way these things happen, I was chatting to a couple of guys who had come to a howling evening. They were part of a group that staged medieval re-enactments and were particularly interested in wolves because the forests of England would have been full of wild wolves in medieval times. They asked what my plans were, and when I told them I was hoping to find some land, they said I should get in touch with a friend of theirs, Stuart Barnes-Watson, an Australian who had just bought fifty acres in north Devon. Another member of the re-enactment group, he too was very interested in history and therefore wolves. He was intending to create a kind of outdoor adventure and education centre for kids to teach them forest skills and about the creatures that used to live there. They gave me his number and said I should give him a call.

I phoned him and very much liked the sound of what he was planning. I told him I had these two wolf pups ear-marked, and he couldn't have been more delighted by the idea of adding wolves to the mix, so I went down to East Buckland to see him and to have a look round the place. It was a beautiful location, with pine forests leading down a valley to a stream at the bottom; and we got on famously. He said I could choose anywhere I liked for the wolves. I went for an area right at the bottom that reminded me of Idaho. It was steep and more thickly forested, and although obviously on a much smaller scale, it was just as picturesque. I could imagine the wolves coming out of the ferns in the early morning mist – and how exciting it would be for the kids camping there – and I loved the way the sun dappled through the tree canopy. It looked like a picture post-card. It wasn't going to be the easiest place to build an enclosure, but I couldn't have dreamt of a more perfect home for the wolves and immediately told Broxbourne that I'd take the pups.

While I was working on the enclosure the pups, which I named Shadow and Pale Face, went to Linton Zoo, a family-run business in Cambridge. They happened to have a spare enclosure for a few months before some lions arrived, and offered to have the wolves, and to house me, free of charge, until we were able to move to Devon. In return, I gave talks when I was there and helped them with the other animals.

My accommodation there and part-time home for the next two months was a Portakabin. It was very basic and the nearest it had to cooking facilities was a microwave oven, so I borrowed a cash-and-carry card and went to the local wholesale store and bought Pot Noodles, which need no cooking and which I had always thought were quite tasty. But because you could only buy in quantity at a cash-and-carry, I had to buy the same flavour and lived off chicken and mushroom Pot Noodles for breakfast, lunch and supper for two months. I never want to see another Pot Noodle as long as I live.

The enclosure was a nightmare to build. I had help from a couple of guys, but it nearly killed us. The only access was down a forest track, and the truck that I'd hired to take the materials and equipment down kept getting stuck in the mud. In the end we had to carry it all down by hand – a distance of about six hundred metres. We dug a trench four feet deep around the entire perimeter in which to sink the wire, because wolves are notoriously good at digging their way out, and fixed the wire to scaffolding poles which we concreted into the ground. That was the basic structure and it couldn't have been sturdier or more secure. I'd got a local welder in Plymouth to bend the top of each pole to a forty-five degree angle, facing inwards, so there was no way any wolf could escape. We successfully begged, borrowed, stole and fund-raised to get the money, but the greatest cost was in blood, sweat and tears.

Stuart had put in an application for a licence to keep dangerous animals at the outset, and when it was finished the various planning inspectors came to look. There was a vet that I'd known at Longleat, someone from the police firearms department and a man from the local council. They tested the fencing, asked to see paperwork about public liability insurance and so on, asked about safety procedures, asked who held firearms certificates and wanted to be sure those people would be on hand in the event of a wolf escaping. They covered everything and went away apparently satisfied, saying we would get their decision in due course. We were confident that the rest was a formality, and I went ahead with arrangements to collect the pups from Linton. Kim Simmons, the owner, was delighted because the lions were arriving any day.

Then on Christmas Eve I had a phone call; the county council had turned down our application. They said there had been objections locally to having wolves in the area. We could appeal, they said, but it would cost £2000. I couldn't believe it. I was in real trouble. I couldn't keep the wolves in Cambridge for much longer; I didn't have the money for an appeal; I didn't even have money to buy decent Christmas presents for my kids. I had nowhere to keep the wolves and no thought about what to do next. It was not a happy Christmas.

Fortunately the local newspaper, *The Journal*, had been interested in what we were doing in South Buckland and when planning was refused, they sent a journalist to interview me. She wrote a big piece highlighting my plight, and the very day the paper hit the streets I had a call from Bob Butcher, who ran the Combe Martin Wildlife and Dinosaur Park near the coast about thirteen miles away. He had read the story and said that he had space, and if I could put up an enclosure for my wolves, which he would pay for, he would give them a home free of charge. You couldn't see me for dust; I went to see him right away, unable to believe my luck. I liked him from the start and was impressed by what he had done on the property and his obvious interest and concern for the animals. The park, set on the edge of Exmoor, was twenty-six acres in all and, as the name suggests, contained a variety of wildlife as well as a display of life-size animatronic dinosaurs that brought children to the park in droves. The wildlife collection was quite modest. He had birds of prey, snow leopards, meerkats, apes, monkeys, sea lions and tropical butterflies, and I think he recognised that the addition of wolves would boost trade, while the research I was known for would boost his credentials. The justification for keeping wild animals in captivity was to protect them and improve their welfare, and he seemed very keen to be doing the right thing.

The space he offered me was less than an acre, much smaller than the previous site and very wet. It had been a pelican pond and, although there were a few trees, there was more pond than earth, but beggars can't be choosers; I could fix that and in other respects it was good. It was near the bottom corner of his property near the monkey house, with fields and open countryside beyond, which was hilly, wooded and unspoilt. I agreed to take it and we shook hands on the deal. In return for his housing the wolves, I undertook to give educational talks about them every day during the season, and he allowed me periods away from the park to further my research.

Kim very kindly agreed to keep Shadow and Pale Face in Cambridge for another couple of months, and I immediately set to work with a digger with a swing-shovel, moving earth from higher up the hill and landscaping an enclosure. Then the hard work started: digging a four-foot trench around the perimeter – by hand. It was backbreaking. We couldn't get the machinery down there so there was no alternative, but every few inches my shovel would hit a massive tree root. There weren't many trees but those that there were had been there for a long time and had gigantic roots that reached over the entire area. I was working with a very entertaining Scottish welder called Arthur, who fixed the heavy-duty metal fencing to the metal posts. The highlight of our day was a huge breakfast in the local pub, the London Inn. But what I remember most about Arthur was that every time I touched the fencing while he was welding at the back of the enclosure, I got a tingle up my arm. I couldn't work it out until I noticed one day that the electric cable to his welding gear that ran from the monkey house was submerged in the pond. I turned to him and I said, 'Arthur, is that all right, mate?' And he said in his broad Scottish accent, 'Aye, there's nay problem there. I do it all the time.'

My first season at Combe Martin was a huge success. At Christmas time the local paper had followed up their story with news about where I was, and people started coming from far and wide to see the wolves. Every afternoon I gave a talk and went into the enclosure and howled and, without fail, the wolves began to howl with me. The children loved it and so did I; it was such a pleasure to see the looks on their faces and a great opportunity to demonstrate to everyone, young and old, that wolves did not deserve their demonic reputation.

The wolves seemed happy in their new home but mine was over eighty miles away, and it was no longer such an enjoyable place to be. My preoccupation with the wolves and building a home for them hadn't helped my relationship with Jan. But looking back I realise that it was probably never a great passion for either of us. It was a relationship that, at the time, suited us both. Each of us provided what the other wanted – companionship, friendship, a home and children – and although we thought we were in love, and were very loving and caring towards one another, I am not convinced that it was ever the real thing. But maybe I never gave our relationship a chance. I was so bound up in my work at that time and so passionate about the wolves and everything I was learning and discovering about them, that I wonder whether any human relationship could ever have come close. If I had had to choose between spending a night in the wolf enclosure or at home, if I'm honest, I would probably have chosen the wolves.

We were together for eleven years in all and had four children – Kyra, Beth, Jack and Sam, who are all great kids. Jan, however, had been playing second fiddle to wolves for too long, and although we never formally brought it to an end, it was clear to us both that the relationship was over. The drive to Plymouth was a good hour and a half and I had been doing it twice a day, so when Bob suggested that I rent a room in the house at the park, which he ran rather half-heartedly as a hotel, it didn't take long to agree. I didn't move my things out of the house in Plymouth and there was never any animosity at that time between Jan and me; it was more a case of separation by default. After a couple of months, the falconer at the park, who looked after the birds of prey, offered to sell me his damp, derelict old caravan that was parked on a piece of land alongside the road, just a short walk up the hill from the wolves, and I moved in there.

I say parked, but its travelling days were done. If you'd tried to move it, it would have fallen apart. I paid £20 for it – and I was robbed! It was tiny, just big enough for a bed and a little gas cooker. It was in a shocking condition with mould growing all over the inside, and there was no toilet so I had to pee into an empty putty bucket, but it was somewhere to lay my head and it was all I could afford. Bob had a shop at the park where visitors bought mementoes, and I sold bits and pieces there which brought in a bit of money, but I no longer had a salary and I had exhausted my savings.

It was fantastic to have my own wolves, to be with them night and day, to be able to freely interact with them, feed them and study their behaviour; this became the sole focus of my life. What I now wanted was a female for them. I wanted to breed a litter to see whether a captive pack would allow me to raise its pups and, if so, whether I could teach them about our world and theirs. Howletts Wild Animal Park in Kent answered my prayers with the offer of a three-year-old female called Elu that needed to be re-homed. It is common practice for wildlife parks to give one another animals that they no longer have space for or that are being picked on by the pack – animals that in the wild would be dispersed and go and find another pack.

She was a gorgeous animal, black in colour, but when I went to see her the first thing that struck me was how skittish she was; none of the wolves she was with had been socialised at all and practically climbed the walls when anyone went near their enclosure. My first thought was: would my fencing be up to it – particularly those bits where the tree roots had defeated me? But she seemed to be a climber rather than a digger and the keepers assured me that provided she had somewhere underground she could hide, she would be fine. Fortunately I had already built a den in the enclosure. I'd made a wooden frame that I covered with plastering mesh and finally plaster, leaving an entrance that was big enough for me to climb through should I need to get inside. I arranged a date to come back and collect her.

Three volunteers made the journey with me; I borrowed a decrepit old van from someone who worked at the park and put a big cage in the back. Two of the volunteers travelled in front with me, and the other followed in a car just in case we broke down. It was a long trip; six hours each way. Howletts were very efficient and professional. By the time we arrived, the vet had been, Elu had been darted, she'd had a full medical examination, she was fit and in good condition and she was on a stretcher ready to go. We carried her to the cage; I gave her an injection to reverse the tranquilliser and bring her round, and covered the cage with a big tarpaulin. Some people keep animals sedated for travel, but in my experience it is better for them to be fully conscious, particularly wolves. We've lost too many animals that way – and if the cage is covered so they can't see what's happening, that usually keeps unsociable animals reasonably calm.

We had driven for about three-quarters of an hour when we started to hear noises from the back – sounds of scuffling and the cage rattling – so we decided to stop for some coffee and investigate, and while the others got the thermos out, I went and checked on the wolf. She was wide awake and badly distressed. She was a pack animal, clearly didn't like being alone and was doing all she could to bite and claw her way out. I wasn't worried about her getting through the cage; Arthur, the Scottish welder, had made it for me – it was so strong it would have held a rhinoceros and it weighed about as much – but we still had more than five hours to drive and she was going to hurt herself unless I found some way to calm her.

Goodness knows what possessed me to do what I did next – but that's been the story of my life. I've done things no sane person would have dreamt of doing. I opened the cage, climbed in and travelled for the rest of the journey to Combe Martin cramped into an area that measured two foot by four foot by five foot with a dangerous animal that had never been in contact with a human being before.

My companions stood watching as I got in, their mouths gaping in disbelief. They then closed the door, pulled the tarpaulin back into place, leaving a little peephole so I had just enough light to be able to see Elu, and set off. The transformation in this wolf was incredible. As I climbed in she moved to the very back of the cage but she didn't try to get away. She became completely calm and spent the next five and a half hours with her head resting on my shin, nibbling at my bootlaces. She was even happy to have me stroke her and gently scratch her back end, as you would a dog. I still have bits of hair that I pulled off her that day as a memento. I was astonished by the trust she showed me – and deeply flattered.

It late at night and dark when we got back, so rather than put her straight in with the boys in the enclosure, not knowing how they would take to each other, I put her into a bigger cage I had up near the caravan; and I went in there with her to keep her company. During the night she started communicating with the wolves down at the bottom which was a really good sign. The next morning we transferred her back into the small cage, and again I went in with her, and the others loaded it – and me – into the bucket of a dumper and drove it down to the enclosure. She went through the open gate, walked straight past Pale Face and Shadow without even looking at them, and and began sniffing and scenting round the perimeter. She showed no signs of wanting to escape, while they followed her drooling like love-struck teenagers. They hadn't met a female since they were pups and she clearly exceeded all their expectations.

Chapter Twenty

POLAND

The biologists I worked with were always sceptical about the value of comparing wolf and dog behaviour. They regarded them as two distinct creatures and didn't share my belief that unless we check it, the wolf will eventually turn into the dog that we know today – and the dog into the stereotype of the wolf. I believe we can use them to help each other. If you look at the behaviour of wolves as they get closer to human populations in countries like Poland and Finland, where there is less space than north-west America, they are developing similar characteristics. Originally they were so frightened of humans they stayed in the forests and the hills and were rarely seen. When they started approaching farms, a farmer could see off a pack of four or five wolves by simply showing himself. The minute they saw him they would turn and run. Nowadays, they are so confident that if a man appears armed with a dustbin lid and a broom, that pack of four or five wolves will hold their ground and growl and may even chase after him.

I became interested in Poland some years ago; a volunteer at the park called Angela, who is sadly no longer with us, asked me to go there, hoping that I might be able to help the local smallholders who were losing livestock to marauding wolves. Having been a research student in the forests of the north-west, she felt passionately that something needed to be done and still had contacts in the region. I had never been to Poland and it was a great opportunity to learn more about European wolves and possibly interact with them. It is one of the few places in Europe where, despite being hunted and persecuted, wild wolves were never quite eradicated. They were hunted for sport in these forests until 1997, when the Polish government gave in to pressure from environmentalists and banned wolf hunting, but the ban was rather feebly policed, so poachers had a field day and not surprisingly there was little change recorded in their numbers. There were two other factors, I was told. The number of prey animals had dropped dramatically and, with Poland's rapid economic growth, what was left of the wolves' habitat had become fragmented.

So in 2002, when the park at Combe Martin was closed for the winter, I left a team of volunteers in charge of the wolves and flew to Poland for the first of several short visits, to learn as much as I could about the wolves, their habitat and what was making them raid the farms. I flew to Gdansk, then took an eight-hour bus ride due east to the Romincka Forest on the Russian border. On the other side of the border it's called the Krasny Les, after the river Krasnaya that runs through it. It was the most amazing sight, a natural forest that looked as though it had never been touched. This truly was a place that time forgot. It was incredible to think that at one time, thousands of years ago, most of central Europe would have been covered in dense forests like this with massive trees, and they would been home, as this one was, to species of wildlife that have become extinct in most other places. Among dozens of other creatures there were elk, wild boar, red and roe deer, red foxes, even the odd lynx and, of course, wolves.

I stayed right in the middle of the forest, in a lodge, busy during the season with people of all nationalities who came to hunt game. The walls were hung with antlers and there were photographs going back over hundreds of years of forest life. The food was fantastic – soups, meats, vegetables and serious cakes all made by the lady who ran the place. It was food designed to keep you going in the forest and none of it was expensive. The price list on the wall made me laugh. It had the price for every nationality and at the top was the German which was a good few euros higher than any other. When I looked quizzically at Romick, my companion, who was one of the foresters, he just grinned.

Romick didn't speak a word of English and I didn't speak a word of Polish, but I had a guide who spoke better English than I did, so between the two of them I discovered everything he knew about the area and the wildlife within it. He was one of several foresters who managed the forest; all of them highly respected men in the community, like local policemen in ours. The jobs were handed down from father to son; they were managers of nature, keepers of the wild, and he was as pleased to join forces as I was. Our aims were very similar: my job was to help manage the creatures within his forest and his job was to manage the forest that gave those creatures a home. Despite the language barrier Romick and I forged a tremendous bond between us. At dusk he would take me up to the high seat he had built in the forest, where we would watch the wolves and all the other wildlife without being seen, and all the way there he would be pointing at things and explaining and I would answer as best I could. We managed to establish a way of communicating that went beyond words; it was the natural world. I respected this man deeply; he was a genuine, honest person, whose word was his bond and whose promise meant everything. That, I discovered, was the culture of these people. A slipped word that means nothing to us means everything to them.

On a subsequent trip, I took along a few colleagues from Combe Martin to give them some experience of wild wolves. One of them, after a very drunken night on the local vodka, invited one of the foresters to come to England – the kind of thing we all do in a friendly sort of way to strangers we're having a good time with; an easy gesture that usually goes no further. The next time I went to Poland, this forester was noticeably standoffish. I was on my own this time and was mystified. I couldn't imagine what I had done to offend him so I asked the guide if anything was wrong. 'Yes,' he said bluntly. 'The last time you were here someone promised him a trip to the UK and it hasn't happened.' That someone who had invited him had long since gone, but I had no alternative but to buy tickets for this man and his son to visit me in Devon for a week. The son had to come because he was the only one in the family that spoke English. They loved the wolves and it turned out to be a good week, but it made me realise just how important it is to respect other people's cultures – and just how dangerous vodka can be.

Meeting one of the farmers who had lost animals to the wolves took me straight back to my childhood and immediately I had great sympathy for the man. Stanislaw had a wife and daughter and a small plot of land which stretched to the edge of the forest on two sides. They owned no more than twenty cattle, and these were so much part of the family and so precious to them that each animal had a name. There were no fancy tractors or machines around, just a utilitarian working farmyard and rather shabby outbuildings. Nervous guard dogs ran around that looked like a cross between a German Shepherd and a Pyrenean Mountain Dog. The wolves had killed some of the dogs as well as the cattle and although he had put studded collars on them for protection, the dogs had still been taken. That didn't surprise me – by the age of six or eight weeks wolf cubs have learnt how to avoid antlers on deer, so for them a studded collar would have been just another pair of antlers to avoid. What was interesting was that the wolves obviously didn't respect the dogs as being their own kind.

Stan and his family lived very simply, in a traditional, two-storey painted brick house. They kept chickens and geese and it was clear that the farm was their life and their entire livelihood. Dressed in bib and braces and a straw hat, he told me through the interpreter what had been happening. For a while a string of flags along the fence-line had kept the wolves away, but that no longer worked and neither did their fences. One of his calves had been attacked just before my visit and he had some video footage, which showed clearly which parts of the calf the wolves had taken.

To a farmer like this, losing a calf was like losing a leg. But losing an adult milking cow or a seasoned bull was even worse. The government paid compensation but no money could replace an animal that had taken years of breeding to reach its peak. On a smallholding like this farmers bred for succession, so that there would always be a younger animal coming through ready to replace one that was too old to work. So if one of them was killed by wolves it could take six or seven generations to replace it.

This man had more reason to hate the wolf than anyone I have ever met, and yet he didn't. You could see in his eyes that he had the utmost respect for them. His father, and his father before him, had taught Stanislaw about the wolf when he was a child. He knew that wolves created balance in the forest and kept the animals in natural harmony; knew that they provided food for others as well as themselves and stripped out disease and illness. Even though they attacked his livestock, which he and his family could ill afford, he knew that he needed the wolf as much as he needed the cattle.

I visited two other farms in the vicinity, with boundaries that went to the edge of the forest. They lived on the same subsistence level as

Stanislaw and his family, and had suffered similar devastating losses, but like Stan they were amazingly philosophical about it. They understood the value of wolves to the forest and said they would be happy to see them deterred rather than shot. One of these farms had a First World War cemetery on its land and they took me to see a calf that had been killed very recently right on the edge of it. While I was examining the remains, we heard a door slam and a car speed off down the track. As we walked back to the house, four puppies came bounding towards us across the field. I was told by my guide that it was not unusual for people with an unwanted litter to dump them, and word had got out that animal experts were in the area. They looked to me as though they were the result of a wolf mating with a domestic dog, which again I was told was a common occurrence. We took them back to the hunting lodge and I gathered later that they kept one for themselves and found homes for the others.

The third farm I visited was the poorest of the lot. It was a mother and son business. She had been on the land all her life and was very old-school in her attitudes; and although she respected the wolf she had had enough. The son had obviously had more education than his mother and seemed to have studied ecology and knew more about the animals in the forest. But what I remember most about this visit were the coffee and biscuits. The Polish are very hospitable people and in every home you go into you are offered food and drink – which you cannot possibly refuse. The old lady handed me one of the most disgusting biscuits I've ever put into my mouth and asked what I would like to drink. Since coffee was the only word I knew in Polish, I asked for 'kawy'. The room fell silent and I wondered what terrible faux pas I'd committed. The others – who'd been given refreshments at this farm before – asked for 'herbata', which I discovered meant tea. My coffee was like pond water and the only consolation was that by comparison the biscuit seemed quite palatable.

What interested me, in looking at the carcasses of the animals that the wolves had killed, was how little of the beast they had taken. I have been with wolves when they were starving and seen how quickly they tear up a carcass; if they are hungry enough they will eat every last bit. These carcasses had not been the centre of a feeding frenzy; they looked as though they had been dissected by a surgeon. In almost every example I examined, either from a recent kill that I saw in the flesh or in one that had been photographed, strips had been taken from the thigh or the shoulder, or an incision has been made in the ribcage and the vital organs taken, or the stomach had been opened and cleaned out and a few choice pieces of meat taken, but the legs were still intact and the bulk of the animal had been left. Meanwhile, surprisingly, parts of the dogs had been eaten.

The evidence simply didn't support the theory that the wolves were attacking domestic livestock for survival because there wasn't enough natural prey in the forest. Besides, the forest was bristling with deer and elk and beaver – all of which I had seen in the scats.

The other common theory was that farmed animals were an easy meal for the wolves. I didn't buy that. I have spent nearly twenty years with these creatures and I have never seen them do anything that could be described as opportunistic. Everything they do has a purpose, and that includes what they seek out to eat. They know so much about regulating their own bodies and about the world they live in and the value to the pack of the animals that share it with them. What they take, and when, depends on a host of variables like the time of year, the weather conditions, when pups are expected, their health, the cohesion of the pack and a whole lot more. They know instinctively what their bodies need. I have even seen a pack of wolves eat the most putrid carcass that was so rotten it was practically liquefied, but they had worms and knew instinctively that eating bad meat would flush the worms out of their systems.

I have seen my own pack in Devon (about which I'll talk later) become practically addicted to the fatty stomach lining from the carcasses of cows and sheep that I fed them on. They suddenly started eating that in preference to the meat. I couldn't understand it, so I ate it myself for four months and I found that during that period I was much better able to cope with the cold. The stomach lining of deer was completely different; it didn't have the fat content of the domesticated animals. They ate what their bodies told them they needed.

If I was right about these Polish wolves hunting according to need, then they were getting something from these cows and sheep – and even dogs – that they couldn't get from any other source. I haven't done enough research to prove it yet, but I suspect that, if the farm animals have been inoculated, the answer could be immunity to disease or even something as simple as wormer that the farmer has dosed his stock with. Or it could be the fat content in the stomach lining, as with my captive pack, that boosted their resilience to the long, cold, snowbound winters.

The irony is that the wolves would have discovered the value of domestic livestock without moving from the forest. For many years they received meals-on-wheels. Hunters used to bring livestock carcasses into the forest to attract the wolves so that they were easy to find and shoot. After wolf hunting was banned, eco-tourism took over, and the practice continued so that tourists could be sure of seeing wolves and getting the photo they'd been promised. It was only when Poland joined the European Union in 2004 that baiting was banned.

The solution to this problem could be simple. Once we know exactly what it is the wolves are missing in their natural diet, we could take the nutrients they need to them in some other form and they would no longer need to attack the cattle. It is early days and a lot of research still needs to be done into the food they are taking but I believe it could be achieved.

There is one other possible explanation for the raids, which is more difficult to remedy. They may not be wolves at all; they may be hybrids – like the four little pups that came bounding over to us on the farm. With wolves now living in such close proximity to human beings in Poland, it's inevitable that they breed from time to time with domestic dogs. It would explain why these creatures that look like wolves and live like wolves are prepared to come into the fields in broad daylight and have no fear of humans.

Chapter Twenty-one

MAKING CONTACT

That first trip told me all I needed to know about the forest, the surrounding area and the farmers. Next I needed to infiltrate a pack to see if there was any other explanation for their taking livestock when there seemed to be plenty of food for them in the forest. The problem was that I didn't have time to do what I did in Idaho because I couldn't be gone from the park for that long. I had to speed up the process and, after the success of my experiment with a tape recorder at Longleat, I thought the method might also work here. This time we would have to convince these wolves that there was a rival pack in the area with more males in it than they had in theirs. My theory was that it would make them want an extra male to boost their defence against the rivals. And that extra male was going to be me.

I didn't get a lot of data from Romick. He knew every pathway and tree in the forest and he knew how many wolves there were, but not whether they were male or female, young or old. So before I could make a convincing tape I had to find out how many male wolves were in the existing packs. I had to get out on the ground and establish contact. On this trip I had colleagues to help, and during the day they would go into the forest and look for tracks and scats and signs of any kill which would help me know which direction I should be heading in at night. I used the technique I had used in Idaho. I went into the forest as a lone wolf, howling to try and establish how many wolves were out there.

The European wolf was a lot more flighty than the wild Timber wolves I lived among in America, probably because they saw many more humans. The Romincka Forest was a national park, so there were nature trails through it and people went there to walk or to study the wildlife. As well as the game and large mammals there were dozens of smaller species, and hundreds of rare birds and plants. The foresters came and went, as did loggers, and during the hunting season there were men with guns. Men, guns and wolves are not a good combination. So the wolves had a lot of interaction with people, but all of it was negative. Even the biologists, collecting data, used snowmobiles to track them down and caught them with lassoes. So where North American wolves were curious about humans these ones were plain frightened and therefore very shy; one sight of you and they were gone. Romick told me through the interpreter that he didn't think I had a chance of even getting close.

I had started preparing about a month before I left England. I adjusted my diet and cut out all perfumes, which meant no soap, toothpaste, deodorant or shampoo. I wanted to look and smell as much like a wolf as possible – all of which went well until I was on the plane and the lady in the seat next to me sprayed perfume all over herself. I began to think that in future the answer might be to travel by sea and lock myself in my cabin. I ate nothing but the food the wolves ate – venison, rabbit and pheasant with some vegetables – and only had water to drink. I ate no carbohydrates and nothing sweet, and obviously I stuck to that when I arrived in Poland – although it took a lot of willpower to resist those gorgeous cakes at the lodge.

Running as a lone wolf there was not as scary as it had been in Idado. I knew the forest quite well by now but it was still pretty hairy to be alone there in the dark. There may not have been bears in Poland but there were wild boar and they terrified me. One night, before I set off on foot, I was in a high seat – a viewing platform on stilts – with a couple of other guys. We had night-vision goggles and were hoping to spot wolves in the forest below. There was no toilet in the seat and as the night wore on I became desperate for a pee; so desperate that there was nothing for it but to climb down and have one in the forest. I told one of the guys to keep the goggles on me and give me a shout it anything untoward appeared. Having held it in for so long, I was down there for quite a long time, enjoying the feeling of relief, confident that I was safe. All of a sudden I heard snuffling noises and the sound of something quite heavy on the ground not far to my left. I wondered what it might be; obviously nothing to worry about because if it had been, my colleague would have yelled at me. Just as I was about to zip up my flies, a huge boar with great tusks appeared in front of me. My feet didn't touch the ground as I ran for the ladder, screaming abuse and shaking like a leaf. 'Why the hell didn't you warn me?' I said, but he didn't hear me; his back was turned. The other one had spotted a light in the forest and the pair of them were staring intently in the other direction having entirely forgotten about me.

The boar were about the size and weight of large sows but with tusks and a ferocious temper; they could be as mean as hell, particularly if they had young. One of the foresters had a 'tame' one that he aptly called Wreck-a-neck which was incredibly aggressive. My fear wasn't illogical. Local children that used the forest didn't worry about wolves but they were afraid of wild boar. Not even wolves would take on a wild boar. They would take a young one if they were lucky, but

I once saw three of them having a go at a female and she just ran at them and they scarpered. I often heard them crashing around at night and my heart would be in my mouth, but I didn't ever come face to face again.

After a week or so I had established what packs were out there and what we needed on a tape. They were very different from the North American wolves. Their packs were much smaller and they didn't stay together, maybe because they were looking for food. There were four packs in the area and two of them were just pairs. The largest pack had five individuals and that included pups. I worked out their territories, which was not hard – the ammoniac smell of their scent was quite eye-watering in places; but they frequently seemed to go outside those areas and travel across the border into Russia. The border was marked by a series of white posts with red tops that stood about two and a half feet above the ground and which in the winter were entirely buried in snow. It was very easy under those circumstances to get lost, and more than once I found myself on the wrong side of the border trying to explain to a vehicle full of Russian border guards, armed with rifles and looking trigger-happy, what I was doing there. I had learnt that the trick was to shout 'Wilk! Wilk! Wilk!' (Wolf! Wolf! Wolf!) at them in my best Polish, while digging quickly through all my layers of warm clothing to find the official piece of paper from the Polish authorities that proved who I was and that I was there studying wolves.

Unhappily the foresters wouldn't allow me to use a tape recorder inside the forest. They would let me howl but they would not let me take in any sound equipment. So my colleagues played it from Stanislaw's farm. Wolves can hear from up to ten miles away but whether they heard it and were influenced by it I will never know for sure. What I do know is that we established sound contact. I heard what I assumed was a lone female calling. I responded and she called back.

Her call went from defensive to locating. She was asking for help and my call indicated my willingness to join her. We called back and forth for the best part of two and a half weeks. During that time I was letting her know my position by scenting and eating food left from the pack's kill, taking what a mid-ranking member would eat, fillet meat and stomach content. I had a feeling that she was ghosting me, watching me, following me; and every now and then I would catch a glimpse of her.

One morning I came round a corner in the forest and there she was on the track ahead of me, not more than six or seven metres away. She stood and stared at me for forty or fifty seconds, which for an animal that had been shot at, chased and persecuted was extraordinary, and then she was gone. She was the most beautiful wolf, in good condition, obviously well fed. There was no doubt in my mind that she was the wolf I had been calling to. And then one morning when I was kneeling over a stream in a clearing, splashing water on to my face and having a drink, I felt aware that I had company. I turned round slowly and there, sitting no more than six feet away, was this glorious female.

Sadly my time in Poland was running out, so I will never know whether I could have got closer to her or infiltrated a pack in the way I did in Idaho, but I viewed this as a tremendous personal breakthrough. It showed me that no matter what human beings have done to them, if you go to wolves on their own terms, as I did with foxes all those years ago, and show them that you mean them no harm, then that trust will gradually return.

It was time for another experiment with tape recordings. I had promised Stanislaw I would try and find a way to keep the wolves away from his livestock, and with this limited knowledge of the wolves in the area, the farms and the forest, I now felt confident I could show him how to help himself. My plan was very simple. I gave him a cheap tape recorder with some speakers; exactly what I had used myself when I had tried to locate the different packs. What we needed to do was persuade the wolves that a rival pack already owned the territory around Stan's farm. If I could do that convincingly enough, my theory was they would leave it alone.

I showed Stanislaw how he must use the equipment. It was very basic. There was no point in coming into this impoverished rural area with complicated technology. It had to be straightforward enough for people to be able to work it and cheap enough for other farmers like Stan to be able to afford it. The tape I gave him had a a series of recordings of a pack with five males in it – one more than any of the packs I had heard in the forest – therefore a potential threat. They were giving a defensive howl, as if making it clear to all comers that the area around Stan's farm was their territory. I explained to Stan that there were different-sounding howls and that before wolves went into an area to hunt they gave a locating howl to make sure they weren't stepping on anyone else's toes. He immediately said he had noticed the different howls; it was gratifying to see how in tune this man was with his environment. Before a raid, he told me, the howls were high-pitched and afterwards they were low. This, I said, was because having made a kill, the pack gives a defensive howl to establish that this area is now theirs.

I told him that whenever he heard the high-pitched call – the locating call – he must turn on the tape and play it until he heard the howls of the wild pack recede, which I felt confident they would. He could see the logic at once and was very keen to give it a go. I next saw Stan two years later when I went back to Poland to film a documentary, and he was delighted by how successful the tape recordings had been. He had used them exactly as I had told him to and there had been no more attacks on his livestock. He was absolutely thrilled.

The great thing about working with the Polish farmers, as opposed to the ranchers in Idaho, was that the Poles fundamentally respected wolves and that a man like Stanislaw was prepared to give anything a go. He didn't want to have to shoot the wolves; he just needed them to stop attacking his livelihood. By contrast the American farmers that I met, sadly, seemed to believe that the only good wolf was a dead wolf.

Before I went home, Romick wanted to show me the primeval Bialowieza Forest, which is the oldest national park in Poland and a UNESCO world heritage site. It was due south of where we were. It was the most incredible place; it has eleven thousand different species of wildlife, including the European bison, and the plant life is equally amazing. But it gets hundreds of visitors and the wolves appeared to be adapting their behaviour in a slightly ominous way. As a consequence, perhaps, the foresters seemed to get closer to the wolves than they did up in the Romincka Forest, and one told me he had watched two wolves walking down a track. At first he thought they must be dogs, because wolves don't normally use tracks, but there was no doubt they were wolves – a male and a female – and while the female walked in a straight line, the male wove in and out of the trees from one side to the other, flushing out prey, which she then took. It was the way dogs hunt; not wolves.

Chapter Twenty-two

A HARSH
LESSON

I didn't really expect Elu, my female back at Combe Martin, to become pregnant that first year, but I decided to move in with the pack two weeks before she came into season, just in case, so I could watch the courtship behaviour and bond sufficiently with her for her to allow me to be nanny to her pups. To my surprise, although Shadow was the dominant male, it was Pale Face that mated with her. At the time that puzzled me, and I had to wait five years for a possible explanation. It turned out that Shadow had a defective heart. He and a female wolf I had recently rescued from Dartmoor Wildlife Park, called Lady Penelope, were on their way to a collector in Oxfordshire, on loan as a breeding pair, when he unexpectedly died in transit. A post-mortem revealed that he had heart disease. It's just possible that he always had heart problems and that was why Elu chose Pale Face to father her pups.

During the nine weeks of her pregnancy Elu showed every sign she was going to be a good mother; although this was the first time, she instinctively seemed to know what to do. She got the boys to help her dig rendezvous holes for the pups. These are small burrows, in the vicinity of the den, that the cubs are taught to dive into if they are in danger. They are two to three feet deep and usually dug beneath a rock or tree root so it is almost impossible for a predator to dig the pup out. My relationship with her seemed to be going well. I mimicked everything I had seen Daisy do at Longleat when she was hoping to be a nanny, and Elu seemed to be responding to me. I had a moment's anxiety after about six weeks when she started digging furiously beneath the roots of the biggest tree in the enclosure. I thought she might be preparing to give birth in there rather than in the den I'd built. If she had taken herself deep underground and something had gone wrong, we could have had a problem. Luckily she didn't use it.

Two days before she gave birth, I had been off on a hunting trip and came back to the enclosure with a few rabbits. It was mid-afternoon; Elu took one of the rabbits and went off into the den, where I had dug a birthing bowl like ones I had seen wild wolves dig, and there she stayed until, in the early hours of the following morning, I heard the low, mournful howls of a wolf in labour. It was unlike any noise I had ever heard a wolf make before. I had no idea what was going on or whether she was in distress and had no way of finding out. Every time I or any others went near the entrance to the den she gave a deep, rumbling growl to warn us off. Judging by where the noises were coming from she had ignored my birthing bowl and dug something for herself beyond that, obviously to be as far away from any threat as possible, and was now completely inaccessible. But the ground sloped and in her digging she had come very close to the surface at one point, and as she had turned some of the earth had been dislodged, leaving a tiny hole above her. I guessed with a torch I might be able to see what was going on beneath.

At first light I heard the first little whimpering sounds. My heart pounding, I quickly ran up the hill to the caravan to find a torch, and when I shone it through the hole I had to choke back tears. I was looking straight down into her birthing bowl and there were four minute pups that all seemed to be wriggling and squirming and therefore were alive and well. Bursting with what felt like paternal pride, I covered the hole with a boulder to stop the rain getting in and sat back patiently to let nature take its course. I wouldn't be on duty to look after them for another five weeks.

On the third day Elu came out of the den and alarm bells started to ring. Normally a mother will stay underground with her pups for a full week. When I was with the wild wolves in Idaho, the mother had been in the den for over a week and was completely emaciated when she came out. I tried to convince myself that it was perhaps different with wolves in captivity, and the weather wasn't as harsh here as it was the Rockies. But newborn pups need their mothers to regulate their temperature – they lose body heat very quickly – and they need feeding at least every two hours. When she was still out after three or four hours I began to panic. I put pressure on her to go back in; I lined the entrance to the den with food, hoping the sound of her pups would rekindle her maternal instincts, but nothing worked, in fact she seemed determined to stay as far away from the den area as she could.

If the pups were to be saved, I had to make a decision, and quickly or there would be nothing to save. I went in and grabbed the tiny creatures; they were like furry little rats with their eyes tightly shut, snuffling and grunting. Three of them were huddled together and were warm and looked reasonably well; the fourth looked quite different and was lying about two feet from the others and felt cold. Elu had clearly not wanted to know her and had pushed her away. They were all suffering from a degree of dehydration, which you can test by pinching the skin. The longer it takes for the pinched skin to stretch out flat again, the more dehydrated the animal. The skin of the fourth little pup stuck up like the crest on a dinosaur.

With the help of volunteers, we quickly took them up the hill to a little breeze-block shed next to my caravan which I'd prepared for a German Shepherd puppy for someone at the park. The floor was already covered in straw, and we rigged up a fake birthing bowl by putting a furry blanket with a heat-mat under it into a box to replicate their mother as much as possible and folded the pups into it. We bottle fed them on a formula milk called Esplac, and the three boys that had been huddled together suckled as though it was going out of fashion, which suggested to me that Elu hadn't fed them for some hours before she'd left the den. The fourth little one, which I named Cheyenne, would barely open her mouth. I had to sit with her tucked into my jacket to keep her warm and painstakingly coax her to take the milk one drop at a time.

It is not unknown for wolves in captivity to abandon their pups. Sometimes the maternal instinct is just not strong enough, and sometimes it's because they've had no role models to learn from. Howletts, where she was born, hadn't wanted any more pups, so they had kept the males and females in separate enclosures and she had never watched other mothers give birth or raise pups. When it happens there are two alternatives. To go in and save the litter, as I did; or to let the pups die in the hope that the mother will learn from her negligence and be a better mother next time around. This does happen, although it sometimes takes the death of three or four litters for the female to realise that she needs to suckle her pups for five weeks if they are to survive; it is nature's way of teaching a harsh lesson. For me there was no choice; I had to go in.

After a couple of days I was needing to devote so much time to little Cheyenne that I needed help with feeding the others. That was fine during the day when there were volunteers around, but at night it was becoming impossible. I appealed to Jan, who came to the rescue, God bless her, by agreeing to help me look after them at home in Plymouth. The children were so excited to have the pups in the house and Kyra loved helping to feed them. I could make it to the house in under the two hours I had between feeds, so I fed them before I left, bundled them into a box on the front seat, covered them up and drove while they slept beside me; and Jan fed the boys at two-hourly intervals throughout the night, while I concentrated on Cheyenne. Come the morning I took them all back to Combe Martin, and repeated the process the next night.

I named the boys Tamaska, Matsi and Yana, and it was interesting to watch them develop their own characteristics. It didn't take long to see that Tamaska was the biggest and greediest. The boys were all doing well, and every now and again Cheyenne would drink half a bottle of milk in one go and I'd think she'd finally turned the corner, but it didn't last and I was forever taking her to the vet. The bills were mounting up and I was beginning to really scrape the barrel financially when a friend who owned a pet shop came to my aid. She generously said I could charge future visits to the vet to her account at the surgery in Plymouth. For two and a half weeks I nursed this creature, willing her to live, but we were making no progress. One day she started making a crackling sound as she breathed, which I knew was never a good sign. The vet said she had pneumonia, and the results of some blood tests he'd done indicated she had no immune system. She died in my arms on the way home. I was heartbroken; but he said the only thing that had kept her alive that long was my round-the-clock care. In the wild, she would never have lived beyond the first day.

It taught me a valuable lesson. Her mother knew that this pup wasn't going to make it and had deliberately pushed her to one side. She didn't have the luxury of helpers to feed the other pups while she concentrated on the weakling. Nature told her to go with the ones that would survive. I was interfering in something I knew nothing about – but I would never do it again. I buried Cheyenne in a box in what is now another wolf enclosure near my caravan and I planted a tree for her. I mourn her to this day.

Chapter Twenty-three

WE ARE WHAT
WE EAT

The three remaining pups now needed a mother and, since Elu had lost interest in them, it was down to me. Having hoped I might be chosen as nanny, I was now facing an altogether different and more difficult role. Was I up to it? I knew I could keep them alive – that was the easy bit; the challenge was to prevent them turning into domesticated wolves. I wanted them to grow up with as many of the instincts and characteristics of their wild cousins as possible, because for me the justification of keeping wolves in captivity was to further our understanding of what makes wild wolves behave the way they do and, by understanding that, to help to prevent them from clashing with humans.

There was a shocking incident in Canada a few years ago where a hiker, a student on his own in the Saskatchewan forest, was attacked and partially eaten by wolves. Some were suggesting that it was an opportunistic kill. As I've already explained, I have never bought the line that wolves do anything because it's the easy option. Humans are fellow predators; they are not prey and everything that wolves have taught me about their world in all this time tells me that these creatures would not take a man – or any food source – just because it happened to be there and was convenient.

The dominant female will direct the hunters to go for the food sources that will provide them with what they need at that particular time in their lives – and that plays an important part in maintaining the social ranking within the pack too: they are what they eat. The richest bits of the kill and the vital organs always go to the alpha pair; and their scent, and therefore authority, is very different from that of the lower-ranking members who eat less well.

The pack is quite capable of ignoring an injured animal that they could effortlessly bring down, and running instead after a healthy creature for a week and a half, if they need what that animal can provide. It might be that there's a rival pack in the area, for example, and they need high-octane food to be able to defend their territory. Equally, if the alpha female is close to delivering her pups she might deliberately select an older animal or one that's not as fit as the rest; this would be because she wants to calm the pack's energy levels so they won't be too boisterous and unruly around her young, which would endanger them. This intelligence is passed down from generation to generation and is amazing to watch in action.

She can identify and select the animal she wants, out of a herd of three hundred, by the scent it leaves on the ground. It might be a moose with a cut on its foot that has become infected. Every time that foot touches the ground it leaves the smell of pus. She knows it has been weak for some time and so she follows it. She smells the grass and the bushes where the animal has stopped to graze and nibble leaves along the way, and she can smell from the scent of its decaying teeth that it's not a young animal. So before she gets anywhere near this moose she has built up a mental picture of it. As she gets closer she switches her attention from the ground to the air. She could still be two miles away but she opens up her nostrils, takes a deep breath and her nose fills with particles of dust mite and hair that are on the wind, and all her senses confirm that this animal is the one she wants. And so they go on to make the kill. She starts to run and the hunters follow, which gets their adrenalin up, and when she draws level with the beast she's chosen she indicates which one it is with her tail and they bring it down – even if other animals in the herd are closer. They obey their alpha.

The pack that killed the hiker were living in an area where a lot of trees had been felled and forests cleared, which meant that the prey animals were losing their habitat. These wolves had started eating migratory salmon instead, which is something wolves enjoy from time to time but it is not part of their regular diet and does not have the properties of meat. I thought this might go some way to explain why they had attacked a man, so I carried out an experiment with my wolves at Combe Martin – which is the value of having animals in captivity. After a few months on a diet of fish, which meant they were all eating exactly the same quality of food, the social structure of the pack fell apart. There were no longer any distinct ranks, so there was no one to make the decisions, no one to do the disciplining and they behaved like unruly hooligans. So I think the most likely explanation for why that pack attacked the hiker is that there was no one to tell them what to do – and what not to do.

That still left the question of why they started to eat him. Both wild and captive wolves will kill other predators. I've seen wolves kill bears and bears kill wolves and wolves kill mountain lion and coyote, but I have very seldom seen them kill a fellow predator for food. They will eradicate a predator if they see it as competition for food and they'll kill to protect their young – and they would kill humans as readily as any other animal under those circumstances, but they wouldn't eat us.

My theory is that maybe they no longer recognise us as fellow predators. It's arguable that because of our modern diet – a lot of which is carbohydrate and junk food, not to mention the people who are purely vegetarian – we smell more and more like prey animals. We behave more like prey too. Our ancestors would never have run away at the sight of a wolf or a bear or a mountain lion; their heartbeat wouldn't have raced, they wouldn't have broken into a sweat, or rolled their eyes like a frightened zebra. These animals were a familiar sight, and because our forebears shared a world – as the Native Americans continued to do for much longer than them – they knew better than to come between a mother and its cub or to walk too close to a den. The smell of fear is very exciting for a predator and it's only prey animals that transmit it so readily. So if there was some confusion about the hiker, and the pack's instincts were telling them they needed meat to restore the ranking system, I can see how they might have started to eat him.

Foresters say the same thing about bears. The first time a bear attacks it is always protecting its young or a food source, but having killed a human once and realised how much it smelt and behaved and even tasted like prey, that bear will see humans as another source of food and kill again.

The problem is that with every advance we make, humans take away a bit of their world. Wolves have all this extraordinary intelligence that is passed down through the generations about how, where and when to hunt, and what to eat, and suddenly they come face to face with mankind, who has upset the balance. The natural food supply they have been living on for hundreds of years disappears and in its place someone builds a farm or a ranch with cattle. It's inevitable that they are going to stay ever closer to man if he is providing the only source of food that is left.

We have taken the role of the dominant creature on this earth and yet we have no idea how to manage the creatures under us. We don't know how to maintain the balance that regulates everything – which animals do naturally. Rats and vermin are fine in the wild. They feed on carcasses and their numbers are limited by the availability of food; nature doesn't allow them to get out of control. Encourage them to come into the cities by throwing food into the gutter and leaving bins overflowing on every street and their breeding, not surprisingly, goes haywire. If we could begin to be responsible, the animals beneath us would regulate themselves.

We are out of control and too comfortable in our ways. We eat too much of the wrong sorts of food – food that is so low in value that we have to eat mountains of it to get any goodness. The Native Americans used to eat nothing but high-value foods and only ever in moderate proportions. There was scarcely a fat one among them and they were some of the strongest, fittest people on earth. Now they are eating white man's food and they are becoming obese like the rest of the western world – and poisoned. The incidence of cancer seems too high to be a coincidence. The basket-weavers who still work in the traditional way, which involves running the reeds through their mouths, are developing cancer of the mouth; and other sorts of cancer are rife.

We could learn so much from the animal kingdom.

Chapter Twenty-four

KNOWING
YOUR PLACE

A full pack of wolves – and one that is eating as nature intended – will always have the alpha pair, who are in their prime, and the accepted wisdom has always been that these are the only members of the pack that breed. They make the decisions for the welfare of the whole family. Then there will be a beta, or enforcer, and a tester, who is the quality controller. After that come mid- to high-ranking wolves and mid- to low-ranking wolves and an omega animal, whose role is to break up fights and diffuse tension within the pack. We tend not to use the alphabetical terminology so much these days because it suggests too big a gap between the top and the bottom, which doesn't truly exist. So the alphas are often now called the decision-makers. They get the job because they have the most experience, and the minute either of them falters, he or she will be replaced – as Daisy was at Longleat. For years people thought that alphas were the biggest and boldest animals in the pack, the ones that came forward, and the dominant ones who ate first and wouldn't let the others near the carcass until they had had their fill. Living with them, I realised that this was completely wrong. They are the thinkers, the most intelligent animals in the pack, and therefore the most valuable.

Most of us are never going to live with wolves, but an awful lot of us live with dogs, and it is useful to translate the social structure to the dog world because, as I discovered with the army dogs, most of the problems we have with Man's Best Friend are caused by our failure to understand the similarities between the two animals. The difference between the DNA of wolves and domestic dogs is 0.2 per cent. After thousands of years of selective breeding we have created every shape, size and colour that man could possibly want, from the St Bernard to the Chihuahua – we now even have a new breed that doesn't inflame our allergies – but underneath the gleaming coats, clipped toenails and adoring brown eyes, those creatures are very similar to the guys I spend so much time with. They have been domesticated, of course, but fundamentally their instincts are the same. They are pack animals, just as wolves are, and we take them out of their world and are surprised and angry when they don't fit perfectly into ours. And usually that's because we buy the wrong animal for our situation or we feed it the wrong food, which interferes with its ability to socialise.

People often think it's good to have an alpha dog, believing the alpha is the bold one that comes to say hello when you go to choose your puppy from the litter. That is not the case. The alphas stay at the back of the kennel because they have a strong sense of self-preservation. They never put themselves in jeopardy. If a situation becomes dangerous – if a bear is marauding around the den, to put it into wolf context – the alphas won't get involved and will watch other members of the pack being killed rather than risk their own lives. They are the breeding pair, and the continuance of the line is all that ultimately matters.

If you take an alpha puppy home with you, he will be a very quick learner, easy to train so that one day, when he sees the time is right, he can take over the pack. And he'll be looking for that day, for a sign of weakness in you that suggests you are no longer capable of doing the job. That could be at six months, nine months or two years, and unless you are constantly one step ahead of him, your lovely biddable dog will turn into a wilful so-and-so who pays no attention to anything you tell him.

Sometimes he will just become 'deaf' out of the house. Owners often say, 'He's fine at home but the minute he gets into the park he doesn't listen to a word I say.' This is because the dog's sensory powers are infinitely greater than ours. He knows exactly what dogs and what people are in the park because he can see further than us, hear things that we can't and smells everything that has passed that way in the last day, so he assumes control, knowing that you are not capable of keeping you both safe.

The beta, or what we now tend to call the enforcer, *is* the puppy that comes boldly over to you when you go to view the litter. He's the disciplinarian, the bouncer, the bodyguard; he is pure aggression. He doesn't think; he just weighs in. He doesn't need to think, because that's not his job; the decision-makers do that for him. His role is to protect the pack and to make sure that pack members keep pack rules and don't take food that doesn't belong to them or behave above their rank. And if the threat is from outside, he will deal with it, fearlessly.

In a wolf pack this animal has one of the most important jobs, but if you choose this puppy to take into your home without being aware of what you have picked, it could be disastrous. You and he may differ in what you view as a perceived threat. It could be another dog in the park, a neighbour, or a child that has come to visit. From your point of view, his aggression will be inexplicable, but he will have picked up something you haven't. He might also take to enforcing what he sees as pack rules in the house. If he's been taught he's not allowed to sit on the sofa or go upstairs, your children may find they're not allowed to either. And if the dog disciplines your child in the way it would discipline another dog, it could result in a serious wound. We don't have the thick fur that dogs and wolves have to protect them. I hate to think how many dogs have been condemned to death for biting someone when the root cause is that the humans in their life failed to understand the pack system and how that particular dog should have been handled.

Then there's the tester within the pack, the quality controller. He is a mid- to high-ranking animal and his job is to keep all the others on their mettle; to make sure that they can do the jobs they say they can; and if they don't come up to expectations, then the enforcer is the one who hands out the discipline. If it reaches the stage where discipline doesn't work and the animal starts to lose his authority and is no longer useful to the pack in any capacity, the beta wolf will banish him. In a dog, the tester can be a very trying pet because he will be pushing and testing your ability on a daily basis, making sure that you deserve to be the one who makes the decisions for you both.

Mid- to low-ranking individuals are naturally nervous and suspicious. Their role in the pack is to keep a lookout for danger; they pace around the den or go high up on to the hillside to give an early warning of anything the alpha pair might need to know to ensure the safety of the pack. They make good pets because they have no need to discipline or teach anyone anything. All they need is a bit of food every now and again and they will be happy, and they will take orders from anyone. These ranks don't come and seek you out when you visit the litter; these are the ones that will be hiding in the corner; they are the good old British underdog. The only problems might be excessive barking and fear aggression, but those can be prevented – as can all these traits that are useful in the wolf pack but a nuisance in human society.

There are three specialist roles within the pack. The hunter, the nanny, who is usually a grandparent, and the diffuser, and these guys all get a lot of respect from the others. The hunter is very often female because they are lighter and faster than the males, although if the quarry is a big animal, such as a bison, moose or elk, the female might run it to exhaustion but it would need the bulk of the male to bring it down. So they often set up an ambush. The hunters do the chasing and the killing but they are not the ones who decide what to kill – that's the job of the alpha female. She runs with the others and selects the beast she wants by singling it out. The hunters then take over and do the deed. In a dog, the hunter is usually a wiry-looking character, lean and muscular, quick on his feet and with great stamina – and he's the one that's always watching for movement, stalking birds and pouncing on leaves or feathers.

Nannies are chosen by the alpha female to look after her pups, and they are usually wolves that have been alphas themselves when they were younger. They can be male or female but are usually female and take over from the mother at between five and six weeks when she goes back to her duties with the pack. The nanny guards the pups, disciplines them and feeds them – in the early stages by regurgitating. She teaches them how to defend their food, how to hunt and how to interact safely with the rest of the pack.

The role of the diffuser, or omega wolf, is to keep the pack on an even keel, to absorb the energy and aggression of the others. Wolves often fight among themselves, and often violently, particularly at meal times and in the mating season – as I discovered to my cost in Idaho – when tension is high and the whole pack is on edge. It's the way they challenge and re-establish the pecking order. The diffuser gets into the middle of the scrum and takes the brunt of it but never loses his cool, never shows aggression himself and eventually calms things down. He doesn't get many thanks for his troubles; he is always the last to eat and has the fewest privileges, but his role is essential to the wellbeing of the pack. In the dog world, if there are dogs fighting in the park, this guy will dive straight in there and might make a lot of noise but will actually break up the fight.

Knowing which of these animals you have given a home to goes some of the way to ensuring a happy life together, but the rest of it comes down to how you handle the particular dog you've bought and how you train it. Most trainers and behaviourists base their methods on wolf behaviour and they acknowledge the importance of the pack, which of course I have no argument with, but as I have said before, to really understand what's going on, you have to be there. Observing wolves from afar can easily lead one to the wrong conclusions, and I think in many cases this is what has happened. Owners have been taught that they must take on the role of the alpha dog and despite the miraculous results in problem dogs that we've all seen on our television screens, this doesn't always work and isn't always a long-term solution for the owners involved.

I don't mean to do down dog behaviourists in any way, but I do passionately believe that it is important to mimic wolf behaviour accurately, and the fact is that not every animal can cope with its owner taking on the alpha role. They may have to adopt a softer approach.

Chapter Twenty-five

BACK TO
BASICS

In the past, scientists have always argued that it is false to make comparisons between wolves and domestic dogs. Given my first-hand experience of both, I profoundly disagree. I feel strongly that what I have discovered about wolves is not just relevant, it's vital when it comes to handling the wolf in your living room.

If you have that nervous, low-ranking animal that hides in the corner and tugs at your heart-strings – the one that most of us are a sucker for – and you behave like an alpha, or even a beta around that dog, you will destroy him. He will fold himself up his own backside, because in his world the distance between the alpha animal and his rank is colossal. He is valued for what he is by the pack, but in the wild the two don't mix with each other. It would be like asking the Queen and a barrow-boy to share a house together. Don't buy that pup just because you feel sorry for him; think long and hard about where and how you live – the reason being that he will be naturally vocal, because in the pack it's his job to alert everyone to danger. So if you live in the middle of a busy town or city he will bark round the clock and drive you and everyone in the neighbourhood mad. Unless you are able to convince him you know what's going on, he will tell you about anything that moves within a three-mile radius of your house – and over flat ground and with the wind in the right direction it can be anything up to ten miles.

It's not impossible to turn this animal into a relaxed city dog, but it is all in the training and the way you manage him from the day you collect him. Ideally you should get him in the summer when the weather is good, the evenings are light and the atmosphere is clear. Take him out as much as you can and as far as you can, expose him to all the sights and smells and sounds and keep him close, reassure him about anything that seems to make him tense, give him long strokes down his back and breathe deeply, which is how his mother would have calmed him. Let him see that there's nothing out there to be afraid of and he will be reassured: a sound that is familiar is not alarming to a dog, or a wolf, or even a human being. Anything he hasn't heard before will set him barking, so put in the work with him when he's young. Otherwise, when a factory alarm goes off five miles away and rings all night, which you can't begin to hear, he will tell you about it.

Don't go down the shouting and screaming route. You'll be wasting your breath and even encouraging him. He'll think you're backing him up with your own barking. Dogs can only hear tone and pitch – the equivalent of the different sounds we hear by tapping a cup that is full, half full and empty. And they only understand the command words they have been taught. These have to be short words like 'sit', 'stay', 'down', 'come', 'leave it' and 'quiet', and they have to be said in a tone and pitch that's authoritative, bearing in mind that tone and pitch can be distorted by the wind and weather if he is some distance away. So when the dog starts to bark you would say 'Quiet!' with a definite sharp cut-off that means stop. If you wanted him to continue doing something, like coming towards you, you would allow your voice to taper. You would teach him by giving him a reward every time he did the right thing. The command reassures him that you can hear the sound that's bothering him, you know what's happening and you are going to make the decision about what action to take. He's only too pleased to hand over the responsibility because decision making is not his job and he doesn't want to have to do it.

The first thing, though, is to establish why he's barking. There might be times when he thinks you need to be warned about a stranger approaching or something unusual happening across the street. The days of thinking a bark is a bark is a bark are long gone. Dogs have a complex language, like wolves, and their bark says different things and can be pitched to carry over many miles. For example, you have a house with a garden, which the dog regards as his territorial boundary. The dog is in the house, and hears someone coming; he gives a deep growl, followed by a single bark, followed by another growl. He's telling you that someone's out there but is still some distance away so there's no need to panic. If the person keeps coming, he'll give you an update – three barks and then a long growl. If you do nothing and the person comes into the driveway and breaches the boundary you get the full machine-gun effect. If, however, you get up before the final stage and go to the window to see who is coming and give the dog the command he will relax. Spending the first six months of the dog's life giving him this sort of training can make all the difference between you and your dog living happily ever after – or not.

Many people, of course, don't get their dogs as pups. More dogs are rescued than are bought from breeders and often they've been mistreated. We look at the crime sheet and discover the animal was chained up, beaten and starved and, being all emotion, we long to give him a new start in life; but as soon as he pees on the carpet or does anything anti-social we don't give him anything of the sort. We put it down to his past and go straight back to that dark place that he was desperate to escape, usually dragging him with us. Humans are always looking back; dogs, like wolves, live in the present. He thinks: new pack, new rules, new leader, I'm happy. And contrary to the saying 'You can't teach an old dog new tricks', I believe you can, by going back to that period in the dog's life when he was at his most receptive to education.

The wolf and the dog develop in small circles. In the beginning that circle is in and around the den or the whelping box where, while suckling, the pup learns the basic principles from his mother – he picks up her calming signals, discovers the reward system, learns his pack value and how to communicate with his own kind. When he stumbles out into the world at five weeks and begins to mix mother's milk with regurgitated meat, that circle of learning increases and he starts to learn how to treat other pack members, how to defend his food, what to do and where to go if he is in danger. As the months go by the circle goes on getting bigger until at nine months he has the social and survival skills he needs.

We have established that diet plays a very important part in wolf society and can entirely alter the nature of a pack, as the fish experiment proved. The alpha female knows this. Before she introduces her pups to the rest of the pack she ensures that the others' energy levels are down by feeding them the meat either of older individuals from the herd or of calves that are still suckling, because the milk content in the stomach of those animals has a calming and soothing effect on everyone. They become placid, gentle and forgiving, almost like overgrown pups themselves. The aggression and fighting that usually breaks out around mealtimes disappears and they tolerate everyone. When you see them like this is not hard to believe the myths and legends about human children being suckled and adopted by wolves. A lactating female, especially one whose pups had not survived, might welcome a surrogate to nurture.

So to re-educate an adult dog you would feed him on the sort of diet he had in his first few months of life, a mixture of milk and minced or very finely chopped meat which would be similar to the regurgitated food he had during that intensive learning period. After a couple of months on that he should be calm and pliable and ready to listen – whereupon you could train him more or less as you would a puppy, heavy on reward and light on punishment. Force should never be used on dogs, in my view, because it doesn't work; and kicking a dog is only likely to make it attack, because kicking is how prey animals defend themselves when they are being hunted.

The most effective way to teach a dog is by example, and the most effective punishment is to deny the animal warmth. That is how dogs and wolves are taught and punished in their own world – they get pushed away from the security of their mother's body.

It is impossible to over-emphasise the importance that diet plays in a maintaining the structure of the pack. Wolves eat three categories of food: that which they take for basic fitness and health; survival foods, which would include animals with a high fat content to keep them warm during harsh weather conditions; and status foods which keep the structure and hierarchy of the pack.

In order to keep their status, the alpha pair have to have a very high percentage of internal organs in their diet, plus some movement meat, such as leg or rump, and a little bit of vegetable matter to keep them healthy, which, because their prey are always herbivores, comes from the stomach content. The beta ranks, the enforcers, eat exclusively movement meat along with some vegetables; the mid- to high-ranking animal, which would be the tester, has a high percentage of non-movement meat from the neck or the backbone with about twenty-five per cent stomach content. The mid ranks have fifty–fifty, meat and stomach; and the mid to low ranks have seventy-five per cent vegetable matter from the stomach and twenty-five per cent meat.

What has happened to the dogs that live in our world is that we have upset the natural balance. We feed them all, irrespective of the rank they hold, the same sort of food – mostly dried all-in-one, or tinned which we mix with biscuit (no canid in the wild has ever eaten wheat) – and therefore confuse the natural pecking order, making it difficult for the animals to differentiate themselves. We compound the problem with our training – such as making a dominant dog sit or lie down in the park in front of lower-ranking animals.

We have also, with our desire for the cosmetically perfect animal, removed the features that in the wild these creatures use to communicate with one another. We have dogs now with no snouts, so they can't be disciplined in the way canids have been for thousands of years. We have dogs with ears that flop over, which deprives them of another vital way of communicating with their fellow dogs. And until recently, when it was banned, we docked the tails of certain breeds, thus taking away an important part of their language, their ability to communicate via scent, which they did by moving their tails.

Chapter Twenty-six

FAMILY
VALUES

After Cheyenne died, I kept Elu's three boys in the shed for the next couple of months, and during that time they moved from milk only to milk and minced meat – I was doing my best to create what their mother might have regurgitated. They lapped that up and very swiftly moved on to mince alone and finally chicken wings, which they instantly defended from one another, growling and snarling. At about this time I realised they needed some space, but there was no way I could put them back in with Shadow and Pale Face and so, with the help of six volunteers, I built a new enclosure of about half an acre up next to the caravan at the top of the park. I put the two boys in there and put the three pups in the enclosure at the bottom, where they had been born, and I moved in with them.

Suddenly I was responsible for everything. In the wild there would be others who would look after the security of the pups while the nanny role was just to help with the education and to mind and monitor them. Now it was down to me to keep them warm and safe and fed, and to drive them into the den at night. I was the responsible adult but not nearly as well equipped to deal with all these things as an adult wolf. Yet it seemed to work, and when I went into the den at night they followed. But there were other ideas I had in their training which seemed like good ones at the time but which, as they became adults, I came to regret. One was a habit I got into with dear old Tamaska, the beta rank who was big and bold and supposedly scared of nothing and always went forward and was a rock among wolves – yet had a complete terror of thunderstorms. As a small pup he would freak at any sign of an electric storm and he would scream like a big baby and come running to me, and I would pick him up – this was in the shed, long before we moved to the enclosure. He would need warmth, and I would hold him in my arms and wear him like a neck scarf, and the warmth from my neck on his belly would calm him down. When he was calm he would wriggle his way down and try to suck on anything that he thought would give him food. Normally that would be the end of my nose, which to him resembled a teat, and he would suck on it for about fifteen or twenty minutes until he fell asleep, at which point I could put him back with the other pups.

When the cubs were three to four weeks old, having a cute, fluffy little bundle sucking on the end of my nose was a wonderful experience and everyone admired it, but what eventually dawned on me was that everything I taught them as their primary teacher would be taken on into adulthood … so even now, as a full-grown adult, weighing something like one hundred and thirty pounds, he can still be found during a thunderstorm sitting on my lap under a tree sucking my nose. Only now he's too big to suck my nose, so he just gets his incisors round it and holds on tight. So what I would say to anyone with a dog is be careful what you teach them when they are small.

There was another thing I might have avoided with the benefit of hindsight … After we had fed, in the early stages, I used to take them underground into the den to keep them warm. By six months or so, they were quite big animals and seemed to cope with the weather better and preferred to lie under a tree. It was only if it had been raining solidly for four or five days and we were all wet through that we would go under cover to dry out and warm up. Each of the pups established his own place underground. Matsi, Yana and I would all go to the back and lie in a huddle and Tamaska, who was the biggest, would lie at the entrance, with his head and shoulders in the open air and his backside towards us. This was fine when he was small, but as he grew and ate more and more raw meat he developed a serious wind problem. When he got going he was breaking wind every fifteen minutes, and with very little air at the back of the den the smell was horrendous. We were between the devil and the deep blue sea: did we stay out in the wet and the cold, or did we get dry and risk being overcome by the noxious smell? Sometimes it was so bad that even he would whip round and sniff, as if to say, 'God, who did that?'

If I had to own up to having a favourite of the three, it would be Tamaska. He was such a character; but they were all family and I tried not to single one out. Even by my own standards my role among them was unusual. I was there to teach each one of them to fulfil their future roles as adult wolves, yet I was never their leader; that was the unusual thing about this experiment. The only individual I would ever be above was Matsi, who was that wary, shy little animal; with the other two, I had to build them up to be above me in the pecking order. I taught by example in the hope that when the time came for them to lead they would remember and be the balanced animal that I had tried to be myself. I didn't chastise them; I just showed them how I expected them to behave, and if ever I did need to discipline them it would be by denial of warmth or food or water, the way pups are disciplined in the wild. Everything I did was designed to teach them how to be wild wolves, not semi-domesticated. If I needed to display my strength, I did it through games, and if ever I felt angry, I would just walk away and lie down. I didn't want my aggression to interfere with my teaching.

I taught them how to defend their food and to recognise that each of them had a particular source of it on the carcass. By six weeks they were already beginning to show signs of the ranks they would eventually hold, and when I started to introduce rabbit at that age, I portioned it and gave each of them a different part of the animal according to the characteristics they were displaying. Matsi as the lowest would have the stomach content; Tamaska, who was clearly destined to be the beta, the thug, would get the movement meat – the legs and rump; and Yana, who undoubtedly had the brains, would have the internal organs. When I brought in a carcass, I did my best to get Yana into the ribcage, so she could get the heart, liver and kidneys, and keep Tamaska on the rump and the shoulder, but he was so greedy he would start eating any bit he could get and I had more than a few battles with him. I had to try and intimidate him by snarling with my lips pulled back to show my teeth – my weaponry – and my tongue protruding, just as the wolves did themselves. If that didn't work I'd snap to the side of his mouth to get him to move over. Everything I did mimicked what I had seen wolves do in the wild; and often he would decide that he didn't like the place he'd been moved to and come back at me. My nose and lips were riddled with puncture marks where his needle-sharp teeth had caught me, and he somehow managed repeatedly to peel strips of skin from my nose with his molars. He once got my entire bottom jaw in his mouth; his bottom teeth had me under the chin and his top incisors were sunk into the soft tissue under my tongue. We were growling and snarling at each other and at the same time I had him round the scruff of the neck; it was a real tussle and battle of wits. Had he been any older I wouldn't have stood a chance, but for that brief period in his life, as nanny, I held a higher rank and he needed to learn where his place was. I used to joke that

Tamaska and I had so many fights you'd have thought we were married.

Another important lesson was how to prevent them from seriously damaging each other in their play-fights. With their weight, strength and jaw pressure, wolves have to be very careful not to kill another member of the pack by accident. The minute they are in pain, they let out high-pitched squeal and a balanced animal will always let go – and I can vouch for the fact that they do; human skin is no match for a wolf's and many are the times I've had to protest. I had to teach these guys to do the same, but it was quite hard for me to inflict pain on them. The only way I could do it was by biting them on the ear or the lip. So we would get into play-fights, and I would nip them just hard enough to hurt. The moment they squeaked I released my grip, pushed them on to their backs to expose their vulnerable underside, and then held my mouth over their throats, in classic wolf pose, to indicate that I was trustworthy.

Balance had to be taught too, which I did through games based on hunting. Dogs go into what we call a play bow; with wolves it's called a prey bow because from that position, crouched low, they can jump six feet in any direction. A lot of our games started with a prey bow, bouncing from side to side and running and chasing each other around, and if things looked as though they were getting too rough, I would drop down into that prey bow position again and everything would stop. This calmed us all down, giving us a chance to make sure it was safe for everyone for the fight to carry on. I was trying to teach them how to switch from high energy to low so that they never went beyond the danger zone. As a family they could have a mock fight but they couldn't end up hurting one another.

What I discovered through all these games and mock fights and mock prey drives was that the intensity of this interaction pushed up our adrenalin and pheromone levels which gave them – and me – an edge over other animals in the pack. If I couldn't make Tamaska move off the kill, I would just have to go and have a mock fight with Matsi for ten minutes. When I came back, Tamaska would move without my having to do anything very much, because my blood was up and he could smell the change in me.

Another very important lesson was self-preservation; they needed to be able to read body posture, to understand vocal communication and to know how to protect themselves. Any sound a wolf makes that is high in tone is encouraging, so if there was danger in the area and I wanted the pups to come to me I would attract them with a high-pitched whimper, and having brought them to me, I would calm them down with a deep whimper. There was another noise that meant danger, which could come from land or air. If a buzzard was soaring overhead, or a helicopter or plane, I would make a staccato 'uff-uff-ing' noise, and they would instantly come running to me for protection. Anything low in tone is discouraging, so at close range a low throaty growl will be a warning, and, as I learnt from the wild wolves, you then need to look at what their weaponry – bared teeth – and body posture are telling you. One of the ways in which the ranks differentiate themselves is by the height at which they carry their weaponry. A high-ranking animal holds his up high and expects to be greeted by other ranks with theirs down, at the level that accords with their rank. If the lower-ranking animal doesn't show the respect he should, the dominant animal will growl. The same thing happens with dogs that meet in the park; they very quickly establish a pecking order, and if one doesn't give the other the respect he should they snap and snarl and sometimes fight. If that lower-ranking wolf still refuses to avert his weaponry, the growl will intensify until finally the dominant animal will snap beside the other one's face. The snap is its last warning before he goes for him and holds him down with his mouth, growling the while. He will then let go, stand back and repeat the growling, by which time the lower-ranking wolf should have lowered his body and be showing signs of submission.

A similar process happens over food. Adult wolves indicate possession with their ear posture. To an outsider watching wolves feeding, it looks as though the teeth are the thing you need to look out for. You'd be wrong; it's the ears. They tell you exactly what you can and can't have. If an animal is standing over a carcass and has his ears flattened like wings out of the side of his head, he is telling you that he is a higher-ranking animal than you, that piece of meat belongs to him and if you come near it you will be in trouble. Dare to move in and he will growl, baring his teeth the while with his tongue thrusting through; if you don't back off the growl will intensify, he will snap as the final warning and then he'll go for you. If, however, an animal that is higher-ranking than him comes in from the right, for instance, he will turn his right ear sideways and back, indicating to that animal that he can come in and feed, while keeping his other ear horizontal to protect his own portion. I needed to teach this to the pups, but this was one of the most difficult lessons of all because I didn't have their ears. I had to cover the meat with my whole head, but they seemed to get the message.

Possibly the hardest lesson for me, as a human with human emotions, was teaching them to prioritise. As a pack, if they are faced with danger, they have to safeguard the highest-ranking members. Faced with a stark choice they will even sacrifice a whole litter of pups, knowing that they can have more pups next year whereas if the highest-ranking wolves die, the whole pack could be doomed. And if it came to it, the highest-ranking pups, as future leaders, had to be safeguarded ahead of the others. It was something I battled over; to a sentimental human it didn't seem right to let a healthy, fit animal perish because another held a higher rank. But this is what I had to teach them. We played games of tag. I would run after them nipping at their backs and their legs, making them twist and turn, as if a rival wolf was after them. I'd use the same sort of game when teaching them to hunt. In this particular lesson, however, I steered them in the direction of the rendezvous holes and the only way they could get away from my nips was by diving underground. Then I'd leave them – not that I had any alternative. The holes were designed for a three-month-old wolf cub, and I couldn't have got them out for love or money. So they learnt that this was where they went to escape. The hardest bit was having to teach them to seek safety in order of priority; keeping Tamaska and Matsi out by heading them off and making sure that Yana went in first.

I was glad it was only a lesson.

Chapter Twenty-seven

A LIFE APART

I lived with these guys continuously for eighteen months; eating with them, sleeping with them and wrestling with them. During that time I didn't have a proper meal, a cup of coffee, or a sandwich; I didn't change my clothes, shower or wash my hair. I didn't lie on anything softer than the hard ground. I peed in the enclosure as they did, using my urine to scent. The only difference was that while their scats were left where they fell, I bagged my poo for the volunteers to dispose of hygienically. My only luxury was toilet paper, which they left for me in the area between the two entrance gates. I didn't once leave the enclosure and I never once wanted to. I was as happy as I had ever been, and totally fulfilled. These guys were my family – I knew them better than my own children, who sadly, I'd seen precious little of since I'd been at Combe Martin. The wolves were all I had and the longer I was with them the less I wanted to leave them. I was a hundred per cent comfortable in their world. They were constantly challenging – as children are – but watching them grow and become more confident, and seeing their characters develop and their different talents and skills come to the fore and knowing that they valued me and that I'd played some small part in all of that was an incredible feeling.

My contact with the outside world was minimal. I had no idea what was going on beyond the wire fence of the enclosure and strangely I had no real interest. I felt as removed from the world as I had in the Rockies, living, once again, for the moment, perpetually on guard, totally focussed on what some would doubtless think was a crazy notion – that I could teach these guys to behave as their ancestors would have done. I had a walkie-talkie so I could communicate with the volunteers, but all I used it for was to discuss when I wanted them to bring food into the enclosure and what sort it would be; that way I could prepare the pups so that they associated our hunting games with the food we ate. And occasionally, if I felt they were getting a bit over-confident, I asked some of the volunteers to howl or to play tape recordings of different-sized packs howling to give mine the impression that we were not alone.

Once they were past the first few months, during which they needed to eat little and often, I had them on a feast and famine diet, which is how they would have lived in the wild. The obsession with teaching them wild ways, when clearly they were destined to spend their lives in captivity, was for a purpose. I hoped that they might teach their own young what I had taught them and so on through generations, so that one day if ever wolves were released into the wild again in Britain, the descendants of these boys might know how to take care of themselves. My dream was that they would know about their world but also enough about ours to be able to survive in it.

In those first eighteen months we ate every two days. Day One was spent preparing for the hunt, playing games and psyching ourselves up, after which we fed either at dusk or at dawn of Day Two. Matsi was the fastest and nimblest of the pups, and showed the greatest interest in our hunting games, so even though he was male I trained him to be the hunter; and I played the role of the alpha female, choosing what I wanted him to hunt. I taught them how to make a food cache, which is a very important part of survival in the wild – as I discovered in Idaho. They know that times of plenty don't last and they need to guard against those times of the year when there's nothing about or the pack can't hunt. I stashed pieces of meat in the mud around the pond beneath the water level, which acted like a refrigerator, and occasionally I would stretch the interval before the next carcass came into the enclosure to three or even four days, but would then show them how to dig up the cached food to eat in between kills. Along with the meat, I buried bits of the carcass – deer antlers and legs, bits of rabbit, cow and sheep, even pheasant wings – to use as learning tools.

On that preparation day, depending on what the volunteers had told me was coming up on the menu, I would dig up a piece of the same type of animal and use it to excite their interest. If it was pheasant, I would hold the wings up in the air and flutter them and dip them up and down so they had to jump for them – anything to try and teach the pups about the food they ate and, in this case, that pheasants couldn't be caught on the ground. When the birds were eventually delivered I would even get the volunteers to throw them over the fence into the enclosure so it looked as though they were flying. If they brought fish, I would take it into the pond and make the pups wade into the water and dive for them. If a local farmer had been out lamping – shooting animals dazzled by spotlights – and had delivered a whole lot of rabbits, I would prepare them by digging up a piece of rabbit fur or a foot or an ear, and dangle that in front of them; or if someone had come in with a venison carcass, I would dig up a deer leg.

The leg would have the hoof attached and was always very well preserved. I would run with it, twisting and turning and changing direction as though I were a prey animal, and they would chase after me, trying to bring me down. In the early days they tried to grab me from behind, in which case I would kick out at them with this hoof, and catch them beneath the jaw, teaching them a valuable lesson: that if they went for a deer or an elk from behind, it would kick them. This would stop them in their tracks and leave them feeling a bit sore – when *I* did it. They needed to know that a powerful kick in the throat from an elk that was fighting for its life would kill them. I used the antlers to teach the pups about the dangers of approaching a quarry from the front or not being fast enough to move out of the way if the deer turns round. I had seen wolf nannies do this in the wild. If they came anywhere within reach, I stuck the sharp horns into their sides. It didn't take them long to work out that the safest way to get me to the ground was by working together and attacking as a unit, and coming in a triangular pattern from both sides at once. Only when they did that, did I give them the meat.

After eating I would teach them to give a defensive howl to protect their kill from any other wolves in the area that might think of muscling in. And to use what they had eaten to scent every few metres around the perimeter of their territory, which was effectively turning the key in the lock. In the wild it would be every few hundred metres. Day Two was spent relaxing and digesting before starting all over again. I fed them at dusk and at dawn to teach them that these were the natural and most successful times to hunt. The minute the volunteers brought that day's kill into the enclosure, my battle to keep them to the areas of the carcass that were rightfully theirs began – and as they grew bigger and stronger, the more of a battle it was and the more bloodied I emerged at the end of it.

I ate what they ate, putting my face into the carcass and ripping out the raw flesh with my teeth alongside Yana, while growling and snapping at Tamaska to keep him off the rib area, which was ours. But after about nine months of eating it raw, I began to worry, after my experience in Idaho, about the effects it might be having on my health. So for the last nine months I got the volunteers to flash-fry my share and put it with some vegetables into a polythene bag and tuck it inside the carcass. The only problem was that I had to be quick in finding it, as the three wolves were very interested in my portion, particularly Tamaska. He was mad about the taste of this cooked meat for some reason and it was a case of the student becoming the master; if he got there first he saw me off, snarling and snapping like a good 'un, and there was no way I could take it from him. He gobbled up my food time and time again, and I'd have no choice but to go back to the raw meat.

After eighteen months I started leaving the enclosure for about an hour at a time, as if going out on hunting trips, as would happen in the wild, returning with a kill. At first I went no further than the top of the hill, from where I could watch what was going on, and I could see they were very agitated by my absence. If they called to me, I called back to let them know where I was and what was going on. The first couple of times they were so distressed that they didn't stop howling, but they soon learnt to associate my disappearance with food. On one occasion Tamaska gave the most extraordinary howl – one that I'd never heard before. It was like four little barks and a howl, but it sounded as though something was wrong, so I went running back to the enclosure. What I found was that there was a white plastic bucket in the primate enclosure nearby that was being blown about in the wind and making a noise he didn't recognise, and distressing him. He was giving a long-range warning call that I hadn't yet taught any of them. He'd learnt the rallying howl and the short-range defensive 'uff-uffing' noise and he had simply put the two of them together to call me back from a distance and tell me there was something wrong.

That was an exciting day for me – once again I felt the student had become the master.

Hard though it was to tear myself away, I knew that these guys had to be a pack on their own, and less dependent on me. So although I continued to live with them for another six months or so, I started spending longer periods of time away from them. And it was on one of those occasions that I met Helen Jeffs and my life took an unexpected turn. I had always thought that there might be someone one day who would drag me away from the animals and back into the human world, but I hadn't expected the pull to be quite so sudden or quite so strong.

One evening when I was out of the enclosure, a mate of mine turned up at the park saying that there was a two-for-one offer on meals at the local pub, the Station Inn, and against my better judgement I agreed to go with him. Helen was there with a colleague of hers. It wasn't a pub she usually went to – in fact she would say she normally wouldn't have been seen dead in it – but they had had a particularly bad day and felt like a drink on their way home. I would call it a chance encounter; she would say it was meant. She recognised me – I was quite well-known in the area, and there weren't too many men around smelling as I did, with more than eighteen months' worth of growth on their chin, long unbrushed hair and scars all over their face. I wasn't wearing the cover-all I wore with the wolves, nor the shoes I wore in the enclosure; I left those outside my caravan during these breaks so that they wouldn't be contaminated by any other smells, but even without them I must have stunk to high heaven.

She was interested in what I was doing with the wolves, so we chatted for an hour or more while our two mates chatted and we agreed to meet again. She was gorgeous, with big blue eyes and long blonde hair, and reminded me of Michelle, my first love back in Norfolk. She was a year younger than me and worked with children in a local school. She was married and had an eight-year-old son, but the relationship with her husband had been over for a long time and although they shared the roof over their heads it was a matter of convenience. Her situation was very similar to mine with Jan. There was an immediate attraction for both of us; and while I was technically still with Jan, and a moment of rash optimism had even brought about a fourth child, the lovely Sam, born shortly before the pups in March 2004, our relationship had been over for a very long time.

Helen lived in a bungalow across the valley from the park, quite a drive by road but no more than a mile as the crow flies, and for the next few months, as my time with Yana, Tamaska and Matsi gradually drew to a close, Helen and I communicated with one another by howling across the valley.

Chapter Twenty-eight

A CURIOUS
COINCIDENCE

Shortly before I moved back to sleeping in my caravan, someone tried to poison the three wolf pups. I went into the enclosure at the end of the day, to spend the night with them as usual, and Yana was behaving as though he was stoned, off his legs, drunk. I had never seen anything like it in a wolf – and if I hadn't been so worried, it might have been funny. He couldn't walk straight; he kept bumping into things and hitting himself. He collided with trees and rocks and the fencing once or twice, and kept wandering in and out of the pond. I pulled him out a few times, because he was standing there shivering, but he just went straight back in as if he were sleepwalking. He didn't respond to me in any way; he didn't even seem to notice that I was there. He was completely out of it; and obviously freezing cold although it was not an especially cold night.

I had no idea what was wrong. I stayed with him that evening, and yet again he wandered into the pond and yet again I had to fish him out. He couldn't hold his temperature, and by the early hours of the morning I was at my wits' end. I suddenly had a hare-brained idea –

it was the only way I could think of warming him up: I picked him up, and with herculean strength born out of panic I managed to get him through the gates, fending off the other two wolves, and carry him up to my caravan, where I put him into bed with me. I put the heater on and lay under the duvet with him, holding him close to my body to try and give him some of my heat. He was a full adult wolf at that stage, in appearance at least, yet he was so out of it he could do nothing but lie limply beside me. Thank goodness no one was there to witness the scene that night. It must have looked like an interesting variation on Little Red Riding Hood!

His body seemed to draw the heat out of mine and within a couple of minutes *I* was freezing, so I had to keep jumping out of bed, wrapping myself in a blanket in front of the heater and, when I had warmed up, getting back under the quilt with him, letting him take my heat again. This went on for the remaining hours of the night until shortly before dawn, when he started to come to and, still not recognising me, tried to bite me. I grabbed his jaws and then had the idea that even if he didn't know who I was, he might know my voice. In the wild I had never used my human voice, and I rarely did with these wolves, but they had heard me talking to volunteers in the park when necessary and speaking on the phone occasionally. It was the only thing I could think of doing, so for the next couple of hours I spoke to him about everything and nothing, I told him about the weather and about what was going on in my life and everything I planned for the future. I exhausted every subject under the sun.

When he did finally come round properly he proceeded to tear apart my home, which was not entirely surprising for a full-grown wolf that was now compos mentis and found himself in a confined space that he didn't recognise. Fortunately, I managed to get a chain around his neck and led him out into the field, where I walked him round and round and round until he was exhausted.

I then took him back to the caravan and gave him buckets of water. He was still a little bit shaky, but I hoped that the water would flush whatever it was in his system out of it – which is what eventually happened. It was after midday when I felt he was safe enough to return to his brothers down in the enclosure. Analysis of Yana's faeces showed a heavy concentration of the barbiturate phenobarbitone, which is widely used as an anticonvulsant for epilepsy. I can only think that someone threw a piece of meat laced with the drug into the enclosure and that Yana, being the alpha male and first to feed, ate the bulk of it.

The Native Americans believe that after an experience like that, Yana and I would have a unique bond. They used to say that if a hunter and a bear spilt each other's blood they would become the same person and the hunter wouldn't be able to shoot that bear, no matter where he saw it. I never really believed that until, a few months later, Helen and I were in bed in the caravan and I had a really sore left hand. I kept rubbing it and examining the fleshy bit by the V of the thumb, expecting to see a cut or a thorn or some kind of explanation, but I couldn't see anything. I asked Helen to have a look for me, but apart from the redness she could see nothing. It felt like one of those thorns that get right under the skin and get so inflamed and so sore that you can't bear to touch them or even try to get them out. The pain got progressively worse as the evening wore on and was so intense that night that I barely slept. The next morning we went down to the enclosure. Helen, who had been slightly ahead of me, came running back up the track.

'You're not going to believe this,' she said. 'Yana's limping; he's holding his left foot up.'

I said, 'He's probably taken a bite in the night,' and went and had a look at him, not giving it a second thought.

When I rolled him over and looked at his foot, he had a thorn in a place on his left front foot that corresponded almost exactly to the place where I had felt the pain in my hand. The thorn was just below the surface, but I managed to get my nails around the top of it and pull it out.

All I'd said to Helen was 'He's got a thorn in his foot.'

I didn't immediately make the connection because I was too busy with him, but she said, 'Oh my God.'

'What?'

'Your hand,' she said. 'Last night. The thorn.'

Now that could have been the biggest coincidence of my life. Or it could support the Native American belief that if you help a creature and look after him you will become as one and share similar feelings.

Chapter Twenty-nine

A SOUL-MATE

My relationship with Helen progressed rapidly, although most of our time together was spent around the wolf enclosure or in my terrible caravan. She was under no illusion about what she was getting herself into, but that didn't seem to faze her – and I admired and loved her all the more for that. She was prepared to spend the night in the caravan, with no hot water, peeing into the putty bucket, and get up to leave at 5.30 in the morning so she could be home for Arran, her son, before her husband left for his shift-work. I was always up at that time anyway to look after the wolves, so it was no problem for me, but it wasn't her idea of fun. She would shower at home, have some breakfast with Arran and the two of them would go off to school together. Her husband had no problem with what she was doing – I had even been up to the bungalow to meet him and Arran, and we were all very friendly – but it made for a very long day for her.

This arrangement couldn't work long-term, and after Helen and I had been away for the weekend to a hotel in Minehead – and I had enjoyed my first bath in years, having had only the cold hosepipe outside the caravan – she decided she had had enough of getting up at 5.30. She needed a place of her own, where she could live with Arran and I could join her on nights when I could get away from the wolves. She rented a chalet in a holiday park in the village, and I went there as often as I could but not as often as I might have liked.

I was very busy at the park. I had been offered two young European wolves that a private collector didn't want – and I suspect would have had put down if I hadn't taken them off his hands. The man had more money than sense; he seemed to me like a rich man with toys. I don't have a problem with people splashing out their money if the toy is driven by an engine, but when it's driven by a beating heart, I do. When I went to see the wolves it was quite clear what had happened. He had a brat of a son who had been kicking a football around inside their enclosure and had induced a prey drive in these young wolves and one of them had finally given him a nip. The names of the disgraced three-year olds were Totto and Nanook. I hastily adapted another enclosure near the caravan for them, so there was no chance of them interbreeding with the Timber wolves, and brought them home to Combe Martin.

They settled in soon enough, but their experience had done them no favours. They were very quick to nip, and for the first week or so I had to go into their enclosure with rabbits and rodents in my hands to teach them that I was the provider of food, not the food itself. Not long afterwards I was offered their brother, Zarnesti, whom I had known at Broxbourne when he was a small pup. He was the one whose mother had rolled or trodden on him soon after he was born and who had the crushed jaw that gave him a comical look, like Goofy. And he was the one who had induced emotion in the disabled child.

That brought the total number of wolves to nine, which I now had in three enclosures: Shadow, Pale Face and Elu were together; the three pups, Yana, Tamaska and Matsi, were together; and there were the Europeans. I was not looking to expand and gave Elu a contraceptive injection for the second year running to ensure she didn't fall pregnant. It was designed for dogs but had worked well on Elu the first year so I used it again. What I hadn't allowed for was the wolf's extraordinary ability to regulate its own body; these are animals that can absorb a litter of pups if they feel the environment is no longer safe to give birth in. Elu worked out what was going on and held her season back until the contraceptive had lost its potency and then she mated. Nine weeks later she delivered exactly what she had had the first time around, only this time the female survived. I called her Cheyenne; and the boys Natta, Tejas and Nanoose.

Elu's maternal skills had not improved, unfortunately. Once again she abandoned the den and I had to go in and rescue the pups, and once again I was up all through the night for the next five or six weeks bottle feeding four hungry mouths. This time, as soon as they were on solids, I handed them over to Yana, Tamaska and Matsi in the hope that they would do a better job than me.

Although the pups had been unwanted, they turned out to be very useful. I had been in touch over the years with Bernard Walton, a television producer who had made the *Talking with Animals* series for the BBC. He now had his own production company, Aqua Vita Films, and when he heard about what I had done with the first set of pups at Combe Martin he wanted to make a documentary about them, and about me and my career and about the research I was doing in Poland. The new pups were perfect for the purposes of reconstruction and we filmed them extensively, as well as travelling to Poland, Finland and America to film wolves and to talk to wolf experts, including Levi Holt. The film was shown on the National Geographic Channel in America as *A Man Among Wolves*, and in the UK on Channel Five as *The Wolfman*. And in the interests of balance

– and to add controversy – Bernard invited a panel of scientists to voice their opinion about my hands-on approach.

Most of the scientists were scornful, if not downright disapproving, which didn't surprise me. The young biologists seemed to be blinkered, frightened of questioning the accepted wisdom and jeopardising their careers – as they always had been – but one of the most rewarding conversations for me was with Doug Smith, who was the biologist in charge of the wolf reintroduction programme at Yellowstone National Park. We sat on the hillside at Blacktail Deer Plateau, looking out over the park in all its glory, and for the first time I felt at ease and hopeful that there might be a middle way. I had never before been able to sit down with a biologist and bat ideas back and forth, and although it was just for a TV programme, at the end of it I felt we could see a mutual glimmer of hope or, as he put it, the silver bullet that we were both striving to find.

He acknowledged that howling and scent were the secrets to wolf behaviour and two of the least researched aspects of it. He knew that each wolf had a different howl, but he didn't seem to know that collectively there were different howls that meant very different things.

Yellowstone was a fantastic programme that had set the standard for other reintroductions, including Idaho, but in my view mistakes were made. They looked at this glorious park with its thousands of acres and picturesque forests, valleys and streams and thought it had everything for the wolf and that the sight of wolves majestically roaming free would be a money-spinner with the public. But setting eight wolves down in all of this was just one part of the equation. When the wolves ran the prey out of the park they had no alternative but to follow into the surrounding countryside, which brought them up against people and livestock. What wolves do in the wild is to fragment into rival packs so that they can bat the prey back and forwards between them, which keeps them and the prey within their own territorial boundaries. And if that can't be done by real packs, my belief is that it can be done by playing tape recordings of packs, which will turn the prey animals and make it unnecessary for the wolves to stray outside the park. It's the same principle as we used in Poland although the wolves there weren't following prey out of the forest, they were going in search of livestock. But it's the scientists that run the reintroduction programmes and they guard their patch jealously; they don't want an unqualified maverick suggesting there might be other ways of doing things.

Doug and I also had a long chat about the similarities between the dog and the wolf, particularly in the social positioning, something that I had brought up time and again in Idaho but which had been a taboo subject. I had always felt that the key to the wolf was the dog and vice versa; that the way to get people to understand and respect the wolf was by comparing it to the animal they had in their living rooms. But the biologists wouldn't listen to me. I was told that they were different animals and there was nothing to be gained from comparing them. Ten or twelve years later here was Doug, one of the most respected wolf biologists in the world, saying much the same as I had said, and he was being taken seriously. It was frustrating to think of the problems that might have been avoided if the biologists had listened ten years before.

The last time I went to the Education Center in Idaho, they were having terrible problems with the captive pack that I had spent so long with. They were down to just three animals, which didn't surprise me. It had become such a celebrated pack that even members of the public knew their names. Years ago, dogs were like wolves, but by bringing them into our homes and domesticating them we changed them. Humans are not intrinsically pack animals. We like to have family but we can survive without them, on our own if we have to, and by associating with us for all these years, dogs have learnt to do the same.

What happened to the dog is now happening to wolves in captivity. They are turning on each other, fighting, sometimes killing each other, and packs are gradually dwindling in numbers because in captivity, where there is no territorial threat and no chance of famine, the wolves have no need of family. In the wild they can't survive without every rank pulling its weight; the pack is all. But because of their increasing proximity to man, even in the wild, wolf behaviour is changing.

The wolf is an adaptable animal – the Nez Perce taught me that. Their people came close to extinction themselves years ago and they looked to the wolf for inspiration and guidance to bring them back from the brink, because wolves had rescued themselves many times before. Nature – wolves – will always find a way. I have to believe that eventually some balance will return and humans will stop dominating and start listening. The biologists have used wolves to get letters after their names; the Nez Perce have always seen them as a symbol of survival and hope. Their attitude was that if the wolves could come back on to the land, then so could they. Just to be sitting there on the plateau with Doug Smith was a breakthrough. He had tried science and discovered that it didn't hold all the answers. Unlike some of his colleagues, he was prepared to listen to other ideas. I had to hope, for the wolf's sake, that more would follow his example.

A Man Among Wolves/The Wolfman was shown in March 2007 and caused quite a stir. It very nearly won an Emmy award but was narrowly beaten by *Meerkat Manor*. For the launch *National Geographic* flew me to America to do a whole lot of publicity, and everywhere I went, people seemed to recognise my face. Helen came with me and we had the time of our lives, staying in a lovely hotel – with the biggest bath I'd ever seen. I spent more time in the bath than anywhere else; I thought I'd arrived in heaven. One evening Helen and I ventured out on our own. We went to see a show on Broadway and as we made our way back to the hotel afterwards, feeling and looking like two fish completely out of water, I could see a gang of young guys in hoodies ahead of us, shouting and gesturing at passers-by. They were heading our way and I began to think of all the TV dramas I'd seen about muggings and rapes on the streets of New York. I told Helen I was going to push her into a doorway and that she must then run and I would do my best to fight them off. As they came level my heart was pounding. There were four, five, six of them. Wild wolves, bears – those were nothing compared to the terror I felt now. The biggest and the meanest-looking brought his face right up close to mine, thumped me on the shoulder and said, 'Yo bro! It's the Wolfman!' And as he gave me a high five and asked how it was going, I smiled with relief but thought, what were you doing sitting in watching the National Geographic Channel on a Friday night? You ought to be out mugging old ladies.

Helen was becoming an indispensible part of my life. The more I saw of her, the more I realised that I had obviously never been in love before. I hadn't understood the meaning of the word. The excitement, the laughter, the need to be with her, to know everything about her, was a whole new experience. We had so much in common. Her passion was for children and mine was for wolves, seemingly two very different subjects, but there were so many similarities in our aspirations and our outlook on life. She was a learning support assistant but her views on child care, especially with disabled children, were almost as alternative as mine were in the study of wolves. She had come up against the educational establishment in the way that I had come up against the scientists, and she had felt some of the frustrations in her job that I had felt in mine.

The more I saw of her, the more I was convinced I had found a soul-mate; someone I wanted to be with – the *only* person I'd ever wanted to be with as much as the wolves.

After several months, Arran expressed a desire to go back home and live with his father. He was a sensitive boy and I suspect he felt that his mum had someone to be with but his dad was on his own. Helen was devastated. I told her Arran was too young to know what he wanted, and that she should make the decision for him, but she wouldn't do that. She had always listened to what he said and respected his views, even though he was a child, and all credit to her, she let him go – although it caused her weeks of heartache. But it was the right decision. I thought it would be a flash in the pan, that he'd be back in a couple of weeks, but not so; he is still living with his dad, but Helen sees him a lot and everyone is very happy.

Once it was clear that Arran was not coming back, we started to think about moving in together. One good thing that came out of the television series was that Bob decided that my tatty old caravan was making the park look untidy and gave me another, larger one with two bedrooms and a shower and toilet. It wasn't the height of luxury; the hot-water system didn't work properly – and eventually stopped completely – and there were no cooking facilities to speak of, but it gave us a little more space and at last we were able to say goodbye to the putty bucket.

Helen was getting more and more involved in the wolves and the work I was doing and getting less and less enjoyment from her job. She spent every spare moment with me in the evenings and at weekends and was such a natural with the animals that after a little while I asked her to come and join me full time. And so she gave up the chalet, with its kitchen, bathroom and hot and cold running water, gave up a good job and security, gave up a normal life and came to live in a caravan with a gas ring and with a man who stank of wolves. I had such admiration for this woman.

By chance – although Helen would say nothing happens by chance – the morning she agreed to join me I had a meeting to discuss ideas for a new television series. Bethan Corney, the commissioning editor of Channel 5, who has always been a great supporter, was looking for two hour-long documentaries to take the story of my life with the wolves further. The question was, how? She had driven down to Combe Martin with Hilary Knight, my newly acquired agent, and Kath Moore, an executive producer with a company called Tigress, based in Bristol, that was to make the films. We were sitting round the table in the caravan nursing coffee mugs when I mentioned that Helen had decided to come on board full time to help at the park. Kath asked what work she'd be doing. I said that first of all I would have to teach her to be with the wolves. Her eyes opened wide and in that moment the theme for *Mr and Mrs Wolf* was born. About three months into the filming Animal Planet in America joined the Channel 5 project and extended the brief for the US market. They wanted twelve half-hour programmes that would go out under the title *Living with the Wolfman*.

Helen always felt that her place was with children. She had worked with them all her life and watched their hierarchy in the classroom and in the playground, and the more we talked, the more we realised how similar they were in this respect to wolves. I felt that if I could train her and make her comfortable with the pack, she would make a perfect wolf nanny. I was interested in discovering whether wolves were gender specific. I guessed they were. The wolves I had the closest interaction with had always been male, and I guessed that Cheyenne might open up to Helen, as another female, in a way she didn't with me. She was coming up to two; if she became pregnant, there was an obvious, irresistible challenge that we all knew would make good television: could I teach Helen enough about the wolves in the nine weeks of the pregnancy to persuade Cheyenne to choose Helen as the nanny for her pups?

Chapter Thirty

THE MIRACLE
THAT IS THE WOLF

The filming started in late February with the courtship, and the males endlessly fighting with one another as they had done in the wild. I had put Cheyenne into the main enclosure with Yana, Tamaska and Matsi, fully expecting her to take Yana, the alpha male, as her mate. He was her half-brother, but wolves breed with their own family members in captivity, as they do in the wild, and there is no evidence that it causes any problems with the bloodline. Her full brothers were in the enclosure next door which had a connecting gate, so we could segregate them if necessary, but at this point they were all running together, a pack of seven animals. Nataa, Nanoose and Tejas were too young to mate and even if they had come close, one of the adult males would have seen them off.

Wolves are so shy about mating – usually doing it either away from the rest of the pack, as I discovered in the wild, or under the cover of darkness – that I had never properly witnessed it before. This time we were hoping to capture it on camera, so as soon as I knew from her behaviour that she'd become receptive, I spent all my time with her watching and waiting – expecting Yana to make his move.

He did nothing of the sort. In the middle of the afternoon, shortly after they had fed, Cheyenne chose Matsi – the lowest-ranking animal in the pack. I couldn't believe what I was seeing. It was a complete shock; it went against everything I had been told. The biologists all say that the alpha will suppress any other hopeful candidates. We were watching something very interesting and I guessed she must have chosen him for a reason. Early the next morning she mated with Matsi again. That night, although it was difficult to see under the trees in the dark, it looked to me as though she was finally allowing Yana his due.

The following morning I was up at the caravan with the film crew, snatching a quick cup of coffee and a bacon sandwich, when Linda and Roger, two members of staff at the park, called my mobile and said, 'Come quick; you're not going to believe this.' We ran down the hill to find Cheyenne and Tamaska, the beta, knotted together. In the space of two days, she had mated with all three possible candidates.

To the best of my knowledge, this has never been witnessed before, and at some stage we will carry out blood tests to find out which males fathered which pups. There is evidence of dogs producing two different breeds in the same litter – some of them pure Labrador and some clearly Labrador–Collie cross, for example – so it must be possible for wolves to do the same. I have a theory that she might have selected her partners because of their rank, knowing instinctively that her young would have exactly the same rank as their father – designer pups, if you like. It could, of course, just have been an inexperienced female; but it could have been something far cleverer – which would turn current thinking on its head.

After all this mating the next big question was whether she was pregnant, which because of the filming schedule, we needed to know.

The most reliable way to tell is with ultrasound, but I wasn't prepared to put Cheyenne through the stress involved, so about fourteen days later we tried two alternatives. We sent a sample of faeces away to a lab, where they normally test lions and big cats but were prepared to see what came up with a wolf, and we tried a human pregnancy test, which again was not guaranteed to be accurate but we felt might give us some idea. When Helen and I went into the chemist in Combe Martin to buy it, everyone looked at us knowingly and we quickly had to explain it was not for us but for a wolf.

Collecting a sample of urine was the next challenge. Armed with a little pot I had to run around after Cheyenne, who had the run of two enclosures, and throw myself on to the ground every time she looked as though she might be about to squat. Against all the odds, I succeeded, and we carefully took the sample up to the caravan and dipped in the testing stick. I thought I detected a faint cross but I couldn't be sure.

We had to wait another three weeks for the results from the lab about the faeces, but in the meantime she was showing all the signs of being pregnant: she had started to put on weight, her teats had begun to swell, and she'd started digging a den and constructing rendezvous sites, as I'd witnessed the alpha female doing in the wild. When the lab finally said they were as sure as they could be that she was in pup, it was all systems go. We had only a few weeks left to convince Cheyenne that Helen was experienced enough to be a nanny.

She had been going into the enclosure in the intervening weeks, but now everything had to be stepped up. Every day I took her down to the expectant mother, her mouth stuffed with little bits of chewed raw beef and mince that she could regurgitate on demand when Cheyenne nibbled her lips – the first thing the pups do to their nanny. I did the same alongside Helen, and Cheyenne had such an appetite and nibbled so greedily at our lips that we both looked as though we had been sucking on a cactus. After weeks of doing this our lips were so sore that we could no longer drink hot coffee from a mug.

Finally the birth day arrived. The den was already fitted out with infrared cameras, positioned at angles to cover every corner she could possibly get herself into. Outside the enclosure, in the little stadium where during the season the public sat to listen to my talks, the film crew had set up a monitor so we could all see what was happening underground. Cheyenne went into the den and was restless, but otherwise there was no sign of activity, and bearing in mind that her mother had gone into the den two days before giving birth, I wasn't expecting much. Helen and Jude, a volunteer who had come to us from primates, took the first shift while I had something to eat. I went down to take over at about 11.00 p.m. At about 1.00 a.m. she started to get restless again and scratched out a birthing bowl, partially covering one of the cameras in the process. I called Helen and Jude, and a little later we started to hear sounds that suggested she was going into labour. We then watched the most incredible sight: she tore the fur away from around her teats to prepare them for the pups. I had never seen or heard of wolves doing this before. We were witnessing something truly extraordinary.

Between 4 and 4.30 in the morning the first pup emerged – a very dark-looking creature, which she picked up rather roughly with her teeth. I had a moment's anxiety and said out loud, 'Ease up, Cheyenne,' but the pup squeaked and she relaxed her grip on it immediately and gently eased it over to her underside, where it started suckling. We all heaved a massive sigh of relief and allowed ourselves to relax. She had one live, healthy, suckling pup and seemed to know what she was doing. Numbers two, three and four arrived with the same ease and we were over the moon. Success. Helen started to do a piece to camera for the video diary she was keeping. Cheyenne was suckling, licking and cleaning up her pups. We could all go and get some sleep; our girl had done good – we had expected four pups and she had delivered. They were textbook births.

And then I realised that Cheyenne had started to push again and was producing nothing. She was becoming distressed. She howled and grunted and moaned, and the noises she made will probably haunt Helen and me until the day we die. She did that for the best part of an hour and a half, but it can take that long for a final pup to be born so I tried not to panic. After two hours and still no sign of anything, I became seriously worried. At first light I decided to try and get her out of the den and walk her around a bit to see if that would get things moving. Helen and Jude called her and she came out and sat on the bank for four or five minutes licking her back end, then went back underground, circled, lay down and started pushing again, getting more and more distressed as she did so. I realised there was a very real possibility that we might lose her. If the pup inside her was dead it would soon start to poison her system, so I called the vet, who took an agonisingly long time to come.

He agreed that the pup still inside her was probably dead and wanted to dart her so he could ease it out and let her return to her live pups. We called her out a second time, and the vet darted her, but it didn't do more than make her groggy. He darted her a second time but she still didn't go down and in her semi-consciousness gave me a nasty bite on the hand. The vet couldn't dislodge the pup manually. He was going to have to do a caesarean section, and that meant taking her to his surgery, which was a twenty-minute drive away.

We had an agonising dilemma. The worst-case scenario was that we would lose Cheyenne; if we didn't, the chances were that she would be gone from the pups for so long during the operation and the travel back and forth that we would lose the pups; and if we removed them and fed them while she was away, she would probably reject them once she came back.

I decided to go in and get the pups and take them with us to the vet. So while Helen and Jude loaded Cheyenne into the cage in the van, I went into the den. Cheyenne had dug six or seven feet beyond the den I had made, exactly as her mother had done before her, making sure nothing larger than her could get at the pups. I had to wriggle through this narrow tunnel, which was a very tight fit. At one point the tunnel dipped down, almost like a U-bend in a drain, possibly dug to catch water and prevent the birthing chamber being flooded. As the ground went down, there was a bulge above which I thought must be concrete. I bumped it inadvertently as I snaked my way beneath and it turned out to be earth that was subsiding after her excavations, which collapsed around my face. I couldn't breathe and I couldn't move. I yelled for help, several times, but everyone was so busy above ground getting Cheyenne loaded that no one heard me – except for Helen's young son, Arran. I could hear the panic rising in his voice as he shouted for someone to come back to the den and, thank God, two of the keepers came and I felt hands pulling my on feet, just as I was beginning to find breathing difficult and to fear I'd never get out. The den had collapsed completely by this stage and I had no option but to dig the pups out of their chamber. I put them into a box, covered them with a jumper to keep them warm, put the box on the front seat of my 4x4 with little banana-shaped bottles of formula milk and raced after Helen, who had had to set off without me because Cheyenne was beginning to come round.

By the time I arrived, Cheyenne was on the operating table, so I left the pups with all our helpers to try to get some milk into them, and went to see how their mum was doing. It was as we expected; she had a large female pup dead inside her and there was no way it could ever have come out naturally. Luckily we had been in time – Cheyenne was still alive and the C-section was successful – but we still had a long way to go with the pups and I was facing at least another twenty-four hours without sleep.

I can't explain why I did what I did next. I reckoned that if the pups had suckled once from their mother a bond would have been created, however fragile. It would be a lot to expect of Cheyenne; she had been through a great deal of trauma, she'd had the worst birthing experience imaginable and her den had been destroyed. Nevertheless, I went back to the park ahead of Helen, taking the pups with me, went into the enclosure and started to re-create a den and to make it as much like the one Cheyenne had made as possible. I was completely shattered by this time. I was running on pure adrenalin, but I couldn't accept offers of help because if my plan was to have any chance of success, the den couldn't smell of anyone but me. I was hoping to put the pups back underground and encourage Cheyenne to join them. The odds on succeeding were not good, but I knew that if the den smelt of anyone else she wouldn't go near it.

One by one I placed the squirming, squeaking little bundles in my newly created birthing bowl, just as Helen was backing down the track in the van with Cheyenne in the back. We manoeuvred the cage into the enclosure and opened the door and a very groggy and blood-stained wolf staggered out, looking very sorry for herself. She tried to run and immediately fell into the pond, so I went in and pulled her out, which meant we were now both soaking wet as well as everything else. The boys were shut in the adjoining enclosure and she desperately wanted to join them. She seemed to have no memory of the pups or of anything that had gone on before the anaesthetic, but just moved shakily back and forth, up and down the fence line. I didn't know what to do. If I opened that connecting gate she would never look at the pups again.

Then I had a flash of inspiration. I went up to her and started whimpering and whining in a high-pitched voice that she knew from all the time I'd been with her. I rubbed myself around her, trying to create a bond in the way that a couple of wolves do when they need each other, and she started to respond. Very slowly I started to back away, calling her all the time, until we were round the back of the pond and halfway to the den. Slowly, slowly we edged forward, getting closer and closer until we were within maybe ten metres of the den entrance, when she turned and ran back towards the boys.

Valuable minutes were ticking away. I couldn't afford to go through that procedure again. I could hear the pups underground, urgently squawking, in need of warmth and food, and knew that if I didn't get her down to them soon, we were going to lose them. If I could only get her close enough, my hope was she would hear them too and their cries might trigger her maternal instinct. So I stayed by the den and whimpered and whimpered until my throat was starting to seize up. I hadn't had anything to eat or drink all day and I still had mud all round my mouth; I had been on my feet for nearly forty-eight hours and I was exhausted. Finally she started to come towards me, and kept coming, coming until she was about one and a half metres away. I backed away, still whimpering, until my head was right by the entrance and she came and put her mouth to mine as if asking for food, and at that moment I saw her hear the pups. Her head tilted to one side and then to the other and her ear flickered, as if listening intently. Shakily she put her head and shoulders inside the entrance and I was willing her to keep going – I was even tempted to give her a push – but she backed out again and went and sat under a tree.

I started up the whimpering a second time and once again she staggered over to the den entrance and licked around my mouth, so I put my head inside and she put her head and shoulders inside with me. Slowly, I backed away. She had her head and neck and shoulders in, and this time I held my shoulder under her back end to try and stop her backing out. The noise of the pups calling was almost deafening by now, and suddenly the pressure against my shoulder vanished, I fell forward and she disappeared underground.

I waited a few seconds. I could still hear the pups calling but I had no idea what was going on; whether she was going to come back out again or lie on them and crush them. My heart was in my mouth and I crossed every finger I had. As I made my way out of the enclosure, Helen came towards me in floods of tears. She had been watching the monitor.

'What's happened?' I asked. 'Has Cheyenne killed them?'

'She's feeding them!' said Helen, laughing through the tears.

I just thought, 'Oh my God.' This is the miracle that is the wolf.

Chapter Thirty-one

PUSHING THE
BOUNDARIES

I had been very excited by the prospect of teaching Helen to interact with the wolves and of her becoming a part of my world. I also
liked the ideas behind the documentary, which would be a great
showpiece for the research work we were doing. But I didn't kid
myself; I knew she and I had a huge mountain to climb. She had to
learn in a matter of weeks what I had taken years to discover, and I
was aware that what kept me safe with these creatures was largely my
experience. In expecting this to work – expecting the pack to be
conned into thinking Helen was more experienced about their world
than they were – I was pushing every boundary, and although I had
spent my life pushing boundaries and doing things that common
sense told me were foolish, it had always been my own neck that I'd
put on the line. This time it was the neck of the woman I loved – and
if, later on, I had been able to turn the clock back, and have those
months over again, I would never have gone through with it.

During those months of filming, I tasted for myself the anxiety
she had suffered in all our time together. Every day she felt sick with

worry about the state I would be in by the end of it, not knowing whether I would be cut, bitten or bleeding and needing to be patched up or even taken to Accident and Emergency for stitches. Quite often I was concussed. If I got a really hard blow to the head – the sort that left me reeling and seeing stars – an hour or so later I'd be sitting having a cup of coffee one minute and then suddenly I'd come round to find Helen hovering over me, ashen faced, asking if I was all right. She'd tell me that I'd been unconscious for the last ten minutes. And many were the times I'd pee blood.

Now I felt that we had reversed roles, and both of us found it unnerving. I became the one that lived with the terror of something going wrong. She was the one facing the daily interaction, and although I was in the enclosure with her for most of the time, and reassuring her that there was no danger, I knew I was bluffing. I was telling her she must lie down on the ground, on her back, and expose her neck and vulnerable underside. I couldn't guarantee that one of the wolves wasn't going to accidentally bite too hard or nick a vein with his canines. If he punctured one of the big veins in the neck she could be dead in seconds.

At the start I had been quite confident, and to begin with things were going well. My plan was to introduce Helen to the wolves in stages. First she met Cheyenne, on her own, because unless she accepted Helen the whole experiment was over; and their first few meetings looked promising. Helen had to show Cheyenne respect as a higher-ranking member of the pack and she did everything I had drilled into her. She then met the young males, Nanoose, Nataa and Tejas. She had to convince them that she was of a higher rank than they were, which was more of a challenge. They were like boisterous teenagers, spoiling for a fight, and she was very frightened, but she managed to hold her own with them and at the end of the day they all howled together to cement the relationship. The wolves that she was going to have to work really hard with were the expectant fathers, Yana, Tamaska and Matsi. To be successful she had to be accepted by the entire pack.

Then something happened which gave me a reality check. I had taken a deer carcass down to the enclosure. Helen had been helping me feed the animals but had not come in with me. She was standing outside chatting to a volunteer. The whole pack's energy levels were up; I think there must have been a bitch on heat in the area that had come close to the enclosure. Whatever it was, the atmosphere around them was very tense – explosive almost. Feed time is always highly vocal, with all the wolves snarling and snapping and defending their own place on the carcass. To anyone unfamiliar with the scene, it looks as though they are out to kill one another but they never are. It's the classic case of their bark being worse than their bite. Until it isn't.

I was in my usual place on the carcass between Tamaska and Yana; both were growling and snarling as they tore at the fur and the ligaments. I was growling as I ripped away at my section, making it clear to all comers that this was mine, and then suddenly, instinctively, I pulled back and raised my head. A split second later Tamaska and Yana went for each other; their jaws locked and their bodies turned into a spinning bundle of black and tan fur. Had I not pulled back when I did, I would have been in the middle of it, and some of the worst injuries I have sustained over the years have come from being caught in the crossfire.

Helen watched with mounting horror. She wanted to know how I had known that such violence was about to erupt and asked me to teach her how to recognise it, so that she could do the same when she was in there on her own. I felt physically sick. I couldn't begin to tell her how to do what I had just done. It was instinctive and came from years of experience. It wasn't something I could teach her and it wasn't something I could do for her. And at that moment I realised what I was putting Helen through was too risky. I had thought I knew enough to be able to keep her safe, but I didn't. I always felt that Steve Irwin, the Australian wildlife expert who was known as 'the Crocodile Hunter', had been killed because he allowed himself to be taken outside his field of expertise. He was killed by a stingray barb, filming in the Great Barrier Reef. I had great admiration for him, but he knew crocodiles, and I thought it was dangerous when he was either tempted or persuaded to move out of his area of expertise. I remember sitting watching him on television one day, and his wife was playing with dingoes on Fraser Island. To the best of my knowledge he knew nothing about dogs, and I thought he was probably out of his depth, but was doing it because of the demands of television. At one point I could see one of these dingoes was about to snap and a moment later it did snap at his wife, and Helen, who was watching with me, said, 'How did you know it was going to do that?' and I couldn't answer. It was just a feeling that came after years of knowing these creatures. The realisation hit me that, television or not, this was Helen's life I was playing with and I needed to play safe.

There were several times during the course of filming when I thought I'd made a big mistake. I was consistently torn between doing what I knew the cameras were looking for – that is, making it authentic, which was important – and what I knew was safe for Helen. Sometimes I deliberately took her by surprise. She was terrified of meeting the older boys; it had built up and up in her mind until it was blown out of all proportion. I knew that if I told her in advance that I planned to introduce her to Matsi in a couple of days, she wouldn't have eaten or slept a wink and would have worked herself into such a state that she would have gone into the enclosure smelling like a different person and giving out all the wrong signals. Matsi is the probably the most unpredictable of all the wolves in the pack because his job, as the tester, is to expose weakness. If he detects the slightest hesitation in another wolf, or a person, he alerts the alpha and she dispatches the beta, the bully boy, to deal with the problem.

So I sprang it on her. She was feeling more confident than at any time, having managed to cope well with the three teenagers, and Matsi was in a good mood. I had spent a few hours with him earlier that morning and he was calm and relaxed; and he had met Helen from the other side of the fence many times so he already had a lot of information about her. It was a beautiful, still day. Everything augured well for a successful encounter. All I needed now was some old-fashioned deception. I told her we were going to meet the young-sters again; when she saw Matsi was in the main enclosure with them, she started to panic. I said all she had to do was lay down some scent so that he could get to know her through that first.

With a hint of hysteria in her voice, she said, 'But what if Matsi comes over to me?' 'He won't,' I lied, 'because the camera crew will be in the enclosure too with all their equipment and he'll be too nerv-ous.' I knew that he would make a beeline for her but gambled that once she was in there she would deal with it, just as she had dealt with the others. I had noticed already that her tendency was to panic a few hours before the event, but to be as cool as a cucumber when the cri-sis was actually upon her. Besides, I was going to be there with them and I wouldn't have let things go too far.

As Matsi came towards her I could see tears begin to well up in her eyes and her bottom lip start to quiver. This was the first wolf that she had truly feared meeting. Not only was he a big, heavy, fully-grown adult male, she had heard the stories about Matsi. Not so long before, there had been an accident in the park. This wolf had taken all the flesh off someone's fingers. It was a member of staff, and what she did was completely out of order, but sometimes the more expe-rienced staff could read the animals and get away with things like this. She put two fingers through the wire fence to give him a scratch, mistakenly thinking Matsi was another, more docile wolf. Matsi, being the tester, had spun round and grabbed the girl's fingers in his mouth. The girl started screaming at him and tried to pull her fingers away, whereupon he closed his teeth round them and pulled against her, neatly stripping them to the bone. I hadn't told Helen the story to frighten her; just to remind her that although these creatures were behind bars, they were still wild animals and you could never afford to be complacent around them. They live for the moment and you can't take anything for granted; you are only as good as the last time you were with them. It doesn't matter that you raised them with a bottle; that was then, this is now, and unless you can prove your worth to them every single time you meet, you are in trouble. Wolves are not sentimental.

'Don't you dare!' I said sternly, as her composure started to slide. She glared at me and her jaw set in the way it did when I knew she was cross. Good, I thought, let her hate me if necessary, just don't let her break down in front of Matsi. My hunch was right. Matsi did leap up at her but she stayed completely calm and held her own, and after giving her a thorough investigation, the tester of the pack turned and walked away. The relief on Helen's face was obvious and I breathed a huge sigh of relief. I don't like gambling at the best of times.

Moments later I was knocked flying by the three adolescents, who all cannoned into me. They were in the midst of a rowdy rough and tumble and I wasn't watching carefully enough. I was in my usual position, down on my haunches, and it was my head that took the brunt of it. Everything went black for a second, and then I saw stars and I felt as though I'd been hit by a steam train. Apart from practically knocking me out, the blow had dislodged my microphone so I had to leave the enclosure briefly to let the sound engineer reattach it. While I was out, Matsi moved in on Helen. I was powerless to help.

Watching her with Matsi's jaw clamped round her throat was, without exception, the most terrifying moment of my life. It wasn't that I didn't trust Matsi. I had absolute faith in him. What I didn't trust was Helen to keep her cool. If that member of staff had kept her nerve and remained quiet and still when Matsi had her fingers between his teeth, he would have let them go without harming her. The damage he did was terrible, but those were just fingers; Matsi had his teeth around Helen's neck. If she had screamed or tried to pull away – if she had moved so much as a muscle – he would have done exactly what he did to that member of staff, but the consequences would have been entirely different. Helen would have been dead.

My biggest fear in this whole exercise was Helen's reactions. Helen is *the* most emotional person I've ever met, and how to turn her emotions off was the single most important lesson I had to teach her during that period and also the hardest. Time and time again in the enclosure I could see the telltale signs. There was a little area between the double gates to the enclosure where she would psych herself up before going in with the wolves, and I could see the transformation come over her as she went from emotional Helen to wolf-pack Helen. I always had to wait for that change, when she'd say, 'OK, go.' Then, as I opened the second gate, I used to say to her, 'Forget human; think wolf!' It was very difficult for her and I was incredibly proud of the way she managed to hold it in, but the minute we came out through that first gate she would collapse into tears or laughter or a mixture of both, and everything she had held back came cascading out.

She held still. I stood at the wire on the outside of the enclosure, powerless as I was to help her, and trying to keep calm, told her not to move. The look of naked fear on her face still haunts me, but by the grace of God she listened, she trusted me and she didn't panic. And having held her throat for what felt like an eternity but was in reality probably no more than a minute, Matsi let her go. Strangely, despite her fear, she didn't realise quite how serious the situation was until she saw the look on my face. That was what really freaked her. But she passed the test: Matsi approved and, despite my fears, he and Helen formed an incredibly close bond; they were similar characters – both deeply suspicious and slow to trust. The next hurdle was Tamaska.

Chapter Thirty-two

BREAKDOWN

The meeting between Tamaska and Helen never happened. Two weeks before the end of the filming schedule Helen collapsed. She had reached a point of total exhaustion. At the outset, we had agreed to film for two or three days a week, which, given everything else that was going on in our lives, would have been doable, but as time went by, pressure came from Animal Planet to get the series made ahead of schedule. That put pressure on Tigress, and they in turn put pressure on us. They were gathering material for twelve half-hour programmes for America and two hour-long documentaries for Channel 5 in the UK. That represented several hundred hours of footage and they needed our involvement in most of it.

Our filming commitment increased to six and sometimes seven days a week. We began at 7.30 most mornings and were frequently still at it until 9.30 at night, by which time we were shattered. The filming placed other strains on Helen. Doing a crash course in becoming a wolf nanny meant a complete change of life for her. She had already adjusted to living in a shoe-box, but now she had to change

251

her diet. Like most people, she enjoyed convenience food such as piz-
zas, pasta and hamburgers, and she loved cakes and sweet things. She
wasn't mad about liver but couldn't get kidney past her throat. In order
to smell acceptable to the pack, she had to eat what a high-ranking
wolf would eat – and that meant liver, kidneys and heart as well as
some good-quality meat and plain vegetables. What's more, she had
to chew the offal, partially cooked, and then keep it in her mouth, so
that she could spit it out for Cheyenne and the pups. And she couldn't
even cheer herself up with a drink.

Another major change: she had to work out at the gym to increase
her body strength. As well as the treadmill, I made her do weights,
pull-ups and press-ups. She hated it; she had never taken this sort of
physical exercise in her life, but it was vital that she did. She had to
be able to hold her own against the wolves for her own safety. I was
strong but even I had to work out and was going for daily runs to
keep up my stamina – as I always had and still do. Without that level
of fitness you don't stand a chance wrestling with a one hundred and
thirty-pound wolf that is all teeth and muscle; and, fit as I am, there's
no guarantee that they are not going to break my neck one day.

Our schedule would have been exhausting enough if filming was
all we'd had to concentrate on, but it wasn't. The filming came on top
of our normal day's work. I still had to do what had previously taken
up all my time. I still had to look after the wolves, check on the
perimeter fences twice a day, maintain a bond with them all – including the European wolves, which were not being filmed – as well as
enriching them with recordings of other packs, feeding them every
few days and organising carcass deliveries; and I still had to under-
take my commitments to Bob Butcher. The filming disrupted the
busiest season at the park and he was putting increasing pressure on
me to be there to meet and greet the visitors, a lot of whom had seen
me on television and came hoping to see me give a talk and do my

normal demonstration. Jan and I were going through a custody battle and I hadn't seen my children for twelve months. I was desperate
to see them. Meanwhile, Helen and I were living life at one hundred
and ten miles an hour, we were working up to seventeen hours a day,
and it was too much. It left us no time for each other; no time to talk.
We had no escape from one another either and no life outside what
we were doing. It placed an unbelievable strain on us both and on
our relationship. We felt as though we were sliding ever closer to the
abyss. Something had to give.

It must have been about three-quarters of the way through the filming when the cracks started to show. Helen was working up to meeting
Tamaska, the enforcer, and she knew that this was the big one. Matsi,
the tester, had been tricky, but the tester doesn't do the disciplining.
His job is simply to highlight your failings to the other animals. It's
only if you panic that he reacts, and that's when the life-threatening sit-
uations arise with him. Her meeting with Yana, the decision-maker,
had its own challenges, as Helen found out, and she had to give him
the respect he deserved as the boss, but he was never going to be the
biggest threat. As the alpha male he was self-preserving and would
always be more likely to threaten Helen with his voice or his body posture and bring in another pack member to do the business.

Tamaska was the one who did the business. He was the one that
she couldn't afford to make a mistake with, because there was no forgiveness in him. Under pack rules he had the right, and he certainly
had the power, to mete out whatever discipline was necessary, and I
had no right to interfere. If he went for Helen, the only hope I would
have to save her would be to distract him momentarily, and get him
to have a go at me. That would have bought her a few seconds to get
out of the enclosure, but no more. I would have had to grab hold of
him, which would have gone against everything I believed about
these animals, and take his bites, which would have been serious and

probably fatal. The more I watched Helen, the less confident I felt about her ability to cope with this final introduction. I was becoming seriously worried. Every day she was looking more and more tired and pressurised. The diet, the fitness training, the emotional strain – everything was getting to her and taking its toll.

It reminded me of the commando training I went through. Anyone with a reasonable standard of fitness could go through one of those tests we did quite easily, but doing it day in day out, sometimes twice a day, over a period of eight to ten weeks, as we did, that's when the cracks would appear and that's what was happening with Helen. The physical and mental exertion of her days with the wolves, coupled with what was going on emotionally between us, was too much, and shortly before she was due to meet Tamaska, it all fell apart.

I can't remember the precise incident that sparked it off. It was something petty and irrelevant, like whether I had flushed the toilet or remembered to buy milk at the shop. Whatever it was, as Helen said later, it was the straw that broke the camel's back. Everything had built up and up and we desperately needed a break. I don't think either of us thought it would be permanent; she said she just needed to get away from the wolves and from everything that went with them. Even though we had been together and she had been a part of my world for nearly three years, we still saw things very differently. Her way of dealing with what had happened was to get back to normal life; mine was to go down to the wolves. We both reverted to the worlds we knew. It felt as if we were in a long dark tunnel and every fragment of light at the end of it had been blocked off. We'd had bigger rows than this before and come through them. This wasn't even a full-blown row. It was just a discussion that couldn't be resolved. Helen went to bed that night, I slept on the sofa, and when things were no better the next morning, we came to the conclusion that we needed a break and some space.

It was September. We had been filming for over seven months and we still had several weeks left to go and, of course, we were under contract. But there was no way we could carry on that day, and when the film crew arrived, ready to go as usual, we told them things had broken down and we couldn't work. I needed to get out of the caravan so I left them to it and went off into town. By the time I came back the crew had vanished and so had Helen. Later, she sent me a text message telling me that she couldn't come back to the caravan; she had to go and sort herself out.

In that time I discovered the horrors of the celebrity world. When the Americans heard about our break-up, their answer was to get the cameras on to each of us as quickly as possible, to stick a microphone into our faces and ask us how we were feeling – which, feeling the way we were, was the last thing either of us wanted. Tigress came to our rescue. They had become good friends by this time – we'd been through a lot together – and their attitude was: that may be what you do in the States, but it's not the way we do things over here. These guys need time to try and sort things out between them, and once they have, we'll pick up the story again. I don't think Animal Planet liked hearing that – they seemed to relish the soap-opera element of our lives – but without that breather I don't think we would have been able to carry on at all. We were given a week.

Helen has since told me that those were the worst days of her life; she didn't know how she was going to get through them. They were unbearable for me too, because I sought solace in the wolves, thinking I would find comfort under the cloak of darkness with them. After she left I spent every night down in the enclosure with them, but they missed her as much as I did. They called for her throughout the night, emitting this haunting, spine-chilling cry for a lost member of the pack; a rallying call showing her the way home. I longed for her reply to come over the valley, as it once had, but nothing came back; there was just silence. They called like this for about five nights, and little by little it broke my heart. I wanted her back. I couldn't face the thought of a future without her. She had shown me a world that I hadn't known existed; a world of love and laughter, a world that Helen inhabited. It was a world I wanted to be a part of, but she had closed the door to it.

Helen and I didn't speak to each other in the intervening time, but Kath Moore contacted both of us separately and we agreed to let Tigress film our split. They would conclude the series for Animal Planet by following Helen on her journey to a new life and show me and my future alone once more with the wolves. That was difficult enough for me, but what was worse was having to film 'pick-ups' together. Filming is not always done sequentially, and there were scenes we had to do together to drop into footage about our lives before the break that they had already partially shot. Pretending to be a couple for the cameras was one of the most difficult things I have ever done. It was agony for both of us.

What we needed more than anything was time apart to come to terms with what had happened. Maybe one day we would be able to salvage something from the relationship, maybe we could be friends, but we wouldn't know that until we had taken time to reflect and allow the wounds to heal. But we weren't afforded that luxury. The filming contract that had seemed so exciting in the beginning had turned into the worst kind of nightmare and was forcing us to be together.

And it wasn't over yet. What the contract also held us to was publicity. We had to travel to America together to promote the launch of *Living with the Wolfman*. So when we finally had a break from filming as the happy couple, we had just a few weeks off before we were sitting laughing and joking alongside each other on the sofas of all the major chat shows in New York. Once again it was all pretence. Helen had to talk cheerfully about the joys of living with the Wolfman, while I had to howl and snarl and generally keep the audience amused. This was because Animal Planet had decided that they wanted to keep the breakdown in our relationship secret. It would come out in the last programme and they intended to use it as a cliffhanger for a second series. Would the split be permanent, or would we be able to patch up our differences? It felt as though our heartbreak was being used to push up the ratings.

Our last trip to New York had been so happy. This couldn't have been less so. It was a strange and confusing time. I don't think either of us really wanted to live without the other, but we just couldn't see a way of ever being together and making it work. Separate cars came and collected us to take us to the airport, although we were coming from just a few miles apart. We travelled separately on the aeroplane, stayed in separate bedrooms in the hotel, and were living separate lives, but in the studio we were chatting together on the sofa as if we were inseparable. Going back, seeing all the old haunts from the last visit and remembering the fun and laughter of that time was unbelievably painful. This was tougher than anything I'd had to cope with in the wild. The battle for survival, the physical pain, the bites and gashes and blows to the head and every other part of my body were as nothing compared with the hurt I was feeling now. In all those years I had kept my emotions hidden away. Now, with Helen gone, they were laid bare. I couldn't see a way forward.

Every day it was a battle to get up and I had to remind myself to breathe in and out. I was more depressed than I had ever been and my mood had a tremendous impact on the wolves. They had never seen me display such emotion and I was worried about how they would react. But they were the ones that pulled me round. They had called and called, but when there was no longer any hope of a response, they stopped calling and started restructuring the pack. They had grieved for their loss, for Helen, but life had to go on. If the pack couldn't recruit, it had to restructure; we all had to move forward.

One morning, soon after we arrived back from New York, I was surprised to get a call from Helen on my mobile phone. She asked whether I would let the dogs out for her. 'Why?' I said. 'What's up?' Her voice sounded strange and she said she couldn't get out of bed. I went straight over and I was shocked rigid when I saw her. She looked like an empty shell and as we talked she seemed to drift – one minute she was with me and the next she was far away in a world of her own. It didn't know what was happening or what to do. I hadn't come across anything like it; this wasn't the Helen I knew lying in this bed; she was like a complete stranger and it was very scary. I dealt with the dogs and then I rang the film crew. We were still making the last episodes of the American series. 'There's no way on this earth that Helen's going to be able to film today,' I said, and that I'd see how she was tomorrow. They said they couldn't keep losing filming days like this. It was costing money; Animal Planet was on their backs, the first two episodes had now been shown and they were running out of time. They said I had to sort it out or call a doctor.

In retrospect, that was the best thing they could have said. I managed to get Helen into the GP's surgery and he took one look at her and sent her up to the hospital to see a specialist. The diagnosis was complete physical and mental exhaustion: her system had shut down.

Helen didn't get out of bed for the next two months. Even the slightest activity exhausted her. I did the odd task for her but otherwise I kept away. I wasn't the person to nurse her; I knew that having me around would only make things worse, and besides I still had filming to do and the wolves to look after. It was Jude who stepped into the breach. They had become good friends and, because she worked at the park, she could act as a go-between Helen and me and would alert me to anything Helen might need.

The last days of filming were very difficult. Helen had made her last appearance – she was flat on her back and going nowhere – so

Tigress had to use clips of her that they had already shot to make the final programmes work. I was worried about Helen and, for my own part, I was just clinging on, existing, but time was now of the essence. We had stretched Tigress and Animal Planet to the limit emotionally and financially, but thanks to everyone pulling together and helping to make the best of a bad situation, we got through it; we had the series and the two one-hour documentaries for the UK in the can. Suddenly, after ten months of pressure, of long days and camera equipment filling the caravan, it was all over, Christmas was looming, and I was on my own.

I had accepted the offer of a free meal from friends who run one of the local pubs, but first of all I celebrated with the wolves. A turkey dealer had delivered a whole lot of substandard birds that he'd been unable to sell, and these were the guys' Christmas treat. The only problem was that they hadn't been plucked and it was very muddy down in the enclosure that day. The pups hadn't seen turkeys before and they went mad, pulling them into pieces, and white feathers flew everywhere. When I came out, with only thirty or forty minutes to go before I was due at the pub, I was so filthy I looked as though I had been tarred and feathered.

The hot water hadn't been working in the caravan for months so I stood under the hosepipe, trying to make myself look respectable enough to go out, on Christmas Day at the age of forty-three, thinking my life has got to change.

The decision to go out was a mistake. When I agreed to go, I thought it would do me good to get out of the caravan, but it was disastrous. Helen and I had been to the pub many times together, so it brought back painful memories, and every other table was taken by couples. They were all laughing and joking and pulling crackers and having a good time. And I was sitting at a table for one, feeling about as low as I had ever been.

Chapter Thirty-three

I HAVE
A DREAM

With the help of a therapist, I learnt a lot about myself in the next few months. The Nez Perce had said that I belonged between two worlds, but what I came to realise was that I had been with the wolves in their world for so long, I had almost forgotten how to be human. My aim had been to bridge the gap between those two worlds, to try and find acceptance for wolves in a society that didn't want them or understand the value they have in bringing balance and prosperity to the natural world. But as the Native Americans said, being able to speak for the wolf is pointless unless you can communicate with the people who need to hear you. I had forgotten how to do that. I was so close to the wolves that I had lost sight of why I was doing it. In order to make a difference in their world I had to regain a foothold in ours.

Helen and I had overstretched ourselves with the filming and that had put unbearable pressure on us both, but I knew that the real cause of the break-up, and possibly even Helen's breakdown, was me. She loved the wolves, she felt almost as passionate about them as I was, and she didn't bat an eyelid when it came to dragging carcasses about or hacking off the heads and hooves of the calves that came from the abattoir. That's what I loved about Helen – her enthusiasm for getting stuck in; the fact that she wasn't squeamish and didn't mind getting filthy. I don't think she even minded living in the caravan, with dead rabbits being flung on to the roof of it in the middle of the night by Derek, the slaughterhouse man, after his lamping expeditions. Whenever I asked him why he did it, he said he was hoping to catch Helen outside one night in her nightdress. I don't think she minded giving up the creature comforts that she'd been used to. What she minded was my inability to give myself completely.

Of the two worlds I lived in, one was a world devoid of emotion; the other was full of it. I knew I turned my emotions off when I was in the wolf world, but I had always thought I turned them back on again when I walked up the track to the caravan. It was clear to me now that I never did; I never truly left the forest. I had been with Helen physically during the years we had been together, but mentally I had always been in the enclosure with the wolves. I realised now that if I wanted to have human relationships in future, whether with Helen or my children or anyone else, I needed to come back to the human world.

I had also become obsessive. I couldn't distinguish between the dangers I knew existed in the wolf world, where life is a constant battle for survival, and the dangers I perceived in the human world. I was like a Vietnam veteran or someone suffering post-traumatic stress disorder. When Helen and I took Arran out for the day, I behaved like a male wolf protecting his pack. I could see danger everywhere, even walking down the streets of Barnstable, the local market town. I'd never settle until they were back in the safety zone of home. I couldn't enjoy the outings we made to the park or the zoo or the beach because I was always on edge, fearful if either of them wandered down to the water's edge without me or ran and played in the sand. I was like a misguided Collie dog that needed to herd everyone together, all the time; to be sure they were safe. I had a morbid fear of not being there when danger struck – which, in the animal world, is the biggest crime a protector can commit because it threatens the whole pack. If Helen was going out I would always need to know where she was going and when she'd be back, and I don't think she could take it any more.

My world was wolves, and I had taken her into it and nearly suffocated her. I didn't have any other needs in my life; she did and I hadn't recognised that. She needed to live a much more normal life than I did; she needed to go out, to see friends, to shop and to go to the beauty parlour from time to time to have her eyebrows plucked or her nails painted. She wanted to have a lie-in every now and then, but I got up before dawn every day so I could run to meet the rising sun as the Nez Perce did. Helen was the love of my life. Growing up I'd always had that romantic dream that one day someone would take my breath away, and when it didn't happen like that, I settled for something different. Finally she had come along – that very thing had finally happened – and I had been so desperate to keep her and protect her that I had almost killed it.

As she rested, and the New Year progressed, she gradually grew stronger and sent me the occasional text. There were various things we needed to discuss and sort out. There were financial issues, also things she had left in the caravan, including clothes, that I needed to return, and she had a suitcase with some of my things in it from when we had last been away together. One day she phoned. She had a problem with one of her dogs, which was playing up, and asked my advice. At the end of the call I said, 'If you ever need the twenty-four-hour dog helpline again just give me a shout,' hoping she would pick up the underlying message – which she did. She then had a long conversation with her mother, thinking through the feelings she still had for me and saying how she hoped that there might be some way we could resolve our problems. She also spoke to Arran, who gave her every encouragement.

We met again for the first time in early February 2009 and had a cup of coffee together; Helen had also been in therapy. Our time was taken up analysing what had gone wrong between us, identifying what had caused the pressure cooker to blow, and we came to the conclusion that even though we shared a mutual interest in the wolves, and a desire to understand and help them, we had not allowed time for our individual needs. We went over this ground again in the next few meetings, acknowledging that although we led abnormal lives we were normal people – Helen more normal than me – and we had normal needs.

For most of that summer it looked as though our love could be salvaged. Helen took a job with the National Health Service and rented a small house in Barnstable, and she saw more of her friends than she did when we were together. We spoke daily and saw each other as often as we could, but we both knew it would be a mistake to go back to where we had been. Secretly I was hoping that in time we would be together again, as a couple, but that hope has now gone. I think I have to come to terms with the fact that I am not very good at human relationships and probably never will be – or maybe it was just that Helen was not the right one. I've known some wonderful women and I have some beautiful children but I've probably disappointed them all. And I regret that.

I rented a small cottage myself. After a long battle in the custody courts, I won the right to see my children every other weekend and I wanted somewhere better than the caravan to accommodate them. Besides, I've lived that life for long enough. Wolves will always be central to what I do but as the pack is growing older my role within it is changing. I will be more use to these creatures in the future as an ambassador for them, teaching those people who are willing to learn about the wonders of their world,

One day I would like to bring my mother down to Devon. I have made contact with her again. I went back to Norfolk at the beginning of 2009, confronted my fears and discovered that they were more manageable than I had expected them to be. I went to visit my grandparents' grave in the churchyard at Great Massingham – and realised just how wrong my memory had been about when they died. I saw old friends, and for the first time I was able to see my childhood through my mother's eyes; to see how hard life must have been for her and how brave she was to have brought me up as a single mother in those days, in that environment. My behaviour must have puzzled and hurt her. She still won't tell me who my father was, but she must have her reasons for that. One day, I would like to introduce Kyra, Beth, Jack and Sam to their half-sister, Gemma. All these years they haven't even known she existed. I'd like to get to know my grown-up daughter too. I have so many regrets about not being there for my children – they paid the ultimate sacrifice for my work – but I am determined to make it up to them.

Meanwhile my long-term plan is to find a property to buy with space for the wolves – an acre of natural forest per wolf, ideally – and to run an education and research centre. My dream is to prove that having wolves roam the forest is beneficial to the environment and therefore to mankind. I would bring in naturalists to record what animal and plant life was in the area before the wolves arrived, and then invite them back in three or four years' time to see how it had changed. I believe we would find that the prey animals had become healthier and had increased in number. Having predators in the area stimulates the females to breed stronger animals and more of them; and being kept on the move stops them decimating any one area, as they do in so many places at the moment. The vegetation would also be flourishing, bringing birds and a wide variety of wildlife into the area.

There is a story the Inuit tell about when their ancestors first started to hunt and kill the caribou, which they believed had miraculously come to them from the sea. The animals sustained them well until the people started to take too many and the herd became weak and diseased. So the Inuit prayed for a creature to safeguard the caribou and keep it healthy, and what came from the sea this time was the wolf. After the wolf had weeded out the old, the sick and the injured, the Inuit were left with strong, healthy animals to hunt – and more of them. Neither animal, of course, came from the sea. The caribou would have been a migratory herd, and wherever the prey goes, there the predator goes too; but thereafter, in their eyes, the wolf had mystical powers.

There is still so much research to be done. No one yet knows what would happen if you released wolves into the wild in the UK. In Scotland they are talking about trying to control two to three hundred thousand head of deer with wolves. Even if we can prove that wolves create more life than they take – as I believe we can – releasing wolves on their own would be futile. You would have to release them as part of a much larger programme along with other predators. More research needs to be done into diet; to find out exactly what effect different food sources have on these animals, and to get to the bottom of what it is that the wild wolves in Poland get from domestic livestock that they don't get from their natural prey. And human beings would have to be prepared to have wolves roaming the forests once again. This is probably still the greatest hurdle: people's fear, which is based on myths and legends that have been instilled in them through centuries. If I walk down the beach with a German Shepherd, people are immediately frightened because it looks like a wolf.

If I have a Jack Russell, everyone thinks how cute. The fact is that the Jack Russell is far more likely to bite than a German Shepherd.

In all the talks I have given at Combe Martin, I have tried to dispel the falsehoods that people believe about wolves. Children need to be taught how to behave around them – to stay calm, never to turn and run – which is exactly how they should behave with dogs. I have a friend in Devon, Charlie Richardson, who breeds a dog called a Saarloos, which is a cross between a wolf and a German Shepherd. These dogs look like wolves and have many of the wolf's characteristics but are better adapted to being around humans. They would be useful at our education centre, where children could learn about them and meet them, or we could take them into schools.

We know that wolves can connect with humans in a way that sometimes no human is able to – as Zarnesti did with the disabled child who had never displayed emotion. I have seen several similar scenes over the years. A tall, thick-set man once came to the wolf enclosure at Sparkwell. He had his wife and three children with him but you would never have known they were together. He stood well apart from them, and while I chatted to the family, I noticed that he and Dakota, the female wolf, had connected. She was staring at him through the fence and silently mimicking him: every move that the man made, Dakota mirrored. He bent over, she went into a play-bow; he skipped to one side, she skipped; it was the first time I'd seen a wolf do this. We all stopped chattering and watched. I was then called away, but when I came back I found the family hugging one another and in tears. The man, I discovered, had been a rugby player, fit and athletic, and had recently had a back injury that meant he would never run again. His sporting life was over and he felt everything he lived for was gone. He had been profoundly depressed and had withdrawn from everything, including his family. He had always loved animals and they had brought him to the park in the hope that it might lift

The Man Who Lives With Wolves

his spirits. Whatever happened between him and Dakota that afternoon, the wolf brought him back. Through his tears he was apologising to his wife and to his children and holding on to them as though his life depended on it.

And it is now becoming clear that wolves, as we have long suspected, can detect illness in humans too. Over the years I have run Wolf Encounter courses, which allow people to come to the park and get closer to the wolves than normal visitors. Before these introductions, I always ask if anyone has an ailment or whether women are pregnant or where they are in their cycle, because all these things can have an effect on the wolves. If a volunteer goes into the enclosure with a cold or an injury the wolves know immediately and their behaviour is more challenging. The same has been reported at centres where the public are able to walk with socialised wolves. The wolves immediately single out people who have any kind of weakness.

Helen brought a middle-aged man down to the enclosure one day, who looked perfectly healthy and had been asked all the usual questions. When he went close up to the fence one of the wolves started trying to nibble and lick his hand through the wire, not in an aggressive way but obsessively, as though he couldn't get enough. This was very unusual, not to say abnormal, and I looked at Helen and asked under my breath, 'Is everything OK with this guy?' She said he hadn't told them about any problems, so I put it out of my mind and just thought the wolf must be having a curious day. When he'd finished, I stayed in with the wolves, while Helen took the man back up the hill, and on the way he became short of breath and started to pant and wheeze. She asked if he was all right and he said that he hadn't mentioned it before, because he didn't think it was relevant, but he had a blood disease which made him very short of breath at times. This sixth sense of theirs could be harnessed.

My dream is also to help the Nez Perce. The American government doesn't believe they can manage the land. I would like to bring some of their people to the UK to give them an opportunity to demonstrate that they can; that their methods of purifying the land work, so that one day they might get back some of what was once theirs. We could have summer camps and they could show children – future generations – how to respect and use the land, how to value nature and how to turn a polluted stream into one that is pure enough to drink from by the use of plants and rocks and animals. I think people have a growing thirst for getting in touch with the land again and finding natural means of healing the planet. I would love to be part of that.

One other important ingredient would be dog training courses to help people understand the creatures they share their lives with. As the old adage goes, there is no such thing as a bad animal, just bad teaching, and so much misery is caused by buying the wrong dog and misunderstanding it. Dogs are no different from wolves and I have seen so many dangerous wolves come through rescue centres. If you get a wolf that has been brought up badly by humans then you have a modern-day werewolf. It looks like a wolf but has all the characteristics of an undisciplined, ill-educated yob.

That is my dream.

I am sorry that so many scientists disapprove of what I have done. I believe their fear that, by infiltrating a wild pack, I would make life more dangerous for the wolves was unfounded. Time and time again during those two years in Idaho, it was clear that knowing me didn't mean the wolves let their guard down. They didn't regard all humans as harmless any more than they regarded all wolves as benign. The cubs were taught to trust only those creatures that were part of the family. They were fearful of other wolves and by the same token they were fearful of human beings. I would argue that the benefits of what

I did far outweighed the dangers for that pack. I discovered more about wild wolf behaviour and communication by eating, sleeping and living alongside those animals in the Rocky Mountains than I could ever have done with binoculars, however powerful. My hope would be that the scientists and I could pool our discoveries and join forces.

The wolves I ran with were all wolves that were likely to come into contact with humans and, therefore, needed to know something about our world. I would never try to infiltrate a wild pack in the Arctic or in the wastes of Russia, where there were no farms or villages nearby, no livestock being attacked and therefore no conflict. There would be no reason to interfere and no justification. Those wolves don't need us and we don't need them. My only interest is where the two worlds collide; in learning how to speak for this noble creature whose language no one else seems to understand. And to hope that one day, we humans, who have lost our way in so many respects, might be able to learn from the animal that once walked alongside us and taught us so much of what we knew about survival, loyalty and family but seem to have forgotten.

AFTERWORD

We have so much to learn from animals. If only we would pay attention they could teach us how to save the planet. We need to go back to being keepers of the wild and learn about their world and heal the wounds we have inflicted on nature. Everything has a place in this world and we can't be naïve enough to think we can safeguard ourselves if we let other species fail. The Native Americans believe that what happens in the wolf world happens in ours and vice versa. They say 'He, me.' We need to work together, and then everything else will fall into place. The animal world works together; nature doesn't have to be cruel. Wolves have rivals but they need their rivals to keep driving the prey in their direction. And no animal kills for fun. I've seen predators and prey peacefully drinking alongside one another at a watering hole; it was as if the animals had agreed a truce so that none of them would be forced to drink when the insects arrived and made life uncomfortable for them all. They were co-operating with each other to such a degree, I expected Noah to turn up at any moment with his Ark.

If only humans could do the same.

ACKNOWLEDGEMENTS

My Native American family believes that our breath is sacred. It connects us to the Great Spirit (Creator). Therefore, our words are just as sacred and should not be used lightly. It is important to choose them carefully and use them wisely.

In honour of my Native American family and the many people that have contributed to this book, I hope I have chosen my words wisely.

Firstly, Hilary and Katie at Hilary Knight Management. For your support and loyalty to duty, also going above and beyond an agent's obligations; thank you.

To Jane Turnbull and Daniel Conaway for their support and help in finding me the right publisher; to Julia Pastore at Harmony Books; and Carole Tonkinson and Kate Latham at HarperCollins; thank you all for showing such faith in this book.

To the dedicated and selfless staff at Wolf Pack Management: Roger Cooke, Linda Cowen, Jude Cross and Wendy Jamieson-Butler. Thank you, my friends, for your endless support. I may not have always been easy but it was certainly worthwhile. And thank you Roger and Linda for your huge generosity in allowing me to use your wonderful photographs. Ditto Bernard Walton and Simon Frazier – you took some amazing pictures, and many thanks for letting me use them.

To Penny Junor for committing my innermost thoughts to paper. I always believed it would be virtually impossible to put my life into words, to re-live the miracle of living with wolves through one man's eyes. You truly are worthy of your reputation amongst authors.

To my family and friends, responsible for shaping my childhood and making me the person that I am today. Grandfather, I hope you are looking down on me and are as proud of me as I have always been of you.

To my mother. Sorry for all the doubt through the years, for not only knowing how hard it must have been for you to raise an angry and unforgiving young boy, but for the sacrifices that you made through the years. I know you can't talk to me of my father but I hope for the short time you were together you loved a lifetime's worth.

To my travelling father: Sir, I have never known you. I feel inside that you are a travelling soul and I know that my mother loved you because of the strength she has found to deal with your absence. Thank you for your wisdom.

To my family: for my children, thank you for making my life complete. Watching you grow and take your place in this world, I know that you will help restore its balance. For smiling through Christmases and birthdays without me and often with home-made presents. Never once did I hear you complain. You are my life!

To my wolf family: I have always said every day with you begins and ends with a miracle. For your patient teachings and sharing with me your family secrets. I hope I never let you down. Give me your wisdom so that I may know how to help your children to live peacefully in this world.

Finally, to Helen: thank you for your strength, my Angel. You always believed in me and had the strength to stand by my side. Without your courage I would never have been able to take the steps that I did. I am sorry if I ever let you down. You and Little Man (Arran) will be in my heart and the children's hearts for ever.

INDEX